Saint Francis of Assisi

Works of the Seraphic Father St. Francis of Assisi

Saint Francis of Assisi

Works of the Seraphic Father St. Francis of Assisi

ISBN/EAN: 9783337300838

Printed in Europe, USA, Canada, Australia, Japan

Cover: Foto ©Lupo / pixelio.de

More available books at **www.hansebooks.com**

OF

THE SERAPHIC FATHER

ST. FRANCIS OF ASSISI,

TRANSLATED BY

A RELIGIOUS OF THE ORDER.

R. WASHBOURNE,
18 PATERNOSTER ROW, LONDON.
1882.

INTRODUCTION.

THE following translation has been made from the edition of the 'Works of St. Francis' published at Cologne in the year 1848. As the work is intended to be a practical and devotional one, no critical notes have been introduced, nor references to the authors from whom Wadding made his collection.

In these pages there will be found neither deep learning nor sublime eloquence, but only the expression of the exquisite simplicity, humility, and charity which filled the heart of the Seraphic Patriarch; and above all, his ardent love for that Poverty which he looked upon as the queen of virtues, because in the perfect renunciation of self, and detachment from the things of this world, he saw the surest means for the soul to attain to the possession of the Supreme Good and the eternal riches of the heavenly kingdom.

And yet under these simple words are concealed treasures of profound wisdom; for although, as St. Bonaventure says, 'St. Francis possessed not the knowledge acquired by study, nevertheless, being illuminated by the rays of the Divine light, he penetrated with marvellous clearness the hidden mysteries of Holy Scripture;' for 'where the learning of the doctor stands without, the affection of the loving soul finds entrance.'

And being thus illuminated and transformed into the image of his Divine Master, the Saint taught to others, both by word and example, the knowledge and love of Christ Crucified, which is indeed foolishness to the world, but ever has been, and ever will be to those who believe and love, 'the power of God and the wisdom of God.'

CONTENTS.

PART I.
LETTERS OF ST. FRANCIS.

LETTERS		PAGE
I.	To all the Faithful of Christ	1
II.	To all the Faithful of Christ	2
III.	To St. Antony of Padua	9
IV.	To the Blessed Virgin Clare, and her Sisters at St. Damian's	9
V.	To the same	9
VI.	To Brother Elias, Vicar-General of the whole Order	10
VII.	To the same	11
VIII.	To the Minister-General of the Friars Minor	11
IX.	To the Provincial Ministers of the Order of Friars Minor	13
X.	To the Second General Chapter	13
XI.	To the General Chapter	14
XII.	To the Priests of the whole Order	16
XIII.	To all Clerics	20
XIV.	To all the Custodes of the Friars Minor	21
XV.	To the Rulers of the People	22
XVI.	To Brother Leo	23
XVII.	To the Lady Jacoba of Settisoli	24

PART II.
THE FIRST RULE WHICH THE SERAPHIC PATRIARCH WROTE FOR THE FRIARS MINOR.

CHAPTER		
I.	That the Brethren ought to live in Obedience, without Property, and in Chastity	25
II.	Of the Reception and Clothing of the Brethren	26

CHAPTER		PAGE
III.	Of the Divine Office, and of the Fast	28
IV.	Of the Order of the Ministers, and other Brethren	29
V.	Of the Correction of the Brethren who offend	30
VI.	Of the Recourse the Brethren should have to their Ministers, and that no Brother may be called Prior	31
VII.	Of the Manner of Serving and Working	32
VIII.	That the Brethren may not receive Money	33
IX.	Of the Manner of Asking Alms	34
X.	Of the Sick Brethren	36
XI.	That the Brethren ought not to be Calumniators nor Detractors, but ought to love one another	37
XII.	That the Brethren must avoid the Sight and Company of Women	38
XIII.	Of the Punishment of Fornication	39
XIV.	In what Manner the Brethren ought to go through the World	39
XV.	That the Brethren may not keep Horses nor ride	39
XVI.	Of the Brethren who go among the Saracens and other Infidels	40
XVII.	Of the Preachers	42
XVIII.	How the Ministers are to Meet together	43
XIX.	That all the Brethren must be true Catholics	44
XX.	Of the Confession of the Brethren and of the Reception of the Body and Blood of Our Lord Jesus Christ	44
XXI.	Of Praising God, and of the Exhortation which all the Brethren may make	45
XXII.	Of the Admonition of the Brethren	46
XXIII.	Prayer and Thanksgiving to God	50
	Exhortation to the Brethren	52

THE SECOND RULE WHICH THE BLESSED FATHER ST. FRANCIS INSTITUTED FOR THE FRIARS MINOR.

I.	The Rule and Life of the Friars Minor	54
II.	Of those who desire to embrace this Life, and how they are to be received	54
III.	Of the Divine Office and of Fasting, and in what Manner the Brethren are to go about in the World	56
IV.	That the Brethren may not receive Money	57
V.	Of the Manner of Working	57
VI.	That the Brethren shall appropriate nothing to themselves; of Seeking Alms, and of the Sick Brethren	58

CHAPTER	PAGE
VII. Of Penance to be imposed on the Brethren	59
VIII. Of the Election of the Minister General of this Fraternity, and of the Chapter of Pentecost	59
IX. Of the Preachers	60
X. Of the Admonition and Correction of the Brethren	61
XI. That the Brethren may not Enter the Convents of Nuns	62
XII. Of those who go among the Saracens, and other Infidels	62
Panegyric on the Rule	63

RULE WHICH THE HOLY FATHER ST. FRANCIS WROTE FOR THE RELIGIOUS OF ST. CLARE.

I. The Rule and Form of Life of the Order of the Poor Sisters	64
II. In what Manner Persons are to be Received	64
III. Of the Divine Office, of the Fast, of Confession and Holy Communion	67
IV. Of the Election of the Abbess	68
V. Of Silence, and of the Manner of Speaking at the Grate, and in the Parlour	70
VI. That the Sisters may not receive any Property or Possessions	71
VII. Of the Manner of Working	72
VIII. That the Sisters shall appropriate nothing to themselves, and of the Sick Sisters	73
IX. Of Penance to be imposed on the Sisters	74
X. Of the Visitation of the Sisters by the Abbess	76
XI. Of the Duties of the Portress	77
XII. Of the Visitor	78

RULE OF THE BROTHERS AND SISTERS OF THE THIRD ORDER OF ST. FRANCIS, CALLED THE ORDER OF PENANCE.

I. Of the Manner of Examining those who wish to Enter the Order	80
II. Of the Manner of Receiving those who wish to Enter the Order	80
III. Of the Form of the Habit, and the Quality of the Garments	81
IV. Of not going to immodest Feasts and Plays, and of not Giving anything to Actors	82

CHAPTER		PAGE
V.	Of Abstinence and Fasting	82
VI.	How often the Brothers and Sisters ought to Confess and Communicate during the Year	84
VII.	Of not Carrying offensive Weapons	84
VIII.	Of the Recitation of the Canonical Hours	84
IX.	That all who can lawfully do so should make their Will	85
X.	How Peace must be Established among the Brethren, and with others	86
XI.	How they should Act when Molested contrary to Justice, and their Privileges	86
XII.	That the Brothers and Sisters should avoid, as much as possible, taking solemn Oaths	86
XIII.	Of hearing Mass, and attending the Assemblies	87
XIV.	Of the sick and departed Brethren	88
XV.	Of the Ministers	89
XVI.	Of the Visitation and Correction of those who Offend	89
XVII.	Of avoiding Lawsuits among themselves or with others	90
XVIII.	How, and by whom, Dispensations may be Granted	90
XIX.	That the Ministers must declare notable Faults to the Visitor	90
XX.	That this Rule does not bind under pain of mortal Sin	91

PART III.

Admonitions of the Blessed Father St. Francis to his Brethren	92
The Praises of Wisdom, Simplicity, etc.	101
Of Perfect Joy	102

MONASTIC CONFERÈNCES OF THE HOLY FATHER ST. FRANCIS.

CONFERENCE		
I.	That the little Flock will be Multiplied	105
II.	Of the Vocation of the Friars Minor, and of Preaching the Word of God	106
III.	Of the Religious who live as Hermits	107
IV.	Of True Obedience	108
V.	On Holy Poverty	109

CONFERENCE

VI. Of Avoiding the Sight and Conversation of Women - - - - - 110
VII. Of Asking for Alms with Confidence - - 111
VIII. Of Discretion in Nourishing the Body - - 112
IX. Of Indiscreet Fervour in Abstinence - - 113
X. Of Bearing with small Discomforts - - 114
XI. Of Rejoicing Spiritually in the Lord - - 114
XII. Of the Humility and Peace to be observed towards Priests - - - - 115
XIII. How to Recognise a Servant of God - - 116
XIV. Whether it is more Pleasing to God to Pray or to Preach - - - - - 117
XV. Of those who Apply themselves to Learning - 118
XVI. Of Vain and Conceited Preachers - - 119
XVII. Of the Marks and Praise of a Good Preacher - 121
XVIII. Of Murmuring and Detraction - - - 122
XIX. The Brethren are not to be called Masters - 124
XX. Of the Benefits that will Accrue to the Order by being subject to the Holy Church - - 125
XXI. Of the Tribulations of the Order, and of those who follow the Rule - - - 125
XXII. Of Conversing with Holiness among the Faithful 126
XXIII. How the Brethren are to Act among Infidels - 127
XXIV. Of the assiduous Meditation of the Passion of Christ - - - - - 128
XXV. Why, having renounced the Office of General, St. Francis bore with the Defects of his Brethren 131
XXVI. Of the Qualities that should Characterise the Minister General - - - - 133
XXVII. Of the Qualities of the Provincial Ministers - 136
XXVIII. What Manner of Life is to be observed at St. Mary of the Angels, and that the Brethren are never to give up that Place - - 136

Maxims of the Holy Father St. Francis - - - 138
Favourite Sentences of St. Francis - - - 145

PART IV.

CANTICLES OF THE HOLY FATHER ST. FRANCIS.

I. Canticle of the Sun - - - - - 147
II. 'Love sets me all on Fire' - - - - 148
III. 'O Love of Charity' - - - - 152

PRAYERS.

	PAGE
Praises of the Most High	164
Prayer to be said before the Divine Office	165
Prayer of the Holy Father at the Beginning of his Conversion	167
Prayer to obtain Divine Love	167
Prayer the Saint was accustomed to say at the Elevation of the Most Holy Body of Christ	167
Prayer in Time of Sickness	167
Prayer when the Saint resigned the Generalship	168
Prayer the Holy Father said Daily	168
Salutation to the Blessed Virgin Mary	168
Prayer to Our Blessed Lady	169
Another to the same	169
Paraphrase of the Lord's Prayer	170
Prayer of the Blessed Father to obtain Poverty	171
Testament of the Blessed Father St. Francis	174

PART V.

Sayings of the Holy Father St. Francis - - - 178

FAMILIAR COLLOQUIES OF THE BLESSED FATHER ST. FRANCIS.

COLLOQUY
I. That Meekness and Patience will Soften the hardest Hearts	202
II. The Friars Minor ought not to Reserve for themselves any of the Goods of the Novices	202
III. That the Friars Minor should not Erect superfluous Buildings	203
IV. That the Praise of all that is Good is to be Referred to God	204
V. Those who are Fools for Christ's Sake are Stronger than the Wise of this World	205
VI. The Poor of Christ should prefer Living on Alms to Feasting with the Rich	206
VII. The Friars Minor should remain in their Humble Vocation	208
VIII. That it is not becoming for Superiors to indulge their Appetite, or make use of Delicate Meats	208
IX. The Rule of the Friars Minor was not Composed by St. Francis, but given him by God	209

Contents.

COLLOQUY		PAGE
X.	It is a great Advantage to the Church that various Religious Orders should Flourish therein	210
XI.	The more Humble the Servants of God are, the more Holy they are	211
XII.	All the Virtues of the Saints come from God, and are to be Referred to Him	212
XIII.	The Saint Complains that certain Superiors of the Order follow other Ways instead of his	213
XIV.	The Religious should Win the Minds of the People by Humility, etc.	215
XV.	What they ought to be who Devote themselves to Study	217
XVI.	How the Convents of the Friars Minor should be Founded	217
XVII.	Some Things must be Borne with on account of Circumstances	219
XVIII.	He who Enters Religion from a wrong Motive Lies to the Holy Ghost	220
XIX.	Favours and Graces will be Granted to those who are Zealous for the Rule	221
XX.	The Afflicted and Tempted are to be Consoled, etc.	221
XXI.	How great should be the Patience of the Friars Minor under Afflictions	223
XXII.	A Religious should never Shake off the Yoke of Holy Obedience	224
XXIII.	That we should gratefully Remember the Benefits of God	225
XXIV.	Religious should not Frequent the Palaces of the Great	227
XXV.	In the Poor we are to Consider the Poverty of Christ and His Mother	228
XXVI.	In Religion we must Follow not our own Judgment, but that of our Superior	228
XXVII.	The Demons are Grieved when we are Joyful	229
XXVIII.	Temptations are Allowed for our Greater Profit	230
XXIX.	The Lord's Prayer is the most Salutary of all Prayers	231
XXX.	The Devils are easily Put to Flight	231
XXXI.	How the Devil Hardens the Hearts of Men	232
XXXII.	Idleness is to be Shunned, and Labour Encouraged	234
XXXIII.	We must Bear a little in this World, to Enjoy the Glory of the Next	234

Contents.

COLLOQUY		PAGE
XXXIV.	Murmuring and Discontent are to be Conquered by Meekness	235
XXXV.	Disobedience comes from the Devil	235
XXXVI.	Against Lying and giving Scandal to the Brethren	236
XXXVII.	Those who Cherish the Friars Minor are Pleasing to God, etc.	237
XXXVIII.	The Bread obtained by Begging for the Love of God is the Bread of Angels	237
XXXIX.	Religious and Learned Men ought to Preach to the People by the Example of a Holy Life	238
XL.	True Obedience is like Death	238
XLI.	What a Precious Treasure is Poverty	239

Some Prophecies of the Holy Father St. Francis - 240
Parables and Similitudes of the Holy Father St. Francis - 252
Blessings of the Holy Father St. Francis - 260

APPENDIX.

DOUBTFUL WORKS OF ST. FRANCIS.

Seven Short Sermons - 267
Six Principal Reasons why Almighty God granted the Order of Friars Minor to His Church - 276
The Ten Perfections of a True Religious and Perfect Christian - 280

WORKS OF ST. FRANCIS OF ASSISI.

PART I.

LETTERS OF ST. FRANCIS.

LETTER I.

To all the Faithful of Christ.

LET us love God, and let us adore Him with a pure heart and a pure mind.

To all Christians, religious, priests, laymen, and women, and to all who dwell in the world.

Oh, how blessed and happy are they who love God, and who act as Our Lord commands in the Gospel: 'Thou shalt love the Lord thy God with all thy heart, and with all thy soul, and thy neighbour as thyself.' Let us therefore love God, and adore Him with a pure heart and mind, for this is what He seeks above all things when He says: 'The true adorers shall adore God the Father in spirit and in truth.' All who adore Him ought to adore Him in spirit and truth. Farewell in the Lord.

LETTER II.

To all the Faithful of Christ.

To all Christians, religious, priests, laymen, and women, and to all who dwell in the world; Brother Francis, their servant and slave, reverently wishes true peace from heaven, and sincere charity in the Lord. I, being the servant of all, am bound to serve all, and to minister to them the most sweet words of my Lord. Wherefore, considering in my mind that on account of my infirmities and of the weakness of my body, I cannot personally visit each one, I desire by this letter to announce unto you the words of my Lord Jesus Christ, Who is the Eternal Word of the Father, and also the words of the Holy Ghost, which are spirit and life.

This Word of the Father, so divine, so holy, and so glorious, was announced from heaven by the holy Archangel Gabriel, and He descended into the womb of the glorious Virgin Mary, receiving from her the true flesh of our frail humanity. And being rich, He, together with His most blessed Mother, desired above all things in this world to embrace poverty. Before His Passion He celebrated the Pasch with His disciples, and taking bread, He gave thanks, and blessed and broke it, saying: 'Take and eat, this is My Body;' and taking the chalice, He said: 'This is My Blood of the New Testament, which is shed for you and for many, for the remission of sins.' Soon after He prayed to His Father, saying: 'Father, if it be possible, let this chalice pass from Me.' And His sweat became as drops of blood falling down upon the ground. But He united His will with that of His Heavenly Father, saying: 'Father, Thy will be done; not what I will, but what Thou willest.'

It was the will of His Father that this most glorious and blessed Son, Whom He gave to us, and Who was born for us, should, by the shedding of His Blood, offer Himself as a sacrifice on the Altar of the Cross, not for Himself, for by Him all things were made, but for our sins, 'leaving us an example that we should follow in His footsteps.' And He desires that we should all be saved by Him, and that we should receive Him with a pure mind and a chaste body. But alas! there are few who are willing to receive Him and to be saved by Him, although His yoke is sweet and His burden light.

Those who will not taste how sweet is the Lord, and who love darkness rather than light, being unwilling to fulfil the law of God, are cursed; for the prophet, speaking of them, says: 'Cursed are they that decline from Thy commandments.' But, on the contrary, how blessed and happy are they who adore Him (as they ought) in spirit and in truth. Let us praise and beseech Him day and night, saying: 'Our Father, Who art in heaven,' etc., for we ought always to pray, and not to faint.

We ought indeed to confess all our sins to a priest, that we may receive the Body and Blood of Our Lord Jesus Christ, because whoever does not eat His Flesh and drink His Blood cannot enter into the kingdom of God. We must also each of us partake of this Sacrament worthily, for 'he who eateth and drinketh unworthily, eateth and drinketh judg ment to himself, not discerning the Body of the Lord.

Let us moreover bear worthy fruits of penance, loving our neighbour as ourselves, and if anyone cannot love him as much as himself, let him at least inflict no evil on him, but do him good.

Let those who have received the power to judge, exercise justice with mercy, as they hope to obtain mercy from God. 'Judgment without mercy to those who show no mercy.' Let us have charity and humility, and give alms, for almsgiving cleanses our souls from the filth of sin. At death we lose all that we have in this world, but we take with us charity and the alms-deeds we have done, and for these we shall receive a great reward from God.

We ought to fast, and to abstain from all vice, and from all that will lead us into sin, as well as from extravagance and superfluity. We should often visit the churches, and venerate and reverence all ecclesiastics on account of their office, and because they distribute the Sacred Body and Blood of Christ, which they offer in sacrifice, receive themselves, and administer to others. And let everyone know and hold for certain that we cannot be saved except through the sacred Words and the Precious Blood of our Lord Jesus Christ, which priests preach, announce, and distribute, and of which they are the sole ministers.

We religious especially, and all who have renounced the world, are bound to do more and greater things; we must give up all that is not necessary, and hate our body with its vices and sins, for Our Lord says in the Gospel: 'From the heart comes forth evil things;' we must love our enemies, and do good to those who hate us; we must observe the precepts and counsels of our Redeemer, denying ourselves and subjecting our bodies to the yoke of obedience. But no one is bound to obey where there is sin or fault, for we came to religion in order to save our souls, and to give good example to others.

Those to whom power is entrusted, and who are considered Superiors, must be mindful to become as the least, and servants of their brethren, and they must show mercy to their subjects as they would wish to have mercy shown to them if they were subjects. Let them not be angry with the brethren on account of their defects, but correct them kindly with all patience and humility, and support and assist them by their counsels.

Let us not be wise and prudent according to the flesh, but simple, humble, and pure. Let us despise our bodies and hold them in subjection, because on account of our sins we have become miserable and corrupt, as the Lord says by the prophet: 'I am a worm and no man.' We should never desire to be above others, but rather to be subject to every human being for the love of God. And the Spirit of God will rest on all those who act in this way, and persevere therein to the end; He will make of them His temple and dwelling-place; they will become the children of the Eternal Father, whose works they perform; the spouses, brothers, and mothers of Our Lord Jesus Christ. We are His spouses because all faithful souls are united to Him through the Holy Ghost; we are His brothers when we do the will of His Father,

Who is in heaven; we are His mothers when we bear Him in our hearts and bodies by love and a pure conscience, and bring Him forth by holy works, which shine as examples to others. Oh, how great and glorious it is to have a Father in heaven! Oh, how holy to have a sweet and loving Paraclete for our Spouse! Oh, how holy, how delightful, how sweet, how peaceful, how amiable, how desirable above all is it to have such a Brother, Who gave His life for His sheep, and Who prayed for us to His Father, saying: 'Father, keep them in Thy name whom Thou hast given Me. Father, all those whom Thou hast given Me in the world were Thine, and Thou hast given them to Me, and the words which Thou gavest Me, I have given to them; and they have received them, and have known for certain that I came forth from Thee, and they have believed that Thou didst send Me. I pray for them; I sanctify Myself, that they may be made perfect in one as We are One. And I will, Father, that where I am, there also My ministers may be, that they may see the glory of My kingdom.'

Therefore let all creatures who are in heaven, on earth, in the sea, and under the earth give praise, honour, glory, and benediction to the Lord, for all He suffered for us, and for all He has done, and will do for each one; for He is our strength and our fortitude, He only is good, He only Most High, omnipotent, admirable, glorious, and most holy, and worthy to be praised and blessed for ever and ever. Amen.

But all those who do not the works of penance, who will not receive the Body and Blood of Our Lord Jesus Christ, but who do the works of sin and death; who follow their own concupiscence and wicked desires; who will not keep what they have promised; who are slaves to the world and to their bodies, and are engrossed by the desires, cares, and anxieties of this life—all these are deceived by the devil, whose children they are, for they do his works. They are blind, for they cannot see the true light, Jesus Christ Our Lord. They have not the wisdom of the Holy Spirit, because the Son of God is not in them, and He is the Wisdom of the Father. It is of these that it is said: 'Their wisdom has been devoured;' they know, and see, and understand how to do evil; knowingly they lose their souls. See, O ye blind, how you are deceived by your enemies, that is the world, the flesh, and the devil, because the flesh finds pleasure in sin, and bitterness in the service of God, for all evils come from the flesh, as Our Lord says in the Gospel. You think to possess the vain joys of this world for a long time, but you are deceived, for the day and the hour are coming of which you will not think, and of which you do not know.

When sickness lays hold of the body, and death approaches, the friends and relations of the sick man come round him saying: 'Settle the affairs of thy house,' etc. And behold his wife and his children, his relations and friends, pretend to weep, and, seeing their tears, his heart is touched, and being moved by the evil spirit, he says: 'Behold, I place my soul and my body and all I have in your hands.' Truly this man is cursed who confides and leaves his soul and body and all he has in such hands. Of him Our Lord spoke by the prophet: 'Cursed is the man who places his hope in man.' Then they call the priest, who says to the sick man: 'Dost thou desire to do penance for thy sins?' He answers: 'I do.' 'Wilt thou make satisfaction out of thy property to all those whom thou hast defrauded and deceived?' He replies: 'No.' 'Why not?' asks the priest. 'Because I have placed it all in the hands of my relations.' And then he loses his speech, and so he dies miserably. But let all know that any man, in whatever place, or of whatever quality, who dies in sin without satisfaction, and who can make satisfaction and will not, is seized upon by the devil, who tears his soul from his body with such anguish and tribulation, that none will believe it unless they feel it. And all the knowledge, the talents, and the powers that he had will be taken from him, and his friends and relations, to whom he gave his goods, will divide them, and then they will curse his soul and say: 'Cursed be he, for he might have given us more, only he would not; he might have made more money,' and so on. His body is eaten by worms, his soul is tormented by the devils, and so he loses both soul and body through the love of this short life.

I, Brother Francis, the least of your servants, desiring to kiss your feet, pray and beseech you by that Love which God is, to receive, keep, and observe these words, and all the words of Our Lord Jesus Christ, with humility and charity. And let all those who receive and understand them, practise them as an example to others. And if they persevere in them to the end, may they be blessed by the Father, the Son, and the Holy Ghost. Amen.

LETTER III.

To St. Antony of Padua.

BROTHER FRANCIS to his beloved Brother Antony, health in the Lord.

I am willing that thou shouldst interpret holy theology to the brethren, in such manner, however, that the spirit of prayer (as I most ardently desire) be not extinguished in thyself or others, according to the rule which we follow. Farewell.

LETTER IV.

To the Blessed Virgin Clare, and her Sisters at St. Damian's.

To his beloved Sister Clare and the other Sisters of St. Damian's, Brother Francis, health in the Lord.

Since, by the divine inspiration, you have made yourselves daughters and handmaids of the most high and sovereign King, the Heavenly Father, and have taken the Holy Ghost for your Spouse, choosing to live according to the perfection of the holy Gospel, I will and promise to have always, by myself and by my brothers, a diligent care and special solicitude for you, as for them. Farewell in the Lord.

LETTER V.

To the same.

To my beloved Sister Clare, and to the other Sisters at St. Damian's, greeting in the Lord.

I, Brother Francis, poor and little, will follow the life and poverty of our most Sovereign Lord Jesus Christ, and of His most holy Mother, and will persevere in the same to the end. And I beseech you all, my ladies, and counsel you to abide always in this most holy life and poverty. And take great care that you never depart from it through the teaching or counsel of anyone. Farewell in the Lord.

LETTER VI.

To Brother Elias, Vicar-General of the whole Order.

To the Reverend Father in Christ, Brother Elias, Vicar-General of the whole Order, Brother Francis sends greeting in the Lord.

Brother, may Our Lord give thee His holy benediction. Be patient and kind in all things. If the brethren offend thee in anything, offer it to God. By this I shall know if thou art a true servant of God, if thou bringest back the erring brethren to God by mercy, and if thou never ceasest to love those who have most deeply offended. And if through any human fear they dare not approach thee, ask them if they wish for pardon. And if anyone, through the persuasion of the devil, should fall into some grievous sin, let him have recourse to the Guardian, who shall send him to the Provincial. And the Provincial must receive him with kindness; and if he seem contrite, he shall say to him: 'Go, and now sin no more.' Farewell in the Lord.

LETTER VII.
To the same.

To the Reverend Father in Christ, Brother Elias, Vicar-General of the whole Order, Brother Francis, greeting in the Lord.

I recommend much to thee, Brother Elias, in all that thou doest great charity and patience; thou must be prepared to suffer much, for the burden laid upon thee is great and heavy, namely, many souls. In the old law, the High Priest bore suspended from his shoulders, and hanging on his breast, the rational of judgment, on which were engraved the names of the twelve tribes of Israel, signifying that as Superiors have to bear their subjects on their shoulders, they must also bear them on their breast, for they cannot bear them if they cease to love them. Our Lord Jesus Christ, before making St. Peter the head of His Church, and giving him the care of His sheep, questioned him as to his love. Take care then that no brother should sin, but if anyone should fall into sin, let him not depart from thee without correction and pardon; and as thou art a physician, offer medicine to the sick man, because, as Our Lord says: 'They that are well need not a physician, but they that are sick.' Watch, admonish, labour, feed, love, wait, and fear. Farewell in the Lord.

LETTER VIII.
To the Minister-General of the Friars Minor.

To the Reverend Father N., Minister-General of the whole Order.

May the Lord protect thee, and keep thee in His holy love. I recommend to thee, my Brother, patience in all thy works, so that no matter what impediments thou meetest with either from the brethren or from others, even if they were to strike thee, thou shouldst receive it as a favour, and desire *that* and nothing else. And thou shouldst love those who act thus towards thee, and not wish them to be different until the Lord grants it for thy consolation. But thou must love them by desiring that they become better Christians. By this I shall know if thou truly lovest God, and me, His and thy poor servant, if thou actest in this manner, namely, that thou never allowest any brother who has sinned, no matter how deeply, to leave thy presence without pardon. And if he will not ask it, thou must ask him if he desire it. And if he should afterwards be brought before thee again, even a thousand times, love him still, even more than thou lovest me, in order to draw him to good; and always be compassionate towards such. Enforce this also on the Guardians as much as possible, telling them thou art determined to act in this manner. And let all the brethren who know him to have sinned be careful not to reproach him for it, nor to speak evil of him, but let them have great compassion on such a one, and keep the sins of their brother secret, for those who are whole do not need a physician, but those who are sick. If any brother, by the instigation of the enemy, should sin mortally, he is bound under obedience to have recourse to his Guardian, and the Guardian is equally bound to send him to the Custos. And this Custos has no power to inflict any further punishment upon a brother who is penitent than this: 'Go, and sin no more.' Do this, and farewell.

LETTER IX.

To the Provincial Ministers of the Order of the Friars Minor.

To the beloved Brethren in Christ, the Provincial Ministers of the Order of Friars Minor.

In your government I beseech you to be careful of two things: first, that you be not respecters of persons; and secondly, that you be not free in commanding in virtue of holy Obedience, for this is unsheathing the sword, which should not be done except after mature deliberation and on great occasions. Be moderate in your commands, merciful to sinners, easy in pardoning, sparing in food, poor in dress, mild in words, and faithful to God and your office. Preach by your works, if you wish your subjects to listen to your words and obey your precepts, and what you command by your mouth, fulfil in your actions. Farewell in the Lord.

LETTER X.

To the Second General Chapter.

To all the Reverend and much-loved Brethren, Brother Francis, greeting in the Lord.

Whenever you hear the Name of God pronounced,

adore it with fear and reverence, prostrate on the ground. God has sent you into the world to bear testimony of Him by your words and works, and to make known to all men that there is no other God. Persevere in discipline and holy Obedience, and be faithful in everything to the promises you freely made to God. I beseech the Minister-General with all earnestness to cause the Rule to be exactly observed by all. Let the Clerks recite the Divine Office with all possible devotion in the presence of God, attending not so much to the melody of the voices as to the harmony of the mind. Farewell in the Lord.

LETTER XI.

To the General Chapter.

To the Reverend and much-beloved Brethren, the Minister-General, and others of the Order of Friars Minor, Brother Francis, greeting in the Lord.

Since those who are of God hear the words of God, it behoves us, beloved brethren, who have been chosen to fulfil all divine offices, not only to hear and practise what God has commanded, but also to watch most carefully over the sacred vessels, and the holy Office-books in which His words are contained, that we may become penetrated with the greatness of our Creator, and show our submission to Him. Therefore I desire and exhort my brethren to show all possible respect to the Divine Scriptures wherever they see them, and if they should be found in any improper place, or scattered about in a disrespectful manner, let them collect and put them in a becoming place as far as possible, in order to show reverence to the words of the Lord. For many things are sanctified by the Word of God, and the mystery of the Adorable Sacrament of the Altar is accomplished by the power of the words of Jesus Christ.

Moreover, I confess all my sins to God, the Father, Son, and Holy Ghost; to the Blessed Mary ever Virgin, to all the saints in heaven and on earth, to the Minister-General of the Order, as my venerable Superior, to all the priests of the Order, and to all my beloved brethren. I have sinned in manifold ways and grievously, especially by not observing the Rule as I promised to God, and by not reciting the Office as that Rule prescribes, either through negligence or on account of my infirmities, or because I am an ignorant, simple man. I therefore earnestly beseech the Minister-General, my lord, to cause the Rule to be strictly observed by all, and to see that the clerics recite the Office devoutly before God, endeavouring to please Him by the concord of their hearts, and not to soothe the ears of the people by the sweetness of their singing; not attending to the melody of the voice, but to the harmony of the mind, so that their voices may be in unison with their hearts, and their hearts with God. As for myself, I promise, by the grace of God, to observe these things faithfully, and I will cause them to be observed by those brethren who are with me, both with regard to the Office, and to other regulations. As for those who will not observe them, I do not look upon them as Catholics, nor my brethren; I will neither see nor speak with them until they have done penance. I say the same of those who wander to and fro, and make no account of the ordinances and precepts of the Rule; for Our Lord Jesus Christ sacrificed His life rather than disobey His Heavenly Father.

I, Brother Francis, a vile man, and unworthy creature of God, command, in the Name of Our Lord Jesus Christ, the Minister-General, all the Ministers-General who come after him, all the Custodes and Guardians present and to come, to have this writing, to keep it carefully, and to practise what it contains. I implore them to have all that is written therein carefully and diligently observed. May those who are faithful to these things be blessed of the Lord, according to the will of Almighty God, now and in future as long as the world exists. May the Lord be with you for ever. Amen.

LETTER XII.

To the Priests of the whole Order.

IN the Name of the most Holy Trinity and Supreme Unity, Father, Son, and Holy Ghost. Amen.

To all his Reverend and much-loved Brothers, the Minister-General of the Order of Friars Minor, and all the other Ministers-General who shall succeed him; to all the other Ministers, Custodes, and Priests of this Brotherhood; to all who are humble, simple, and obedient in Christ; to the greatest and the least, —Brother Francis, a poor, miserable man, your little servant, health in Him Who has redeemed us and washed us in His Blood, Jesus Christ, the most glorious Son of God, blessed in all ages. Amen.

Hearken, my lords, my children, and my brethren; listen to my words. Incline the ears of your heart and obey the voice of the Son of God. Keep His commandments with your whole heart, and fulfil His counsels with a perfect mind. Praise Him, for He is good, and exalt Him in your works. The Lord God offers Himself to us as to His children. Wherefore, O my brethren, embracing your feet with all the love of which I am capable, I conjure you to show all the reverence and honour possible to the Body and Blood of Our Lord Jesus Christ, in Whom everything in heaven and on earth has been restored to peace, and reconciled with Almighty God.

I also beseech in the Lord, all my brethren who are, or who shall be, or who desire to be priests of the Most High, that whenever they wish to celebrate Mass, they be pure, and offer with purity and reverence the true Sacrifice of the most holy Body and Blood of Our Lord Jesus Christ with a holy and perfect intention; not from any earthly motive, nor for the fear or love of any creature, as though desiring to please men; but let every will (according to the grace given) be directed solely to the most High God, and do you desire to please Him alone, for He alone works in this holy Sacrifice according to His good pleasure, as the Lord has Himself said: 'Do this in remembrance of Me:' and he who does otherwise becomes a traitor like Judas. Remember, O priests, my brothers, how it is written in the law of

Moses, that those who transgressed even in corporal sacrifices were condemned by God to death, without any mercy. What a far more terrible punishment will he deserve, who tramples under foot the Son of God, and treats the Blood of the New Testament by which he is sanctified as a vile thing, and offers insult to the Holy Ghost! A man stained with sin despises and tramples on the Lamb of God, when, as the Apostle says, not discerning the sacred Bread, which is Christ, from other food, he eats unworthily by being guilty of unworthy actions; for the Lord has said by His Prophet: 'Cursed is the man who does the work of God with negligence or fraud.' And on account of those priests who will not lay these things seriously to heart, we are condemned, when Our Lord says: 'I will curse your blessings.'

Hearken, my brethren. If the Blessed Virgin Mary is honoured, as she well deserves, for having borne our Saviour in her most holy womb; if St. John the Baptist trembled, and did not dare to touch the forehead of his Lord; if the Holy Sepulchre in which this same Lord reposed for a short time is so venerated—how holy, how just, and how worthy ought not he to be who touches with his hands, receives into his mouth and heart, and gives to others, this God Who is now no more to die, but Who will live and be glorified for ever, on Whom the angels desire to gaze! Understand your dignity, O priests, my brothers, and 'be ye holy, because He is holy.' As God has honoured you more than all others through this Mystery, do you love, reverence, and honour Him through this Mystery. It is a great misery, and a deplorable weakness, when you have Him thus present, that you should care for anything else in the whole world. Man should be seized with fear, the earth should tremble, and the heavens rejoice exceedingly, when Christ the Son of the living God descends upon the altar in the hands of the priest. O admirable greatness! O stupendous condescension! O humble sublimity! the Lord of the universe, God, and the Son of God, so abases Himself that for our salvation He hides Himself under the form of a morsel of bread! See, O my brethren, the lowliness of your God! pour out your hearts before Him and humble yourselves, that you may be worthy to be exalted by Him. Do not keep back anything of yourselves, that He Who gives Himself to you without reserve may receive your entire being.

Moreover, I recommend and exhort you in the Lord that in the houses where the brethren dwell, there be only one Mass celebrated each day, according to the rite of the holy Roman Church. If there be many priests in one place, let them charitably be contented to hear the Mass of one, for Our Lord Jesus Christ fills all with His grace who are worthy of it, both those who are present and those who are absent. Although He is present in many places, He is still undivided, He changes not; but He works ever according to His blessed Will, in union with the Father and the Holy Ghost, the Paraclete, for ever and ever. Amen.

LETTER XIII.

To all Clerics.

To my Reverend Masters, all the clerics of the whole world, who live according to the rules of the Catholic Faith, little Brother Francis, their least servant, greeting, with all possible reverence, and humbly kissing their feet.

Since I am become a debtor to all, but cannot now, on account of my infirmities, address you personally, I implore you to receive with all love and charity this admonition and instruction, which I write to you in few words. Consider, O clerics, the great sin and ignorance of which some are guilty towards the Sacred Body and Blood of Our Lord Jesus Christ, His holy Name, and written Words, by which His Body is consecrated; for we know that the Body of Jesus Christ is not present until His Sacred Words are pronounced. We have nothing, and can see nothing corporally of God in this world, except the Body and Blood of Jesus Christ, His holy Name and Words, by which we were created, and by which we have been restored from death to life. Let all those who minister in these most holy Mysteries, and especially those who do so carelessly, consider well within themselves whether the chalices, corporals, and linen which are used in the most adorable Sacrifice of the Body and Blood of Christ, be in a becoming state; whether Our Lord is not left in an improper place, carried about disrespectfully, received unworthily, and indiscreetly given to others. Sometimes even His holy Name and His written Word are trampled under foot, for the animal man cannot understand the things of God. Shall we not be moved to grief by this when we consider that this sweet Lord places Himself in our hands, and that we daily touch Him and receive Him in our mouth? Do we not know that one day we shall fall into His Hands? Let us then at once courageously correct ourselves of these faults and others; and wherever we find the Sacred Body of Our Lord kept disrespectfully and neglected, let us remove It thence, and securely place It in a carefully prepared tabernacle. And in like manner, if we find the Name or the written Words of Our Lord in unclean places, let us at once collect them, and put them away respectfully. And let us remember that we are bound to observe these things by the commandments of God, and the constitutions of our holy Mother the Church. And let him who neglects this know that he will have to give an account thereof before Our Lord Jesus Christ in the day of judgment. That this writing may be the better observed, let those be blessed by God who cause copies to be made of it. May Our Lord Jesus Christ fill you all, my Masters, with His grace and strength. Amen.

LETTER XIV.

To all the Custodes of the Friars Minor.

To all the Custodes of the Friars Minor who shall receive these letters, Brother Francis, the least of the servants of God, wishes health and peace in the Lord.

Know that there are things great and sublime in the sight of God, which are often considered vile and despicable by men, and there are others considered by men as very precious and important, but which God looks upon as worthless and contemptible. I beseech you, therefore, very earnestly to deliver to Bishops and other ecclesiastics the letters which treat of the most holy Body and Blood of Our Lord, and to bear well in mind the recommendations I have given on that head. I also desire you to give another letter, which I send you, to all governors, councillors, and magistrates, to make at once many copies of it, and to be very assiduous in propagating it among those to whom it is addressed, that so the divine praises may be heard by the people in the streets and public squares. Farewell in the Lord.

LETTER XV.

To the Rulers of the People.

To all those who are in authority, to councillors, judges, and governors of all countries in the world, and to others who may read this letter, Brother Francis, their little unworthy servant, wishes health and peace in the Lord.

Consider and think that the hour of death approaches. I implore you, therefore, with all respect, not to forget the Lord, and not to decline from His commandments on account of the cares and solicitudes of the world which weigh upon you; for those who forget Him, and neglect His commandments are cursed and will be forgotten by Him; when the day of death comes, all that they have will be taken from them, and the wiser and more powerful they have been in this world, the greater torments they will have to endure in hell. For this reason I strongly advise you, my lords, to put aside all worldly cares and solicitudes, and to receive with good dispositions the Sacred Body and Blood of Jesus Christ in remembrance of Him. Watch carefully over your people, and cause them to honour this Lord, and every night let them be reminded by a messenger, or by some other sign, to offer their praises and thanksgivings to God, the Lord of all things. If you neglect this, know that you will have to render an account of it at the day of judgment to your Lord Jesus Christ. Those who keep this writing and put it in practice will assuredly be blessed by God.

LETTER XVI.

To Brother Leo.

BROTHER LEO, thy Brother Francis salutes thee and wishes thee peace.

I speak to thee, my son, as a mother, for all that we said on the road is contained briefly in that one word. If later on thou dost wish to come to me for counsel, I advise thee to come. Whatever thou thinkest thou canst do to please the Lord God, and to follow His example and His poverty, thou mayest do, with the blessing of God and my permission. And if, for the good of thy soul or thy consolation, thou dost wish to come to me, my Leo, come. Farewell in the Lord.

LETTER XVII.

To the Lady Jacoba of Settisoli.

To the Lady Jacoba, handmaid of the Most High, Brother Francis, the little poor one of Jesus Christ, wishes health, and the fellowship of the Holy Ghost in Our Lord Jesus Christ.

Know, my beloved, that Christ the Blessed has revealed to me by His grace that the end of my life is close at hand. If, therefore, thou dost wish to see me alive, hasten as soon as thou hast read this letter to come to St. Mary of the Angels, for if thou come later than Saturday thou wilt not find me in this world. Bring with thee a coarse cloth or shroud in which to envelope my body, and some wax tapers for my burial. I also beg thee to bring some of the food thou wert accustomed to give me when I was ill in Rome.

PART II.

*THE FIRST RULE WHICH THE SERAPHIC PATRIARCH WROTE FOR THE FRIARS MINOR.**

In the Name of the Father, and of the Son, and of the Holy Ghost. Amen.

THIS is the Form of life that Brother Francis besought Pope Innocent to grant and confirm for him, and which the said Pope accordingly granted and approved for him and his brethren both present and future. Brother Francis, and whoever may be at the head of this Order, promises obedience and reverence to our Lord Pope Innocent, and to his successors.

CHAPTER I.

That the Brethren ought to live in Obedience, without Property, and in Chastity.

THE Rule and Form of life of these brethren is this: to live in Obedience and Chastity and without Property,

---

* This First Rule was approved verbally by Pope Innocent III., and afterwards by the Holy Council of Lateran in the year 1215. It did not, however, long remain in force, but was replaced by the Second Rule in the year 1223.

and to follow the doctrine and example of Our Lord Jesus Christ, Who says: 'If thou wilt be perfect, go and sell all that thou hast, and give it to the poor, and thou shalt have treasure in heaven, and come, follow Me.' And: 'If any man will come after Me, let him deny himself, and take up his cross and follow Me.' And again: 'If any man come to Me, and hate not his father, and mother, and wife, and children, and brethren and sisters, yea, and his own life also, he cannot be My disciple. And every one that hath left house, or brethren, or sisters, or father, or mother, or wife, or children, or lands, for My Name's sake, shall receive an hundred-fold, and shall possess life everlasting.'

CHAPTER II.

Of the Reception and Clothing of the Brethren.

IF anyone, moved by the divine inspiration, come to our brethren, desiring to embrace this manner of life, let them receive him charitably, and if he be firmly resolved to undertake our life, let them take great care not to meddle with his temporal concerns, but let them send him as soon as possible to the Minister. Let the Minister receive him kindly, and encourage him, and diligently explain to him the tenour of our Rule. This being done, if he be willing and able, with safety of conscience and without impediment, let him sell all his goods, and endeavour to distribute them to the poor. But let the brethren and their Ministers be careful not to interfere in any way in his affairs. And let them not receive any money, either by themselves or by any person interposed. If, however, they are in want, the brethren may accept other things, money excepted, for the relief of their necessities, like other poor. When the candidate returns, let the Minister grant him the habit of probation for a year; that is to say, two tunics without a hood, a cord, drawers, and a caparon* reaching to the girdle. The year of probation being finished, let him be received to Obedience, after which it shall not be lawful for him to pass to another Order, nor to go about without permission, according to the commandment of our Lord the Pope. If, however, anyone should present himself who cannot without difficulty give away his goods, but has the will to relinquish them, it shall suffice. No one shall be received contrary to the form and institution of our holy Mother the Church.

Those who have promised Obedience may have one tunic with a hood, and one without, if necessity require it, and the cord and drawers. And let all the brethren be clothed with mean garments, and let them be permitted to mend them with sackcloth and other pieces, with the blessing of God, for our Lord says in the Gospel: 'They that are clothed in soft garments are in the houses of kings.' And although they should be called hypocrites, let them not cease to do good. Let them not desire costly garments in this world, that they may be clothed gloriously in the kingdom of heaven.

* The caparon is a hood, not fastened to the habit, and with a piece of cloth attached to it, which hangs down over the chest. This is to distinguish the novices from the professed religious, whose hoods are sewn on to the habit.

CHAPTER III.

Of the Divine Office, and of the Fast.

OUR Lord says: 'This kind of devil is not cast out but by prayer and fasting.' And again: 'When you fast, be not like the hypocrites, sad.' For this reason let all the brethren, both clerics and lay-brothers, recite the Divine Office, the praises and prayers to which they are bound. The clerics shall perform the Office, and say it for the living and the dead, according to the custom of clerics. To satisfy for the defects and negligences of the brethren, let them also say every day the Psalm *Miserere mei Deus*, with *Pater noster*, and for the departed brothers, the Psalm *De Profundis*, with *Pater noster*. And they may have the books necessary to perform their Office. The lay-brothers who know how to read the Psalter may have one. But those who do not know how to read, may not have a book. The lay-brothers indeed shall say: *Credo in Deum*, and twenty-four *Pater nosters* with *Gloria Patri*. For Tierce, Sext and None, for each of these Hours, seven *Pater nosters* with *Gloria Patri;* for Vespers, twelve; for Compline, seven, and *Credo in Deum* with *Gloria Patri;* for the dead, seven *Pater nosters* with *Requiem æternam;* and for the defects and negligences of the brethren, three *Pater nosters* every day.

The brethren shall likewise fast from the Feast of All Saints to the Nativity of Our Lord, and from Epiphany, when Our Lord Jesus Christ began to fast, until Easter. At other times they are not bound to fast according to this Rule, except on Fridays; and they may eat of whatever food is placed before them, according to the holy Gospel.

CHAPTER IV.

Of the Order of the Ministers, and other Brethren.

IN the Name of the Lord: The Friars who are appointed Ministers and servants of the other brethren, wherever they may be, should place them in the Convents where they are to dwell, and should often visit and spiritually console and admonish them. But let all my other blessed brethren diligently obey their Superiors in those things which belong to the salvation of their souls, and are not contrary to our Form of life. Let them observe among themselves what Our Lord says: 'Whatsoever you would that men should do to you, do you also to them,' and what you do not wish done to you, do it not to others. And let the Ministers and servants remember what Our Lord says: 'I came not to be ministered unto, but to minister,' and that to them is committed the care of the souls of their brethren, of whom, if any be lost through their fault and bad example, they will have to give an account to Our Lord Jesus Christ in the day of judgment.

CHAPTER V.

Of the Correction of the Brethren who offend.

THEREFORE take well care of your own souls, and of those of your brethren, for 'it is a fearful thing to fall into the hands of the living God.' However, if the Ministers should command one of the brethren anything contrary to our Rule and the salvation of his soul he is not bound to obey, because that is not obedience in which a fault or sin is committed. Nevertheless, let all the brethren who are subject to the Ministers and Servants of the Friars Minor, consider uprightly and diligently whether they see any one of them walking carnally and not spiritually, according to the perfection of our Rule; and if after three admonitions such an one will not amend, let them, without allowing anything to prevent it, denounce him to the Minister and Servant of the whole Fraternity in the Chapter of Pentecost. Again, if among the brethren, wherever they may be, there should be found one who desires to live according to the flesh, and not according to the spirit, let the religious with whom he dwells admonish, instruct, and correct him humbly and diligently. And if after three admonitions he will not amend, let them send him, or make the matter known to his Minister, who must do with him what he deems most expedient before God. But let all the brethren, as well the Ministers as the others, take care not to be angry nor troubled at the fault or bad example of anyone, for the devil desires to corrupt many by the sin of one; but let them endeavour, as much as possible, to help him who has sinned, remembering that 'he that is whole needs not a physician, but he that is sick.' In like manner let not the brethren desire to have power and authority, especially among themselves, for as Our Lord says in the Gospel: 'The princes of the Gentiles lord it over them: and they that are the greater exercise power upon them.' It shall not be so among the brethren, but whosoever will be the greater among them, let him be their Minister and Servant, and he who is the first, let him be as the last. Let not any brother say or do anything against another, but let them rather in the spirit of charity willingly serve and obey each other. This is the true and holy obedience of Our Lord Jesus Christ. And let all the religious, who in any way whatsoever decline from the commandments of God, and wander from obedience, know that they are cursed out of obedience as long as they remain consciously in that sin. And when they persevere in the commandments of the Lord as they have promised according to the holy Gospel and their Rule, let them know that they stand fast in true obedience, and are blessed by God.

CHAPTER VI.

Of the Recourse the Brethren should have to their Ministers, and that no Brother may be called Prior.

LET the brethren, in whatsoever place they may be, if they cannot observe our manner of life, have recourse as soon as possible to their Minister, making known to him their necessity. And the Minister must endeavour to provide for them, as he would wish to be provided for, if he were in the like case. And let no one be called Prior, but let all in general be called Friars Minor, and be willing to wash each others' feet.

CHAPTER VII.

Of the Manner of Serving and Working.

IN whatever places the brethren may reside for work, or the service of others, let them never be keepers of the chamber, nor cellarers, nor overseers in the houses of those whom they serve, and let them not undertake any employment which might cause scandal, or be injurious to their souls; but let them be inferior and subject to all who are in the said house. And let the brethren who know how to work, labour and exercise themselves in the art they understand, provided it be not unbecoming, nor contrary to the salvation of their souls. For the Prophet says: 'For because thou shalt eat the labour of thy hands, blessed art thou, and it shall be well with thee;' and the Apostle says: 'If any man will not work, neither let him eat.' Let everyone therefore keep steadfast to the art or trade in which he is skilled; and in payment of their labour they may receive all necessary things, but not money; and if they be in want, let them seek for alms like other poor. They may have the tools and implements required for their work. Let all the brethren be diligent in good works, for

St. Jerome says : 'Be always busy in some good work, that the devil may find thee occupied ;' and again, it is written : 'Idleness is an enemy to the soul.' Therefore let the servants of God always persevere in prayer or in some other profitable labour. Let the Brethren take care that wherever they may be, whether in hermitages or in other houses, they never appropriate any place to themselves, nor maintain it to be theirs, and whoever comes to them, either a friend or an enemy, a thief or a robber, let them receive him courteously. Wheresoever the Brethren dwell, let them frequently visit one another, and show respect to one another without murmuring. And let them take care not to appear sad and gloomy like hypocrites, but let them be joyful and contented in the Lord, and becomingly courteous.

CHAPTER VIII.

That the Brethren may not receive Money.

THE LORD commanded His Apostles : 'See that you keep yourselves from all malice and avarice, and from solicitude about the affairs of this world, and the cares of this life.' Therefore let none of the Brethren, wherever they may be, or whithersoever they may go, take or receive money in any manner, nor cause it to be received, either for their clothing, or for books, or as the price of their labours, or, in short, for any reason, except the urgent necessities of the sick Brethren. For we ought to have no more esteem of money than of stones, and the devil seeks to blind those who desire or value it. Let us therefore take care, lest, after having renounced all things, we lose the kingdom of heaven for so small a matter. If we should chance to find money in any place, let us no more regard it than the dust we tread under our feet, for it is 'vanity of vanities, and all vanity.' And if perchance, which God forbid, any religious should have or procure money, except, as before said, for the necessities of the sick, the Brethren shall hold him for a false Brother, a thief, a robber, and one having a purse, unless he become truly penitent. And let the Brethren in nowise receive money, nor cause it to be received, seek it, nor cause it to be sought, for any houses or places, nor let them go with men that seek it for them. But in the places where they are, the Brethren may perform other services which are not contrary to our Rule, with the blessing of God. Nevertheless, in case of manifest necessity, the Brethren may ask alms for the lepers; but let them be very wary of money, and let them likewise take great heed not to search the world for filthy lucre.

CHAPTER IX.

Of the Manner of Asking Alms.

LET all the Brethren strive to imitate the poverty and humility of Our Lord Jesus Christ, and let them remember that we ought to have nothing else in the whole world, as the Apostle says: 'Having food and raiment, let us therewith be content.' And they ought to rejoice when they converse with persons who are mean and despised by the world, with the poor and the weak, with the infirm and lepers, and those who beg in the streets. When it is necessary let them go for alms, and not be ashamed thereof, but rather remember that Our Lord Jesus Christ, the Son of the living and Omnipotent God, set His face as a hard stone, and was not ashamed, but became poor, and a stranger, and lived on alms together with the Blessed Virgin and His Disciples. When men treat them with contempt, and deny them an alms, let them give thanks for this to God, because for these reproaches they shall receive great honour before the tribunal of Our Lord Jesus Christ; and let them know that the injuries they undergo shall not be imputed to those who suffer them, but to those who offer them. Alms is a right and an inheritance due to the poor, and which Our Lord Jesus Christ purchased for us. The Brethren who labour in seeking alms will have a great recompense thereof, and they will procure merit for those who give to them; for all that men do in this world shall perish, but for their charity and alms-deeds they will be rewarded by God.

Let the Brethren make known their wants to one another with confidence, in order that they may relieve and minister to one another. And let everyone love and nourish his Brother as a mother loves and nourishes her own son, in so far as God gives them grace to do so. 'Let not him that eateth, despise him that eateth not; and he that eateth not, let him not judge him that eateth.' And when necessity shall arise, it is lawful for all the Brethren, wherever they may be, to eat of any such food as men can eat, as Our Lord said of David, who ate the bread of Proposition which it was only lawful for the priests to eat. Let them also remember what Our Lord says: 'Take heed to yourselves, lest perhaps your hearts be overcharged with surfeiting and drunkenness, and the cares of this life: and that day come upon you suddenly. For as a snare shall it come upon all that sit upon the face of the whole earth.' Nevertheless in time of manifest necessity let them all act as their need shall require, and as Our Lord shall inspire them, for necessity has no law.

CHAPTER X.

Of the Sick Brethren.

IF one of the Brethren fall sick, wherever he may be, let the others not leave him alone, but let there always be with him one or more Brothers, according to necessity, who may serve him as they would wish to be served. But in case of urgent necessity, they may commit him to some person who will take care of him in his infirmity. And I beseech the sick Brother to give thanks to his Creator for all things, and to desire to be as God wills him to be, whether sick or well; for those whom the Lord hath predestined to eternal life, are ordinarily disciplined by Him with the rod of afflictions and infirmities, and the spirit of compunction; as He says in the Apocalypse: 'Such as I love I rebuke and chastise.' If, however, he be disquieted and angry either against God or against the Brothers, or eagerly seek for remedies, desiring too much to deliver his body which is soon to die, and which is an enemy to the soul, this comes from an evil source; he is carnal, and seems not to be one of the Brethren, because he loves his body more than his soul.

CHAPTER XI.

That the Brethren ought not to be Calumniators nor Detractors, but ought to love one another.

LET the Brethren take care not to calumniate anyone, nor to contend in words, but let them study to keep silence as far as God gives them the grace. Let them also not dispute among themselves nor with others, but let them be the first to answer with humility, saying: 'We are useless servants.' And let them not be angry, for 'Whosoever is angry with his brother shall be in danger of the judgment. And whosoever shall say to his brother, Raca, shall be in danger of the council. And whosoever shall say, Thou fool, shall be in danger of hell fire.' But let them love one another, as Our Lord says: 'This is My commandment, that you love one another, as I have loved you;' and let them show their love by the works they do for each other, according as the Apostle says: 'Let us not love in word and in tongue, but in deed and in truth.' Let them not speak evil of any, nor murmur, nor be detractors, for it is written: 'Whisperers and detractors are hateful to God.' Let them show modesty and meekness to all men, neither judging nor condemning any. And, as Our Lord says, let them not pay attention to the small sins of others, but rather let them ponder on their own in the bitterness of their soul. Let them strive to enter in at the narrow gate, for Our Lord says: 'How narrow is the gate, and strait is the way that leadeth to life, and few there are that find it!'

CHAPTER XII.

That the Brethren must avoid the Sight and Company of Women.

LET all the Brethren, wherever they may be, carefully avoid any unbecoming looks, and company of women, and let them never converse with them alone. The priests may speak with them modestly, in order to give them penance and spiritual counsel. Let no woman whatsoever be received to obedience by any Brother, but he may give her spiritual counsel to do penance where she wills. Let us all carefully watch over ourselves, and keep our members in subjection, for the Lord says: 'Whosoever shall look on a woman to lust after her, hath already committed adultery with her in his heart.'

CHAPTER XIII.

Of the Punishment of Fornication.

IF any Brother, by the instigation of the devil, commit a sin of the flesh, let him be entirely deprived of the habit which he has defiled by his crime, and let him be altogether expelled from our Order, and let him go to do penance for his sins.

CHAPTER XIV.

In what Manner the Brethren are to go through the World.

WHEN the Brothers travel through the world, let them carry nothing by the way, neither bag, nor purse, nor bread, nor money, nor a staff. And into whatever house they enter, let them first say, 'Peace be to this house;' and abiding in the same house, let them eat and drink what things are there. Let them not resist evil, but if anyone strike them on one cheek, let them turn to him the other; and if anyone take away their garment and tunic, let them not forbid him. Let them give to all who ask of them, and if anyone despoil them of what they have, let them not ask it of him again.

CHAPTER XV.

That the Brethren may not keep Horses nor ride.

I COMMAND all my Brothers, both clerics and lay-brothers, that when they travel through the world, or reside in any place, they never keep in any way whatever, either with them, or with others, any kind of beast of burden; nor is it lawful for them to ride unless compelled by infirmity or great necessity.

CHAPTER XVI.

Of the Brethren who may go among the Saracens and other Infidels.

OUR LORD said: 'Behold I send you as sheep in the midst of wolves. Be ye therefore wise as serpents, and simple as doves.' Therefore, if any of the Brethren, moved by divine inspiration, should wish to go among the Saracens and other infidels, let them go with the permission of their Minister. And let the Minister not refuse, but give them leave, if he sees they are fit to be sent, for in this matter he will have to render an account to God if he acts indiscreetly. The Brethren who go, may conduct themselves in two ways among the infidels. The one is not to contend or dispute with them, but to be 'subject to every human creature for God's sake,' yet confessing themselves to be Christians. The other way is, when they see it is pleasing to God, to preach the Divine Word, and teach men to believe in Almighty God, Father, Son, and Holy Ghost, the Creator of all things, in Our Lord the Redeemer and Saviour, and that they should become Christians by being baptized; because, 'unless a man be born again of water and the Holy Ghost, he cannot enter into the kingdom of heaven.' These and other truths they may teach them, as it shall please God, for Our Lord says in the Gospel: 'Every one therefore that shall confess Me before men, I will also confess him before My Father Who is in heaven;' and 'he that shall be ashamed of Me and My Words, the Son of Man also will be ashamed of him, when He shall come in the glory of His Father with the holy angels.' Let all the Brethren, wherever they may be, remember that they have renounced themselves, and have given their bodies to Our Lord Jesus Christ; and, therefore, for the love of Him, they ought to expose themselves to their enemies both visible and invisible, for Our Lord says: 'He that shall lose his life for My sake shall save it. Blessed are they who suffer persecution for justice' sake, for theirs is the kingdom of heaven. If they have persecuted Me, they will persecute you. If they shall persecute you in one city, fly to another. Blessed are ye when they shall revile you, and persecute you, and speak all that is evil against you, untruly, for My sake; be glad and rejoice in that day, for your reward is very great in heaven. I say to you, my friends, Fear not them that kill the body, and after that have nothing more that they can do. Yea, I say unto you, fear them not. In your patience, you shall possess your souls. He who shall persevere to the end shall be saved.'

CHAPTER XVII.

Of the Preachers.

LET no Brother preach contrary to the form and institution of the holy Church, nor without the leave of his Superior. And let the Superior take care that he does not grant this leave indiscreetly. Nevertheless, let all the Brethren preach by their works. Let no Minister or Brother appropriate to himself the office and ministry of preaching, but let him give it up without any contradiction immediately he is commanded. I beseech (in the charity which God is) all my ¡Brethren, whether they preach, pray, or labour, whether they be clerics or lay-brothers, that they study to humble themselves in all things, and that they never glory, nor rejoice, nor inwardly exalt themselves for their good words and works, nor indeed for any good which God may sometimes say or do, or operate in them or by them, according to what Our Lord says: 'In this rejoice not, that the spirits are subject unto you.' Let us know for certain that nothing belongs to us but our vices and sins, and we ought much more to rejoice when we fall into divers temptations, and bear some afflictions of soul or body in this world, for the sake of eternal life. Let us, my Brethren, avoid all pride and vainglory. Let us keep ourselves from the wisdom of this world, and the prudence of the flesh. The spirit of the world cares much for words, but little for works; and it seeks not religion and sanctity of the heart, but a religion and sanctity which may appear before men; and these are they of whom Our Lord says: 'Amen I say unto you, they have received their reward.' But the spirit of the Lord wishes the flesh to be mortified and despised, and to be considered vile, abject, and contemptible; it seeks for humility and patience, and pure simplicity, and true peace of heart, and desires above all things to have Divine fear, and Divine wisdom, and the Divine love of the Father, Son, and Holy Spirit. And let us refer all good to the most High and Supreme God, let us acknowledge that all good belongs to Him, and let us give thanks for all to Him from Whom all good proceeds. May He, the Most High and Sovereign, Only and True God have and receive all honour and reverence, and all praises and benedictions, and all thanks and all glory, for to Him all good belongs, Who alone is Good. And when we see or hear any evil said or done blasphemously against God, let us bless and thank and praise Him Who is Blessed for ever and ever. Amen.

CHAPTER XVIII.

How the Ministers are to Meet together.

THE Provincial Ministers may assemble their Brethren in some convenient place every year on the Feast of St. Michael the Archangel, that they may treat together of what regards the service of God. And let all the Ministers who are in countries beyond the sea and beyond the Alps come once in three years, and the other Ministers once every year, to the Chapter on the Feast of Pentecost, at St. Mary of the Angels, unless it be otherwise ordered by the Minister-General.

CHAPTER XIX.

That all the Brethren must be true Catholics.

LET all the Brethren be Catholics, and live and speak in a Catholic manner. And if anyone should err from the Catholic Faith and morals in word or in deed, and will not amend, let him be altogether expelled from our Fraternity. Let us acknowledge all priests and religious as our Superiors in what regards the good of souls, if they do not proceed against our Rule, and let us reverence their office and order and administration in the Lord.

CHAPTER XX.

Of the Confession of the Brethren and of the Reception of the Body and Blood of Our Lord Jesus Christ.

LET my Brethren, blessed of God, both clerics and lay-brothers, confess their sins to priests of our Order, and if they cannot do this, let them confess to any other discreet and Catholic priests, believing and hoping firmly that from whatever priests they may receive penance and absolution, their sins will undoubtedly be pardoned, provided they take care to perform humbly and faithfully the penance enjoined them. If, however, they cannot have a priest, let them confess their sins to a Brother, as the Apostle St. James says: 'Confess your sins one to another;' but let them not on this account fail to have recourse to a priest when they can, for to priests alone is given the power of binding and loosing. And being thus contrite, and having confessed, let them receive with great humility and reverence the Body and Blood of Our Lord Jesus Christ, calling to mind what He Himself says : ' He that eateth My flesh and drinketh My Blood hath everlasting life,' and ' Do this for a commemoration of Me.'

CHAPTER XXI.

Of Praising God, and of the Exhortation which all the Brethren may make.

THIS praise and exhortation all my Brethren may make, with the blessing of God, whenever they please, and with whatever persons they may be. Fear, honour, praise, and bless God. Give thanks and adore the Lord God Almighty in Trinity and Unity, Father, Son, and Holy Ghost, the Creator of all things. Repent and bring forth worthy fruits of penance, for know that we must soon die. 'Give and it shall be given unto you; forgive, and you shall be forgiven ;' and if you do not forgive, the Lord will not forgive your sins. Blessed are they who shall die penitent, for they shall enter the kingdom of heaven, but woe to those who die impenitent, for they shall be the children of the devil whose works they have done, and they shall go into everlasting fire. Beware, and abstain from all sin, and persevere in good to the end.

CHAPTER XXII.

Of the Admonition of the Brethren.

LET us all, my Brethren, give heed to what Our Lord says: 'Love your enemies, and do good to them that hate you.' For Our Lord Jesus, Whose footsteps we ought to follow, called His betrayer 'Friend,' and offered Himself willingly to His executioners. Therefore all those who unjustly inflict upon us tribulations, anguish, shame and injuries, sorrows and torments, martyrdom and death, are our friends whom we ought to love much, because we shall gain eternal life by those things which they make us suffer. And let us hate our body with its vices and sins, because by living in pleasures it wishes to rob us of the love of Our Lord Jesus Christ and eternal life, and to lose itself with everything else in hell. Through our own fault we are corrupt, miserable, and averse to good, but prompt and willing to do evil; for, as Our Lord says in the Gospel: 'From within, out of the heart of men, proceed evil thoughts, adulteries, fornications, murders, thefts, covetousness, wickedness, deceit, lasciviousness, an evil eye, blasphemy, pride, foolishness.' All these evil things come from the heart of man, and these are what defile the soul. But now, after having renounced the world, we have nothing else to do but to endeavour to accomplish the Will of God, and to please Him. Let us take great care that we be not like the wayside, or the thorny or stony ground, according to what the Lord says in the Gospel: 'The seed is the word of God. And they by the wayside are they that hear: then the devil cometh, and taketh the word out of their heart, lest believing they should be saved. Now they upon the rock are they who, when they hear, receive the word with joy;' but when tribulation and persecution arise on account of the word, they are immediately scandalised, 'and these have no roots,' but are mere time-servers, ' for they believe for awhile, and in time of temptation they fall away.' 'And that which fell among thorns are they who have heard the word of God, and the cares and solicitude of this world, the vanity of riches and the desire of other things entering in choke the word, and it becomes unfruitful. But that on the good ground, are they who, in a good and very good heart, hearing the word keep it, and bring forth fruit in patience.' For this reason, my Brethren, let us, as Our Lord says, 'leave the dead to bury their dead,' and let us be much on our guard against the malice and cunning of Satan, who desires that man should not give his heart and mind to the Lord his God, but goes about seeking to seduce him under pretext of some reward or benefit, to efface the words and precepts of God from his memory, and to blind his heart by the cares and business of the world, so that he himself may dwell there, as Our Lord says: 'When the unclean spirit is gone out of a man, he walketh through places without water seeking rest, and not finding, he saith: I will return into my house whence I came out. And when he is come he findeth it swept and garnished. Then he goeth and taketh with him seven other spirits more wicked than himself, and entering in they dwell there. And the last state of that man becomes worse than the first. Therefore, let us watch diligently that we do not separate our souls from God for the sake of any gain, or favour, or business; but I beseech all the Brethren, both the Ministers and others, in the charity which God is, that, overcoming all obstacles, and putting aside all care and solicitude, they strive in the best manner they are able, to serve, love, and honour the Lord God, with a clean heart and a pure mind, which is what He desires above all things. Let us always make in our hearts a tabernacle and dwelling-place for Him, Who is the Lord God Omnipotent, Father, Son, and Holy Ghost, Who says: 'Watch, therefore, and pray at all times that you may be found worthy to fly from all the evils that are to come, and to stand before the Son of Man.' And when you pray, say, 'Our Father Who art in heaven,' and let us adore Him with a pure heart. 'We ought always to pray and not to faint,' for the Father seeks for such adorers. 'God is a Spirit, and they that adore Him, must adore Him in spirit and in truth.' Let us have recourse to Him as the Father and Pastor of our souls, for He says: 'I am the Good Shepherd, Who feed My sheep, and I lay down My life for My flock.' You, indeed, are all Brethren. 'And call none your Father upon earth: for One is your Father Who is in heaven. Neither be ye called Masters, for One is your Master, even Christ. If you abide in Me, and My words abide in you, whatever you wish you shall ask, and it shall be done unto you. Wheresoever two or three are gathered together in My Name, there am I in the midst of them. Behold I am with you always, even unto the consummation of the world. The words that I speak unto you are spirit and life. I am the Way, the Truth, and the Life.' Let us therefore hold fast this true way, the life and doctrine and holy Gospel of Him, Who deigned to manifest to us His Father and His Name, saying : 'Father, I have manifested Thy Name to the men Thou gavest Me, for the words Thou gavest Me I have given to them, and they have received them, and have known truly that I came forth from Thee, and they have believed that Thou hast sent Me. I pray for them, not for the world, but for them whom Thou hast given Me in Thy Name, that they may be one, as We are One. These things I have spoken in the world that they may have joy in themselves. I have given them Thy word, and the world hath hated them, because they are not of the world, as I am not of the world. I pray not that Thou shouldst take them out of the world, but that Thou shouldst keep them from evil. Sanctify them in truth. Thy word is truth. As Thou hast sent Me into the world, I have sent them into the world, and for them do I sanctify Myself, that they may be sanctified in truth. And not for them only do I pray, but for them also who through their word shall believe in Me, that they may be made perfect in one, and that the world may know that Thou hast sent Me, and hast loved them, as Thou hast also loved Me. I have made known Thy Name to them, that the love wherewith Thou hast loved Me may be in them, and I in them. Father, I will that where I am, they also whom Thou hast given Me may be with Me, that they may see Thy glory in Thy Kingdom.'

CHAPTER XXIII.

Prayer and Thanksgiving to God.

ALMIGHTY, most holy, most High and Supreme God, holy Father and just Lord, King of heaven and earth, we give Thee thanks because by Thy holy Will, and by Thy only Son and the Holy Ghost, Thou hast created all things spiritual and corporal, and having made man to Thy image and likeness, didst place him in Paradise, whence he fell by his own fault. And we give Thee thanks because, as by Thy Son Thou didst create us, so by the love with which Thou hast loved us, Thou didst cause Him, true God and true Man, to be born of the most blessed ever-Virgin Mary, and didst will that He should redeem us by His Blood and by His death. We give Thee thanks likewise, because this Thy Son will come again in the glory of His Majesty to condemn the wicked, who have not known Thee, nor done penance for their sins, to eternal fire, and to say to all who have known and adored Thee doing penance, 'Come, ye blessed of My Father, receive the kingdom which has been prepared for you from the beginning of the world.' And since we miserable sinners are not even worthy to name Thee, we humbly beseech Thee that our Lord Jesus Christ Thy beloved Son, in whom Thou art well pleased, and the Holy Ghost, the Paraclete, may give Thee thanks as it pleases Thee and Them, for all Thou hast done for us. Alleluia. And we earnestly beg the glorious and ever-blessed Virgin Mary, blessed Michael, Gabriel, and Raphael, with all the Choirs of the blessed Spirits, Seraphim, Cherubim, Thrones, Dominations, Principalities and Powers, Virtues, Archangels, and Angels; Blessed John the Baptist, John the Evangelist, Peter, Paul, the blessed Patriarchs and Prophets, Innocents, Apostles, Evangelists, Disciples, Martyrs, Confessors, Virgins, blessed Enoch and Elias, and all the Saints who have been, are, and shall be, for Thy love's sake to give worthy thanks for all these things to the most High, Eternal and Living God, together with Our most Blessed Lord Jesus Christ, and the Holy Spirit, for ever and ever, Amen. Alleluia. And we, the Friars Minor, their useless servants, humbly entreat and beseech all who wish to serve God in the holy Catholic and Apostolic Church, priests, deacons, sub-deacons, acolytes, exorcists, lectors, door-keepers, and all clerics; all religious men and women, all youths and children, the poor and needy, kings and princes, labourers and husbandmen, servants and masters, all virgins and married people, laymen and women, young men and old, sick and healthy, small and great, and all tribes and tongues and nations, all men in all the earth, who are and shall be; to persevere in the true Faith, and in doing penance, without which no one can be saved.

Let us all love with all our heart, with all our soul, with all our mind and with all our strength, with all our understanding and with all our powers, with all our might and all our affection, with all our faculties, our desires, and our will, the Lord God, Who has given, and gives to us all, our body, our soul, and our life, Who has created and redeemed us, and by His pure mercy saved us, Who has done and does nothing but good to us, although we are most miserable, wretched, vile, ungrateful, ignorant and wholly evil. Let us desire nothing, wish for nothing, and let nothing please or delight us but our Creator, Redeemer and Saviour, the only and true God, Who is all Good, perfect Good, entire Good, the true and supreme Good, Who alone is good, merciful, kind and gracious, gentle and sweet, Who alone is holy, just, true and upright, Who alone is benign, pure, undefiled, from Whom, through Whom, and in Whom is all mercy, all grace, all glory of all penitents and just men, and of all the Saints rejoicing in heaven. Let nothing therefore hinder us, let nothing separate us, let nothing come between us and God. Therefore let us all, at all times and in all places, daily and hourly, firmly believe, and humbly hold in our hearts, let us love, honour, adore, serve, praise and bless, glorify and exalt, magnify and thank the Most High, Supreme and Eternal God, Three in One, the Father, Son, and Holy Ghost, the Creator of all who believe in Him, hope in Him, and love Him, Who is without beginning or end, immutable and invisible, ineffable, incomprehensible, blessed and worthy of praise, glorious, exalted, sublime, most high, sweet, amiable, lovable, and wholly desirable for ever and ever. Amen.

Exhortation to the Brethren.

IN the Name of the Omnipotent God, I beseech all the Brethren that they understand the tenor and sense of those things that are written in this Rule for the salvation of our souls, and frequently recall them to mind. And I pray to God that He Who is Almighty, Three and One, may bless all who teach, learn, remember and fulfil those things which are there written for our salvation. And I, humbly kissing their feet, entreat all greatly to love, keep, and lay to heart these things; and on the part of Almighty God, and of our Lord the Pope, and by virtue of obedience, I, Francis, strictly command and enjoin that no one diminish anything that is written in this form of life, nor add anything thereunto, and that the Brethren have no other Rule.

Glory be to the Father, and to the Son, and to the Holy Ghost.

As it was in the beginning, is now and ever shall be, world without end. Amen.

THE SECOND RULE, WHICH THE BLESSED FATHER ST. FRANCIS INSTITUTED FOR THE FRIARS MINOR.*

*In the Name of Our Lord,
Here begins the Rule and Form of life of the Friars Minor.*

CHAPTER I.

THE Rule and life of the Friars Minor is this: To observe the holy Gospel of Our Lord Jesus Christ, living in Obedience, without Property, and in Chastity. Brother Francis promises obedience and reverence to Our Lord the Pope Honorius III., and his successors canonically elected, and to the Roman Church; and the other Brothers are bound to obey Brother Francis and his successors.

CHAPTER II.

Of those who desire to embrace this Life, and how they are to be received.

IF any one wishes to embrace this life and comes to our Brethren, let them send him to their Provincial

---

* On the return of the Brethren from the missions on which they had been sent after the General Chapter of 1219, the holy Patriarch, desiring above all things to provide for the stability of his Order by having it more solemnly approved by the Holy See, and understanding it to be the Will of God that the Rule should be abridged, retired to Mount Columbo, near Rieti, where, observing a rigorous fast for forty days, he received by express revelation from Our Lord Himself the following Rule, which was confirmed by Pope Honorius III., and has ever since been observed by the Friars Minor.

Minister, to whom alone, and to no others, is permission granted to receive the Brothers. And let the Minister examine him carefully concerning the Catholic Faith and the Sacraments of the Church. And if he believe all these things and will faithfully confess and steadfastly observe them to the end, and moreover if he have no wife, or if, having one, she has already entered into a Convent, or has given him permission with the authority of the Bishop of the diocese, she having previously made a vow of continence, and being of such an age that no suspicion can be raised against her; then the Minister shall address to him the words of the Holy Gospel:—that he go and sell all that he has, and endeavour to distribute it to the poor; which if he cannot do, his good will shall suffice. And let the Brothers and their Ministers take care not to be solicitous about his temporal affairs, that he may freely dispose of his property as Our Lord may inspire him. If, however, he require counsel, let the Minister have power to send him to some persons fearing God, by whose advice his goods may be distributed to the poor.

Then let them give him the habit of probation—that is, two tunics without the hood, the cord and drawers, and the *Caparone* reaching to the cord, unless it shall sometimes seem good to the Ministers to act otherwise. The year of his probation being finished, let him be received to Obedience, promising always to observe this Rule and Form of life. And according to the commandment of our Lord the Pope, under no pretext whatsoever shall it be lawful for him to leave this Order; for according to the Holy Gospel: 'No man having put his hand to the plough and looking back, is fit for the kingdom of God.' Let those who have already promised Obedience have one tunic with the hood, and another (if they wish) without the hood. And those who are compelled by necessity may wear shoes and stockings. All the Brethren shall be clothed with mean garments, and they may mend them with sackcloth and other pieces, with the blessing of God. And I admonish and exhort them not to despise nor judge those whom they see dressed in soft and gay clothing, and who use delicate food and drink, but rather let everyone judge and despise himself.

CHAPTER III.
Of the Divine Office and of Fasting, and in what manner the Brethren are to go about in the world.

LET the clerics recite the Divine Office according to the custom of the holy Roman Church, except the Psalter; wherefore they may have Breviaries. But let the lay-brothers say twenty-four *Pater nosters* for Matins, and five for Lauds; for each of the Little Hours, viz.: Prime, Tierce, Sext, and None, seven, for Vespers twelve, and for Compline seven, and let them pray for the dead. Let the Brethren fast from the Feast of All Saints until the Nativity of Our Lord. But with regard to the Lent that begins at the Epiphany and lasts for the forty days which Our Lord consecrated by His own fast, let those who keep it voluntarily be blessed by God, and let those who will not keep it, not be obliged. But all shall fast during the other Lent, until Our Lord's Resurrection. At other times they are not bound to fast, except on Fridays, but in time of manifest necessity the Brothers are not bound to corporal fasting.

I counsel, exhort, and admonish my Brothers in Our Lord Jesus Christ, that when they go about the world they neither contend nor dispute, nor judge others; but that they be meek, peaceful and modest, gentle and humble, speaking courteously to everyone, as is becoming. They must not ride unless compelled by manifest necessity or infirmity. Into whatsoever house they enter, let them first say : ' Peace be to this house;' and according to the Holy Gospel they are permitted to eat of whatever food may be set before them.

CHAPTER IV.
That the Brethren may not receive Money.

I STRICTLY command all the Brothers that they by no means receive money, either by themselves or through the medium of others. Nevertheless, the Ministers and Custodes, and they only, shall take special care to provide for the necessities of the sick, and the clothing of the Brethren, through the means of their spiritual friends, according to seasons, places, and cold climates, as they shall see to be expedient ; this always excepted, that, as before said, they may not receive money.

CHAPTER V.
Of the Manner of Working.

THE Brothers to whom God has given the grace of

manner, that avoiding idleness, which is an enemy of the soul, they do not extinguish the spirit of devotion and holy prayer, to which all temporal things ought to be subservient. In payment for their labour they may receive things necessary for the support of the body, both for themselves and their Brethren, but not money; and this they should do humbly, as becomes the servants of God, and the followers of most holy Poverty.

CHAPTER VI.

That the Brethren shall appropriate nothing to themselves; of Seeking Alms, and of the Sick Brethren.

LET the Brothers appropriate nothing to themselves, neither house, place, nor any other thing, but as pilgrims and strangers in this world, serving the Lord in poverty and humility, let them go for alms with confidence. Nor ought they to be ashamed thereof, since Our Lord made Himself poor in this world for our sakes. This is the sublime height of most holy Poverty which has constituted you, my beloved Brethren, kings and heirs of the heavenly kingdom, has made you poor in temporal things, and has exalted you in virtue. Let this be your portion, which will lead you into the land of the living, to which, beloved Brethren, strictly adhering, never desire to have anything else under heaven, for the sake of Our Lord Jesus Christ.

Wherever the Brethren may be, or may meet with other Brothers, there let them mutually serve one another, and confidently make known their wants to each other; for if a mother loves and nourishes her son according to the flesh, how much more diligently ought everyone to love and nourish his spiritual Brother. And if any of them fall sick, the other Brothers ought to serve him as they would wish to be served themselves.

CHAPTER VII.
Of Penance to be imposed on the Brethren.

IF any Brother, by the instigation of the enemy, sin mortally in any of those sins which the Brothers are ordered to refer to the Provincial Ministers, the said Brother is bound to have recourse to these Superiors as quickly as possible, and without delay. And if the said Ministers be priests, they shall mercifully enjoin him penance; but if they be not priests, they shall cause it to be enjoined him by others who are priests of the Order, as in the sight of God shall seem to them most expedient. And they shall take care not to be angry or troubled at the sins of anyone, for anger and trouble hinder charity in themselves and others.

CHAPTER VIII.
Of the Election of the Minister General of this Fraternity, and of the Chapter of Pentecost.

THE Brethren are obliged always to have one of the Friars of this Order for the Minister General and Servant of the whole Fraternity; and him they are strictly bound to obey. When he dies, his successor shall be elected by the Provincial Ministers and the Custodes in the Chapter of Pentecost, at which Chapter the Provincial Ministers are always bound to assemble, wherever the Minister General shall appoint. And this they shall do once in every three years, or at other periods longer or shorter according as the aforesaid Minister shall ordain. And if at any time it shall seem to all the Provincial Ministers and Custodes, that the aforesaid Minister General is not qualified for the service and general welfare of the Brethren, the said Brothers to whom the election is committed are bound to elect another in the Name of the Lord. Moreover, after the Chapter of Pentecost, the Provincial Ministers and the Custodes may each, if they wish, and deem it expedient, convoke a Chapter of the Brethren in their Custodies once in the same year.

CHAPTER IX.

Of the Preachers.

LET the Brethren not preach in the Diocese of any Bishop, when the said Bishop has opposed their doing so. And let no Brother by any means dare to preach to the people unless he have been examined and approved by the Minister General of this Fraternity, and the office of preacher have been bestowed upon him. I also admonish and exhort these same Brothers that in the sermons they preach, their words be well-considered and simple, for the benefit and edification of the people, and that they speak to them of vices and virtues, of punishment and glory in few words, because Our Lord when on earth used brevity of speech.

CHAPTER X.

Of the Admonition and Correction of the Brethren.

LET the Brothers who are the Ministers and Servants of the other Brethren visit and admonish them, and humbly and charitably correct them, not commanding them anything contrary to the good of their soul or our Form of life. But let the Brothers who are subject remember that for the love of God they have renounced their own will. Therefore I strictly command them to obey their Ministers in all things which they have promised the Lord to observe, and which are not against their own soul and the Rule. And in whatever place those Brothers may be, who know and acknowledge that they cannot observe the Rule spiritually, they may and ought to have recourse to their Ministers. Let the Ministers, indeed, receive them kindly and charitably, and show themselves so familiar with them, that they may speak and act with them as masters with their servants ; for so it ought to be, the Ministers ought to be the servants of all the Brethren. I exhort and admonish my Brothers in the Lord Jesus Christ, that they carefully avoid all pride, vainglory, envy, avarice, care and solicitude for the things of the world, detraction and murmuring. Let those who cannot read not seek to learn, but let them consider that they should above all things desire to have the spirit of the Lord, and its holy operation, to pray to Him always with a pure heart, to have humility and patience in persecutions and infirmities, and to love those who ill-treat, reprove, and contradict them, for Our Lord says: 'Love your enemies, and pray for those who persecute and calumniate you. Blessed are they who suffer persecution for justice' sake, for theirs is the kingdom of heaven. He who perseveres to the end, the same shall be saved.'

CHAPTER XI.

That the Brethren may not enter the Convents of Nuns.

I STRICTLY command all the Brethren that they do not hold any suspicious intercourse or counsel with women, nor enter the Convents of nuns, except those to whom special licence is granted by the Apostolic See. Nor shall they be godfathers to men or women, lest on this account any scandal should arise among the Brethren or concerning them.

CHAPTER XII.

Of those who go among the Saracens, and other Infidels.

ANY of the Brethren who, moved by the Divine inspiration, desire to go among the Saracens and other infidels, must ask leave from their Provincial Ministers. But the Ministers shall give permission to none but those whom they deem fit to be sent. I command the Ministers under obedience that they ask of our Lord the Pope one of the Cardinals of the holy Roman Church, who may be the governor, protector, and reformer of this Fraternity, that being always subject and submissive at the feet of the same holy Church, and steadfast in the Catholic Faith, we may observe the poverty and humility of Our Lord Jesus Christ, and the holy Gospel, as we have firmly promised.

PANEGYRIC

Which the Holy Father St. Francis made on the Second Rule of the Friars Minor.

MY Brothers and most dear Children! God has bestowed on us a signal favour in granting us this holy Rule; for it is the book of life, the hope of salvation, the pledge of glory, the marrow of the Gospel, the way of the Cross, the state of perfection, the key of Paradise, and the bond of an eternal alliance. No one among you is ignorant of the advantages of holy Religion. As the enemy and adversary of our souls is so exceedingly clever in inventing and executing his malicious designs, and in laying all sorts of snares to injure us, there are many whom he would lead into great danger, unless they were defended by the shield of Religion. Study well, then, your holy Rule, as well to sweeten your trials, as to remind you of the vow you have made to keep it. Entertain yourselves often with it in the interior of your hearts, and in order to accomplish it carry it always with you, and, above all, hold it in your hands at the hour of death.

RULE WHICH THE HOLY FATHER ST. FRANCIS WROTE FOR THE RELIGIOUS OF ST. CLARE.*

CHAPTER I.

In the Name of Our Lord. Amen.

HERE begins the Rule and Form of life of the Order of the Poor sisters, which is this: to observe the holy Gospel of Our Lord Jesus Christ, living in Obedience, without Property, and in Chastity.

Clare, unworthy handmaid of Christ, promises Obedience and reverence to the Lord Pope Innocent, to his successors canonically elected, and to the Roman Church. And as, in the beginning of her conversion, she with her Sisters promised Obedience to Brother Francis, so does she promise to observe the same inviolably to his successors. And the other Sisters are bound always to obey the successors of Brother Francis, and likewise Sister Clare, and all other Abbesses, who, being canonically elected, shall succeed her.

CHAPTER II.

In what Manner Persons are to be Received.

IF anyone, moved by Divine inspiration, present herself to the Sisters, desiring to embrace this form of life, let the Abbess be bound to ask the consent of

---

* This Rule is almost exactly the same (*mutatis mutandis*) as the 2nd Rule of the Friars Minor. A few verbal alterations were made in it by St. Clare after the death of the holy Patriarch.

all the Sisters; and if the greater part give their consent, she may receive her, with the permission of the Lord Cardinal Protector. If it seem fitting to receive her, let the Abbess examine her carefully, or cause her to be examined, concerning the Catholic Faith and the Sacraments of the Church; and if she believe all these things, and is resolved faithfully to confess and steadfastly to observe the same to the end; moreover, if she have no husband, or, having one, if he, with the authority of his Diocesan Bishop, have already entered some religious Order, and have made a vow of chastity; and, in fine, if she be not too advanced in age, nor subject to any infirmity or weakness of mind which might be an impediment to her observance of this manner of life; then let the tenour of your Rule be clearly explained to her. If she be found capable, let the words of the holy Gospel be proposed to her, that she go and sell all that she hath, and endeavour to distribute it to the poor; which if she cannot do, her goodwill shall suffice. Let the Abbess and her Sisters take care not to be solicitous about her temporal goods, in order that she may freely do with them what Our Lord shall inspire her. If, however, she should ask their advice, let them send her to some prudent persons who fear God, by whose counsel her goods may be distributed to the poor.

Then, her hair having been cut off round, and her secular dress laid aside, let them grant her three tunics and a mantle, after which time let her not be permitted to go out of the Convent, except for a profitable, manifest and reasonable cause. When the year of probation is expired, let her be received to Obedience, promising to observe perpetually your Form of life and poverty. No one shall receive the veil during her year of probation. The Sisters may also have little mantles for the convenience and propriety of their service and labour; and, in fine, let the Abbess provide them discreetly with suitable garments, according to the quality of the persons, places, seasons and cold climates, as she shall see it to be expedient.

Let the young persons who are received into the Convent before they have attained the requisite age have their hair cut off round; and having laid aside their secular dress, let them be clothed with the same cloth as the religious, according to the discretion of the Abbess; and when they have attained the proper age, let them take the habit, and make their profession as the others do. Both for these and for the other novices the Abbess shall carefully provide a mistress from among the most discreet of the whole Convent, who shall diligently instruct them in holy conversation and edifying manners, according to the form of your profession. The above-mentioned form shall be observed in the examination and reception of the Sisters who serve outside the Monastery, and these Sisters may wear shoes. No one may reside with the Sisters in the Convent, unless she has been received according to the form of your profession.

I admonish, beseech and exhort my Sisters, for the love of the most Holy and Sweet Child Jesus, Who was wrapped in poor swaddling-clothes and laid in a manger, and for the love of His most holy Mother, that they be always clothed with poor garments.

CHAPTER III.

Of the Divine Office, of the Fast, of Confession and Holy Communion.

THE Sisters who are acquainted with letters shall recite the Divine Office according to the custom of the Friars-Minor, wherefore they may have Breviaries, and they shall read their Office without singing. Those who at times for a reasonable cause cannot read their Office, may say it in *Pater-nosters*, like those Sisters who cannot read. They shall say twenty-four *Pater-nosters* for Matins, five for Lauds, seven for each of the Hours, Prime, Tierce, Sext and None, twelve for Vespers, and seven for Complin. For the Office of the Dead they shall also say seven *Pater-nosters* with *Requiem æternam*, *etc.*, for Vespers, and twelve for Matins. The Sisters who can read are bound to recite the Office of the Dead, and when any religious of your Monastery departs this life, they shall say fifty *Pater-nosters*. The Sisters shall fast at all times; but on the Nativity of Our Lord they may take two repasts, on whatever day it falls. The Abbess may, nevertheless, when she judges it expedient, charitably dispense with the young, the weak, and those who serve outside the Monastery; but in time of manifest necessity the Sisters are not bound to corporal fasting.

Let the Sisters, with the leave of the Abbess, confess at least twelve times in the year, and then let them take care not to mingle any words which do not regard confession and the salvation of their souls. Let them communicate six times in the year, namely, on the Nativity of Our Lord, on Maundy Thursday, on Easter Sunday, on the Assumption of the Blessed Virgin, and on All Saint's Day.* The Chaplain may enter the Monastery in order to communicate the sick Sisters.

CHAPTER IV.

Of the Election of the Abbess.

IN the election of the Abbess, the Sisters are bound to observe the canonical form. They shall endeavour to have present the Minister-General, or the Provincial of the Friars Minor, who, with the word of God, may exhort them to a perfect concord, and to seek only the common good in the election. No one shall be elected who is not professed; and if such an one were elected, or otherwise appointed Abbess, let the Sisters not obey her unless she first make profession of the form of your poverty; and when the Abbess dies, they shall elect another in her place. If at any time it shall seem to all the Sisters that the Abbess elected is not qualified for their service and the common good, they are bound to elect another as Abbess and Mother as soon as possible, according to the above-mentioned form.

Let her who is elected consider well the burden she has taken upon her, and Who He is to whom she must render an account of the flock committed to her

---

* It must be remembered that in the time of St. Francis, the custom of frequent Communion did not exist in the Church. The religious of St. Clare now communicate much more frequently.

care. Let her endeavour to surpass the others in virtue and holy behaviour, rather than in her Office, that the Sisters, animated by her example, may obey her more through love than fear. Let her avoid particular friendships, lest by showing too much affection for some, she should cause scandal among the others. Let her console the afflicted, and be the last refuge of those in tribulation; lest the weak, if they do not find comfort from her in their troubles, should be overcome by the sadness of despair. Let her conform to the Community in all things, but especially in the church, dormitory, refectory, infirmary, and in her dress; and let her Vicaress be obliged to do the same.

Let the Abbess be bound to assemble her Sisters in Chapter at least once a week, where she, as well as they, ought humbly to accuse themselves of their public faults and negligences. Then also let the Abbess confer with her Sisters concerning those things that are necessary to be treated of for the welfare and spiritual advantage of the Community, for Our Lord often reveals to the least what is best to be done. Let no important debt be contracted without the consent of all the Sisters, and for a manifest necessity, and that by means of a procurator. Let the Abbess and Sisters take care not to receive any deposit in their Convent, for scandals and troubles often arise from so doing.

In order also to preserve the unity of mutual love and peace, all the Officials of the Monastery shall be elected by the common consent of all the Sisters; and in this manner they shall choose eight at least of the most discreet, with whom the Abbess is bound always to take counsel in those things which require it in your Form of life. The Sisters may, and even ought sometimes, if it shall seem to them useful and expedient, to change those in office, and the discreets, and to elect others in their place.

CHAPTER V.

Of Silence, and of the Manner of Speaking at the Grate, and in the Parlour.

LET the Sisters keep silence from the Hour of Compline until Tierce, except those who serve outside the Monastery. Let them also continually keep silence in the church, dormitory, and refectory, during the repast only, but not in the infirmary, where the Sisters may always speak discreetly for the consolation and service of the sick. They may even, at all times and in all places, say what is necessary, briefly, and in a low voice.

It is not lawful for the Sisters to speak in the parlour or at the grate without the permission of the Abbess, or her Vicaress. Those who have leave to speak in the parlour may not do so except in the presence of two Sisters, who must hear what is said; but with regard to the grate, let none presume to go there unless there be present at least three Sisters, appointed by the Abbess or her Vicaress, and chosen from among the discreets who have been elected by all the Sisters for the council of the Abbess. The Abbess and Vicaress are bound to observe this manner of speaking as much as possible. They shall speak very rarely at the grate, but at the door it shall never be permitted. At the grate a curtain shall be placed within, which must never be removed, except when the Word of God is being preached, or when a Sister speaks to some one. There must be also a wooden shutter securely fastened with two different locks, and iron bolts and bars, which, in the night principally, shall be locked with two keys, one of which the Abbess shall keep, and the Sacristan the other. This shutter shall be kept always fastened, except during the Divine service, and for the causes mentioned above. No Sister may speak to any person at the grate before sunrise, or after sunset, in any manner whatsoever. In the parlour there shall always be a cloth within, which shall never be removed. No one may speak in the parlour during St. Martin's Lent, nor during the great Lent, except to the priest for confession, or for some other manifest necessity, which must be left to the discretion of the Abbess or her Vicaress.

CHAPTER VI.

That the Sisters may not Receive any Property or Possessions.

LET the Abbess and all the Sisters be careful to observe the holy poverty which they have promised to the Lord our God, and let all future Abbesses and Sisters be likewise bound to observe the same inviolably to the end; that is, in not receiving or having any possession, or property, either by themselves or through the medium of any person, nor anything that can reasonably be called property, except so much ground as necessity may require for the convenience and renovation of the Convent, and this ground may not be cultivated except as a garden to supply the wants of the Sisters themselves.

CHAPTER VII.

Of the Manner of Working.

LET the Sisters to whom God has given the grace of working employ themselves faithfully and devoutly after the Hour of Tierce in those occupations which belong to the welfare and common good of the Convent, in such a manner that, banishing idleness, which is an enemy to the soul, they do not extinguish the spirit of devotion and holy prayer, to which all temporal things ought to be subservient. The Sisters are bound to present the works of their hands to the Abbess or her Vicaress in Chapter before all the Community. Let the same be done with regard to the alms that are sent by any persons for the necessities of the Sisters, in order that in common they may recommend these benefactors to God; and let all these things be then distributed for the good of the Community by the Abbess or Vicaress, with the counsel of the discreets.

CHAPTER VIII.

That the Sisters shall Appropriate nothing to themselves, and of the Sick Sisters.

LET the Sisters appropriate nothing to themselves, neither house, nor lands, nor anything; but, serving God as pilgrims and strangers here below in all poverty and humility, let them send for alms with confidence. Neither ought they to be ashamed of so doing, since Our Lord made Himself poor in this world for us. This is the perfection of that most sublime poverty, which has made you, my very dear Sisters, heiresses and queens of the kingdom of heaven; rendering you poor in temporal things, in order to enrich you with virtues. Let this, then, be your portion, which will lead you into the land of the living, to which, beloved Sisters, strictly adhering, never desire to possess anything else under heaven, for the love of our Lord Jesus Christ.

It is not lawful for any Sister to send letters, nor to receive nor give anything out of the Convent, without the permission of the Abbess; nor to have anything which the Abbess has not given or permitted her to have. If anything be sent to a Sister by her relations or other persons, let the Abbess give it to her, and let her use it if she stand in need of it; if not, let her give it in charity to any other Sister who may require it; and if money be sent to anyone, let the Abbess, with the counsel of the discreets, provide the Sister with what is necessary for her.

With regard to the sick Sisters, let the Abbess be strictly bound, either by herself or by others, to inquire carefully into their necessities, as well in respect of food, as of other things which their state of sickness may require, and to provide for them charitably and tenderly, according to the possibility of the place, for all are obliged to serve and attend their sick Sisters, as they would wish to be served if they were sick themselves. Let them make known their wants to one another with confidence; for if a true mother loves and cherishes her daughter according to the flesh, with how much more care ought a religious to love and cherish her spiritual Sister. The sick may lie on sacks of straw, and have feather pillows under their heads, and those who have need of woollen socks and mattresses may use them. The said sick, when they are visited by those who enter the Convent, may each answer briefly with edifying words those who speak to them. But the other Sisters who have permission to speak to those who enter, may not presume to do so except in the presence and hearing of two discreets, appointed by the Abbess or her Vicaress. The Abbess herself, and the Vicaress, are bound to observe this manner of speaking.

CHAPTER IX.

Of Penance to be Imposed on the Sisters.

IF any Sister, by the instigation of the enemy, sin mortally against the form of our profession, and being admonished two or three times by the Abbess or the other Sisters, will not amend, for as many days as she continues obstinate, she shall take bread and water on the ground in the refectory before all the Sisters, and even undergo greater penance if the Abbess judge it necessary. During all the time that her obstinacy lasts, let them pray that it may please God to enlighten her mind to do penance, but the Abbess and other Sisters must take care not to be angry at the fault of any one; for anger and trouble injure charity in themselves and others. If it should happen (which God forbid) that any occasion of scandal or trouble should arise between the Sisters, let her who was the cause of it immediately, before she offers to God the sacrifice of her prayer, not only humbly prostrate herself at the feet of the other Sister, asking pardon, but let her also earnestly beseech her to intercede for her with Our Lord, that He may forgive her. But let the other, remembering the words of our Saviour: 'If you do not forgive from your heart, your Heavenly Father will not forgive you;' freely pardon her Sister every wrong she may have done her.

The Sisters who serve outside the Convent, shall not remain outside longer than manifest necessity requires. They should behave modestly and speak little, so as always to give edification to those who see them, and they must carefully avoid all suspected company and familiarity with any one. They may not be godmothers to any person, male or female, lest thereby might arise any occasion of scandal or trouble. Let them not presume to relate in the Convent the news of the world; and let them be strictly bound not to repeat outside, anything that is said or done within, which might be a cause of scandal. If anyone through simplicity offend in either of these two points, let it be left to the discretion of the Abbess to enjoin her penance with due regard to mercy; but if she do so through an evil habit, let the Abbess, with the counsel of the discreets, enjoin her a penance proportioned to the gravity of her fault.

CHAPTER X.
Of the Visitation of the Sisters by the Abbess.

LET the Abbess admonish and visit her Sisters, and correct them with humility and charity; not commanding them anything which may be contrary to the good of their souls and the form of their profession. But let the Sisters who are subject remember that they have renounced their own will for the love of God, and that consequently they are strictly bound to obey their Abbess in all that they have promised to observe, and that is not contrary to their salvation and profession. Let the Abbess, on her part, be so familiar with them that they may freely act and speak with her as mistresses with their servants; for thus it ought to be, the Abbess ought to be the servant of all the Sisters.

I also admonish all the Sisters, and exhort them in Our Lord Jesus Christ, carefully to avoid all pride, vainglory, envy and covetousness; all care and solicitude about the things of the world; all detractions, murmuring, dissensions and divisions. But let them be always attentive to preserve among themselves the union of mutual charity, which is the bond of perfection. Let those who have little instruction not be solicitous to learn; but let them consider that they ought to desire above all things to have the Spirit of God and His holy operation, to pray always to Him with pure hearts, to have humility and patience in tribulations and infirmities, and to love those who correct and reprehend them ; for Our Lord has said : 'Blessed are they who suffer persecution for justice' sake, for theirs is the kingdom of heaven ;' and ' He that shall persevere to the end shall be saved.'

CHAPTER XI.
Of the Duties of the Portress.

LET the Portress be of mature character, discreet, and of a suitable age. Let her remain during the day-time in an open cell without a door. Let a fit companion also be assigned her, who may be capable of supplying her office in all things when it is necessary. Let the door be very strongly fastened with two locks, and divers iron bars and bolts, and in the night especially let it be locked with two keys, of which the Portress shall keep one, and the Abbess the other. During the day it shall never be left without guard, but be always firmly locked with one key. Let them take the greatest care that the door may never stand open when it can conveniently be avoided, and let it by no means be opened to anyone wishing to enter without the permission of the Sovereign Pontiff, or of the Lord Cardinal Protector.

The Sisters shall not allow any one to enter the Convent before sunrise, nor to remain within after sunset, except for manifest, reasonable and unavoidable causes. If any Bishop have permission to celebrate Mass within the Convent, either for the benediction of the Abbess, or to consecrate any religious, or for any other reason, let him deign to content himself with as few attendants as possible, and these the most virtuous. Whenever it is necessary for any persons to enter the Convent to do some work, let the Abbess take care to appoint a suitable person at the door, who shall open it to those destined to do the work and to no others; and let all the Sisters carefully avoid being seen by those who enter.

CHAPTER XII.

Of the Visitor.

LET the Visitor of the Sisters be always of the Order of Friars Minor, according to the will and commandment of the Lord Cardinal; and let him be such that his virtues and integrity be well known. His office shall be to correct in the head as well as in the members the faults committed against the form of your profession. Being in an open place, so that he can be seen by the other Sisters, he may speak with several, or with each one in particular, of those things which appertain to his office of Visitation as he shall judge most expedient. As they have hitherto had from the charity of the Friars Minor a chaplain with a companion-clerk of good reputation and great discretion, and two lay-brothers of holy conversation and lovers of virtue to assist them in their poverty, let them ask this favour of the said Order. The chaplain may not enter the Convent without his companion, and when they do so they shall be in a public place, where they can be seen by each other, and by the Sisters. They may enter to hear the confession of the sick who cannot go to the parlour, to give them Holy Communion and Extreme Unction, and for the recommendation of a departing soul. The Abbess may also, according to her discretion, allow a suitable number of persons to enter for the funeral, to celebrate Mass for the dead, and to open and prepare the grave.

Finally, the Sisters are bound to have always for governor, protector, and reformer, the same Cardinal of the holy Roman Church who shall be appointed by the Sovereign Pontiff for the Friars Minor, that being always subject and submissive at the feet of the same holy Roman Church, we may remain steadfast in the Catholic Faith, and observe perpetually the poverty and humility of our Lord Jesus Christ and of His most holy Mother.

RULE OF THE BROTHERS AND SISTERS OF THE THIRD ORDER OF ST. FRANCIS, CALLED THE ORDER OF PENANCE.*

In the Name of Our Lord. Amen.

CHAPTER I.

Of the Manner of Examining those who wish to Enter the Order.

IF any wish to embrace this manner of life, and are to be admitted, they shall, before their acceptance or admission, be subjected to a close examination concerning the Catholic Faith, and their obedience to the Roman Church. And if they sincerely profess and truly believe these things, they may be admitted or received with all safety. But great care must be taken never to admit to this manner of life anyone who is a heretic, or suspected of heresy, or a person of bad reputation. And if it should happen that such an one were admitted, he must be denounced as soon as possible to the Inquisitors, in order that he may be punished for his heresy.

CHAPTER II.

Of the Manner of Receiving those who wish to enter the Order.

WHEN anyone is desirous of entering this Fraternity, the Ministers who are deputed for the reception of

---

* This Rule is given in its original form. The points which have become obsolete, or have been modified, on account of the altered state of society, are explained in all Manuals of the Third Order.

such persons shall make careful inquiries respecting his employment, state, and condition, clearly explaining to him the obligations of the said Fraternity, and especially that of restoring the goods of others. This being done, if he wishes it, he may be clothed with the habit in the usual form, and he shall take care, if he has in his possession the goods of others, to make restitution either in ready money, or by giving proper security; and he must also take care to be reconciled with his neighbour. After having fulfilled all these things, and after the space of one year, he may, by the advice of some discreet Brethren, if they think him worthy, be admitted to make his profession in this manner; viz., that he promise to keep all the Divine commandments, and to make suitable satisfaction for the faults he may commit against this form of life, as the Visitor may think fit. This promise, made by him, must be registered by the public secretary. No person may be received by the Ministers in any other manner, unless, after mature deliberation, they see fit to act otherwise on account of the condition or earnest solicitation of the person.

Moreover, we order and decree that no one, after having entered this Order, may leave it to return to the world. Nevertheless, they may be freely permitted to pass into any other approved Order. Married women may not enter this Order without the permission and consent of their husbands.

CHAPTER III.

Of the Form of the Habit, and the Quality of the Garments.

THE Brethren of this Fraternity must commonly be clothed in a woollen garment, humble as to price and colour, being neither black nor white, unless the Ministers should dispense with anyone for a time, and for some legitimate and manifest cause. Their mantles also and furred dresses must be without collars, clasped and not open, as decency requires, and the sleeves must be closed.

The Sisters also must be clothed with a tunic and mantle of the same coarse cloth, or at least they must wear with their mantle a black or white skirt, or a long robe of hemp or flax made up without any plaits. Nevertheless, with regard to the coarseness of the cloth and furs of the Sisters, a dispensation may be granted should their position or the custom of the place require it. They may not use silk ribbons or cords, but both the Brothers and Sisters having, according to the salutary counsel of the Prince of the Apostles, laid aside the vain ornaments of the world, shall have only common furs, purses of leather, and girdles simply made, without any silk.

CHAPTER IV.

Of not going to immodest Feasts and Plays, and of not Giving anything to Actors.

THE Brothers and Sisters are absolutely forbidden to be present at immodest feasts, plays, public meetings, and dances. They must not spend anything on actors, nor in seeing vain shows; and they must take care to forbid anything being spent on such things by their family.

CHAPTER V.
Of Abstinence and Fasting.

ALL the Brothers and Sisters shall abstain from eating flesh-meat on Mondays,* Wednesdays, Fridays, and Saturdays, unless prevented by illness or weakness. Those who have been bled may eat meat for three successive days, and the same is allowed to those who are travelling.† The use of meat is also permitted on solemn feasts, when according to ancient custom other Christians make use of it. On other abstinence days when no fast is observed, they may eat cheese and eggs, but when they are with other religious in their Convents, they may eat what is set before them, and let them be contented with dinner and supper, unless they are weak or sick or on a journey. Let those who are in good health be moderate in eating and drinking; for the Gospel says, 'Take heed that your hearts be not made heavy with surfeiting and drunkenness.' They may not dine or sup without first saying *Pater noster*, and this they must repeat after the repast, adding *Deo gratias*. If this be omitted they must say three times *Pater noster*.

They must fast on all Fridays throughout the year,

---

* Pope Clement VII., in his Bull *Ad uberes fructus*, of the 15th of March, 1526, granted the secular Tertiaries a general exemption from abstinence on Mondays.

† These dispensations are only granted on the days of abstinence prescribed by the Rule alone.

unless they be dispensed on account of sickness or some other lawful reason, or unless the Feast of our Lord's Nativity should occur on that day. From the Feast of All Saints until Easter they shall fast on all Wednesdays* and Fridays, and they must also observe the other fasts commanded by the Church, or prescribed by the Bishops for public causes. During the Lent, from the Feast of St. Martin until the Nativity of our Lord, and from Quinquagesima Sunday until Easter, they shall fast every day except Sundays, unless prevented by sickness or any other necessity. Women with child may, if they choose, abstain from all corporal austerities, but not from prayer, until the day of their churching.

Those who are obliged to labour, may on account of their fatigue take their repasts three times a day from Easter until the Feast of St. Michael. And when they are employed at work in the houses of others, they may eat whatever is set before them on all days except Fridays, or any other fast-day appointed by the Church.

CHAPTER VI.

How often the Brothers and Sisters ought to Confess and Communicate during the Year.

ALL the Brothers and Sisters must confess their sins and devoutly receive the Holy Eucharist three times in the year; viz., at Christmas, Easter, and Pentecost,

---

* Pope Paul III., by the Bull *Ad uberes fructus*, of July 3rd, 1547, dispensed the secular Tertiaries from this fast on Wednesdays.

taking care first to be reconciled to their neighbour, and to restore the goods of others.

CHAPTER VII.
Of not Carrying offensive Weapons.

THE Brothers may not carry offensive arms, unless it be for the defence of the Roman Church, the Catholic Faith, their own country, or with the permission of their Ministers.

CHAPTER VIII.
Of the Recitation of the Canonical Hours.

ALL the Brothers and Sisters must say daily the seven Canonical Hours; viz., Matins, Prime, Tierce, Sext, None, Vespers, and Complin. Clerks who know how to recite the Psalter must say for Prime *Deus in nomine tuo*, and *Beati immaculati* as far as *Legem pone, etc.*, and the other Psalms of the Hours with the *Gloria Patri*, according to the rite of the clergy.* When they cannot go to the Church they must be careful to say for Matins the Psalms that clerks say, or those used in the Cathedral Church, or at least they must not fail to recite, like those who cannot read, twelve *Pater nosters* with the *Gloria Patri* for Matins, and seven for each of the other Hours. At the Hours of Prime and Complin they shall add the *Credo* and the Psalm *Miserere mei Deus*, if they know them. But if they fail to recite the appointed Hours

---

* That is, the Roman rite, which St. Francis was the first to spread through the world by adopting it in his Order.

they must say three times the *Pater noster*. Those who are sick are not bound to recite these Hours unless they wish. During St. Martin's Lent, and also during the great Lent, they should endeavour to assist at Matins in the parish churches where they dwell, unless they are dispensed for some legitimate cause.

CHAPTER IX.
That all who can lawfully do so should make their Will.

ALL those who have the right and power to do so, must make their will within three months of their entrance into the Order, and shall arrange and dispose of their goods, lest any of them should happen to die intestate.

CHAPTER X.
How Peace must be established among the Brethren, and with others.

SHOULD any dissension occur among the Brothers and Sisters, or even among other persons, the Ministers shall take what means they think best to re-establish peace, having recourse, if necessary, to the counsels of the Diocesan Bishop in this matter.

CHAPTER XI.
How they should Act when Molested contrary to Justice, and their Privileges.

IF it should happen that the Brothers or Sisters are assailed with persecutions contrary to justice and their privileges by any persons in power, or by the magistrates of the places where they dwell, the Ministers shall take care to have recourse to the Bishop or Ordinary of the place, that they may act in such cases according to his advice and direction.

CHAPTER XII.
That the Brothers and Sisters should avoid, as much as possible, taking solemn Oaths.

THE Brothers and Sisters must abstain from taking solemn oaths, except through urgent necessity in cases permitted by the Holy See; viz., to establish peace, to justify faith, to refute a calumny, to bear witness, and even to make a contract of buying, selling, or donation, when deemed necessary.

They must avoid, as much as possible, oaths in common conversation, and if anyone should be surprised into an oath through heedlessness (which generally happens to great talkers), let him, on the night of the same day, when he ought to examine what he has done, say three *Pater nosters* in satisfaction for such idle oaths.

And let everyone remember to exhort his family to serve God faithfully.

CHAPTER XIII.
Of hearing Mass, and attending the Assemblies.

ALL the Brothers and Sisters, to whatever place they belong, who are in good health, must hear Mass every day if they can do so conveniently; and they must also assemble once a month in the Church, or place appointed by the Ministers, and assist at a solemn Mass which shall be celebrated therein. Each one shall give a piece of current money to the treasurer, who, having collected it, will distribute it, according to the advice of the Ministers, among the Brothers and Sisters who are poor, especially those who are sick, and such as are known not to have the means for funeral expenses, and afterwards to other poor according to their wants.

Moreover, out of the said money an offering must be made to the Church where the Mass has been celebrated. They shall also be careful to procure, if it can be done conveniently, some religious man well instructed in the word of God, to exhort, admonish, and induce them to do penance, and to perform works of mercy.

Each one must be careful to keep silence during Mass and the sermon, and let them be assiduous in prayer, and in saying the Office, unless prevented by the common good of the Brotherhood.

CHAPTER XIV.

Of the sick and departed Brethren.

WHEN one of the Brethren is sick, and has notified the same to the Ministers, they are bound either themselves or by others to visit the sick person at least once a week. They shall earnestly exhort him, as they may judge it expedient and beneficial, to receive the Sacrament of Penance, and shall furnish him with those things that are necessary out of the common purse. If the said sick person die, notice must be given to the Brothers and Sisters living in the town or place where he died, that they may assist at the obsequies, from which they must not withdraw until the Mass is finished and the body interred. The same rules are to be observed with regard to sick and deceased Sisters.

Within a week after the death of any member, the Brothers who are priests shall say one Mass for the repose of the soul; those who know the Psalter shall each say fifty Psalms, and those who cannot read shall say as many *Pater nosters*, adding at the end of each *Requiem æternam, etc.* Besides this, they will have three Masses celebrated every year, for the Brothers and Sisters both living and dead; those who know the Psalter will say it, and the others will not fail to recite one hundred *Pater nosters*, adding at the end of each *Requiem æternam, etc.*

CHAPTER XV.

Of the Ministers.

EVERYONE on whom may be imposed the ministerial or other offices expressed in this present Rule, must accept such office with devotion, and fulfil it with fidelity. Each office shall be limited in its duration, and no Minister may be appointed for life, but only for a certain space of time.

CHAPTER XVI.

Of the Visitation and Correction of those who Offend.

THE Ministers and Brothers and Sisters of each place and city shall assemble for the general Visitation in some religious house or Church, if they have no more convenient place, and choose for a Visitor a priest belonging to some approved religious Order, who shall impose a salutary penance on such of the members as may have committed any fault. No other person can exercise this office of Visitor.

This Visitation shall be held only once a year, unless some urgent necessity requires that it be held oftener. Incorrigible and disobedient members shall be warned three several times, and if they will not reform, they shall, with the advice of the Council, be altogether expelled from the Congregation.

CHAPTER XVII.

Of avoiding Lawsuits among themselves or with others.

LET the Brothers and Sisters as much as possible avoid lawsuits among themselves; but should one happen to be begun against them, let them endeavour to stop it; and if they fail, they must carry the matter before those who have the power of judging in such cases.

CHAPTER XVIII.
How, and by whom, Dispensations may be Granted.

THE local Superiors or the Visitor can dispense the Brothers and Sisters from abstinence, fasts, and other austerities for a legitimate cause, and when they judge it necessary.

CHAPTER XIX.
That the Ministers must declare notable Faults to the Visitor.

THE Ministers shall declare to the Visitor the notable faults of the Brothers and Sisters, that they may be punished. But if any should be found incorrigible after they have been warned three several times, the Ministers, with the advice of some discreet Brethren, shall denounce him to the said Visitor, that he may cut him off from the Order, and announce the same at the next assembly of the whole Congregation.

CHAPTER XX.
That this Rule does not bind under pain of mortal Sin.

FINALLY, we will not that the Brothers and Sisters of this Order be bound under pain of mortal sin to observe the things above mentioned, unless they are already bound thereto by the Divine commandments or the precepts of the Church; but let them accept with prompt humility the penances imposed on them for their transgressions, and endeavour faithfully to fulfil the same.

PART III.

ADMONITIONS OF THE BLESSED FATHER ST. FRANCIS TO HIS BRETHREN.

I. OUR LORD said to His Disciples: 'I am the way, and the truth, and the life. No man cometh to the Father but by Me. If you had known Me you would surely have known My Father also; and from henceforth you shall know Him and have seen Him. Philip saith to Him, Lord, show us the Father, and it is enough for us. Jesus saith to him, Have I been so long a time with you, and have you not known Me? Philip, he that seeth Me seeth the Father also.'

The Father dwells in light inaccessible. God is a Spirit, and no one ever saw God; therefore it is only by the spirit we can see Him, for the spirit giveth life, the flesh profiteth nothing. For neither can the Son, inasmuch as He is equal to the Father, be seen, as the Father and the Holy Ghost cannot be seen; therefore all those who saw Our Lord Jesus Christ according to His Humanity, but did not see and believe according to the spirit and the Divinity that He was the Son of God, were condemned.

II. In like manner, all those who behold the Sacrament, which is sanctified by the Word of God upon the Altar in the hands of the priest, under the appearances of bread and wine, but who do not see and believe according to the Spirit and the Divinity that It is really the most holy Body and Blood of Our Lord Jesus Christ, are condemned. He, the Most High, has declared it, when He said: 'This is My Body, and the Blood of the New Testament;' and 'They who eat My Flesh and drink My Blood shall have eternal life.' He who has the Spirit of God, Who dwells in His faithful servants—he it is who receives the most holy Body and Blood of the Lord; but all others who presume to receive Him not having this spirit, eat and drink judgment to themselves. Wherefore, 'O ye sons of men, how long will you be dull of heart? why do you love vanity and seek after lying?' Why will you not know the truth, and believe in the Son of God? Behold, every day He humbles Himself as when He descended from His royal throne in heaven into the womb of the Virgin Mary; every day He comes to us with like humility; every day He descends from the Bosom of His Heavenly Father upon the Altar in the hands of the priest. And as 'He appeared in true flesh to His holy Apostles, so now He shows Himself to us under the form of bread. And as they with the eyes of their body saw only His flesh, but contemplating Him with their spiritual eyes, believed Him to be their Lord and their God; so we, who see only bread and wine with our bodily eyes, believe most firmly that It is His most holy Body and true and living Blood. And in this way Our Lord is always present with His faithful servants, as He said: 'Behold, I am with you all days, even to the consummation of the world.'

III. God said to Adam: 'Of every tree in paradise thou mayest eat; but of the tree of knowledge of good and evil thou shalt not eat.' Adam might eat of every tree in paradise, because as long as he was obedient he did not sin. That man eats of the tree of knowledge of good and evil, who acts according to his own will, and prides himself upon the good which the Lord has given him and works in him; and thus through the suggestion of the devil and his own transgression, this good becomes to him as the apple of the knowledge of evil. Therefore it is necessary that he should suffer punishment.

IV. Our Lord said in the Gospel: 'He who does not renounce all he possesses, cannot be My disciple,' and 'He that will save his life shall lose it.' That man renounces all he has, and loses his life, who places himself by obedience entirely in the hands of his Superiors, and always does and says those things that are agreeable to their wishes (provided that the things he does are good). This is true obedience. And if a subject thinks that something would be better and more profitable to his soul than what his Superiors command, let him sacrifice his will to God, and endeavour to accomplish the work enjoined him. This is charitable obedience, which causes him to sacrifice himself for God and his neighbour. If, however, a prelate orders a subject to do anything that would be injurious to his soul, he may refuse to obey, but he must not on that account leave his Superior. And if, for this cause, he suffer persecution from Superiors, he should love them the more in the Lord. Now he who would rather suffer persecution than separate himself from his Brethren, practises perfect obedience, for he gives his life for his Brethren. There are many religious who, under pretence of doing a greater good than what is commanded by their Superiors, look back, and return to the vomit of their own will. These are murderers, for they cause the loss of many souls through their fault.

V. Our Lord says : 'I did not come to be ministered unto, but to minister.' Those who are appointed to be over others, should glory in this office only as much as if they had been chosen to wash the feet of their Brethren ; and if they are more disturbed at the loss of their dignity, than they would be at the loss of that lowly office, they may be sure their soul is in danger, and in proportion to the disturbance they feel is the greatness of their peril. Think, O man, how great is the excellence God has bestowed on you, for He created and formed you to the image of His beloved Son according to the body, and to His own likeness according to the spirit. And all creatures under heaven, according to their nature, know, serve, and obey their Creator better than you ; the devils did not crucify Him, but you, incited by them, have crucified Him, and still crucify Him when you delight in vice and sin. Of what then can you glory? For if you were so wise and clever that you knew all things, and could interpret all languages, and penetrate all heavenly mysteries with the greatest clearness, you could not glory in all this, for one demon knows more of heavenly, and even of earthly things, than all men put together, although some have been endowed with special wisdom by God. Again, if you were richer and more beautiful than all others, nay, even if you could work miracles and put the devils to flight, still all these things are contrary to your nature, and in no way belong to you. In all this you cannot glory, but in one thing we may glory, that is in our infirmities, and in bearing daily the holy Cross of Our Lord Jesus Christ. Let us all, my Brethren, consider the Good Shepherd, Who bore the suffering of the Cross to save His sheep. The sheep of the Lord followed Him in tribulation and persecution, in shame and hunger, in infirmity and temptations, and other sufferings, and for this they have received eternal life from the Lord. Therefore it is a great shame to the servants of God, that the Saints should do the works, and that we should expect glory and honour for preaching and reciting the works they have performed.

VI. The Apostle has said: 'The letter killeth; the Spirit giveth life.' Those are killed by the letter who desire to know the words only that they may be reputed more learned than others, and that they may acquire great riches to bestow on their relations and friends. Those religious are killed by the letter, who will not follow the spirit of the Divine teaching, but only care to know the words and to interpret them to others. And they are enlivened by the spirit of the Divine teaching, who offer all their knowledge, and all they wish to know, to the great God, from Whom is all good, for they do not live by the body only, but by the words and examples of the Holy Scriptures.

VII. The Apostle says: 'No one can say, the Lord Jesus, except by the Holy Ghost,' and 'There is none that doeth good, no, not one.' Therefore, whoever envies his Brother for the good which God says or does in him, commits a sin like unto blasphemy, for he envies the Most High Himself, Who is the Author of all good words and works.

VIII. The Lord says in the Gospel: 'Love your enemies, do good to them who hate you, and pray for those who persecute you,' etc. They really love their enemies who do not grieve for the injury done to themselves, but for the sin committed, on account of the love they bear to God, and who show this love by their works.

IX. There are many who, if they commit sin, or suffer any injury, immediately blame their neighbour or their enemy. But this is not just, for each one has his enemy in his power, namely, his body, by which he sinned. Therefore blessed is the man who having this enemy in his power always keeps it chained, and wisely defends himself from it, for if he do this, no other visible enemy can hurt him.

X. Nothing but sin should be displeasing to the servant of God. And no matter in what way a person sins, if the servant of God is disturbed and angry at it (unless it be for the love of God,) he commits a fault and deserves punishment. The true servant of God is not troubled or angry about anything; he lives justly and seeks not himself. Blessed is he who keeps nothing back, but who renders 'to Cæsar the things that are Cæsar's, and to God the things that are God's.'

XI. The servant of God may know whether he has the spirit of God, if, when the Lord works some good through him, he is not puffed up in body or mind, knowing that in himself he is contrary to all good, but rather appears viler in his own eyes, and esteems himself more miserable than other men.

XII. It cannot be known how much humility or patience a servant of God has, when he has everything according to his wishes or necessity. But when the time comes that those who ought to befriend him turn against him, then he has as much humility and patience as he shows, and no more.

XIII. 'Blessed are the poor in spirit, for theirs is the kingdom of heaven.' There are many who recite long offices and prayers, who afflict their bodies with abstinences and penances, but who are scandalised and disturbed by a single word, or by any injury done to them, or by the loss of anything belonging to them. These are not truly poor in spirit, for he who is truly poor in spirit hates himself and loves others, even if they strike him on the cheek.

XIV. 'Blessed are the peace-makers, for they shall be called the children of God.' Those are truly peace-makers who in all the sufferings of this life keep their body and soul in peace for the love of our Lord Jesus Christ.

XV. 'Blessed are the clean of heart, for they shall see God.' Those are truly clean of heart who despise the things of earth and aspire to those of heaven, and who never desist from adoring and contemplating the living God with a pure heart and mind.

XVI. Blessed is that servant who is not more exalted on account of the good God says and works by him, than for that which He says and works by others. That man sins who wishes to receive more from others than he is himself willing to give to the Lord his God. Blessed is the man who bears with the weakness of his neighbour, as he would wish others to bear with him in like case.

XVII. Blessed is the servant who gives and attributes all good to the Lord God, for he who retains anything for himself hides the money of the Lord his God, and all that he seems to have shall be taken from him. Blessed is that servant who does not think himself better when he is praised and exalted by men, than when he is despised and considered simple and good-for-nothing, for what a man is in the sight of God, that he is and no more. Woe to that religious who is placed in a high position by others, and is not willing to descend from it. And blessed is that servant who is elevated by others against his will, and who always desires to be under the feet of all.

XVIII. Blessed is the religious who takes pleasure only in holy words and works of God, and who thus leads men to the love of God, with joy, happiness, and exultation. But woe to that religious who delights in vain and idle words, and by these tempts men to laughter. Blessed is that servant who does not speak for the hope of reward, who does not manifest all his thoughts, nor speak with eagerness, but who wisely considers what he should say and answer. Woe to that religious who does not keep secret the good which God does in him, manifesting it to others only by his works; but who, for the hope of the reward, is more anxious to speak of it to men than to show it to God; he may indeed receive the recompense he seeks, but those who hear him will derive but little benefit.

XIX. Blessed is that servant who bears discipline, accusations, and reprehensions from others as patiently as from himself. Blessed is the servant who mildly yields to reproof, obeys with modesty, humbly confesses his fault, and willingly makes satisfaction. Blessed is the servant who is not quick in excusing himself, and who humbly bears the shame and reprehension for sin when he has committed no fault. Blessed is that servant who is as humble among his Brethren and inferiors as among his Superiors and Prelates. Blessed is the servant who always remains under the rod of correction. He is a faithful and prudent servant who in all his offences does not delay to punish himself interiorly by contrition, and exteriorly by confession and works of satisfaction.

XX. Blessed is the servant who loves his Brother as much when he is ill and cannot do anything for him, as when he is well and can be of use to him. And blessed is he who loves his Brother as much when he is at a distance from him as when he is near, and who would say nothing about him behind his back, that he could not with charity say before his face. Blessed is that servant who trusts in the priests who live justly, according to the rules of the holy Roman Church, and woe to those who despise them; for even if they were sinners, still no one ought to judge them, for God reserves to Himself alone the right of doing so. For as their charge is greater than that of any others, namely, the administration of the most holy Body and Blood of Our Lord Jesus Christ, which they receive, and which they alone can give to others, so the sin of those who offend against them is greater than against anyone else in the world.

XXI. Where charity and wisdom are, there is neither fear nor ignorance. Where patience and humility are, there is neither anger nor perturbation of mind. Where joyful poverty is found, there is neither cupidity nor avarice. Where there are quietness and meditation, there is neither solicitude nor dissipation. Where the fear of God guards the house, the enemy can find no entrance. Where mercy and discretion are, there is neither superfluity nor parsimony.

XXII. Blessed is the man who treasures up for heaven the good things which the Lord shows him, and who does not desire to manifest them to men through the hope of reward, for the Most High will Himself make manifest his works to whom He pleases. Blessed is the servant who keeps the secrets of his Lord in his heart.

These are the words of life and salvation, and whoever chooses them and fulfils them, shall find life and receive salvation from the Lord. Amen.

The Praises of Wisdom, Simplicity, Poverty, Humility, Charity and Obedience.

O QUEENLY Wisdom, the Lord save thee with thy Sister, pure and holy Simplicity. O Lady holy Poverty, the Lord save thee with thy Sister holy Humility. O Lady holy Charity, the Lord save thee with thy Sister holy Obedience. O all ye holy virtues, may the Lord, from Whom you proceed, save you! There is absolutely no man in the whole world who can possess one of you unless he first die to himself. He who possesses one virtue, and does not offend against the others, possesses all; and he who offends against one, possesses none, and offends against all, and confounds altogether vices and sins. Holy Wisdom confounds Satan and all his malice. Pure and holy Simplicity confounds all the wisdom of this world and the prudence of the flesh. Holy Poverty confounds cupidity and avarice and all worldly cares. Holy Humility confounds pride, and all men and all things that are in the world. Holy Charity confounds all carnal and diabolical temptations and all earthly fears. Holy Obedience confounds the carnal and natural will, and keeps the body under subjection to the spirit and to Superiors; it is submissive and docile to all men, and not to men only, but even to wild beasts, who may do with it whatever they will, according to the power God gives them from above. Thanks be to God. Amen.

Of Perfect Joy—that the most Precious Gift which we can receive from the Holy Ghost, is Strength to conquer Self, and to bear Reproaches patiently for the Love of God.

ALTHOUGH the Friar Minor should give good example of great sanctity and edification throughout the whole world, still that is not perfect joy. And even if the Friar Minor should give sight to the blind, cure the paralysed, cast out devils, cause the deaf to hear, the lame to walk, the dumb to speak, and what is still greater, restore to life one who has been dead four days, still this is not perfect joy. And if the Friar Minor should know all kinds of languages, and all sciences, and the Scriptures, so that he could prophesy and reveal not only things future, but even the secrets of consciences, this would not be perfect joy. If the Friar Minor were to speak with the tongues of angels, if he knew the courses of the stars and the virtues of herbs, if all the hidden treasures of the earth were revealed to him, and if he understood the virtues and properties of all birds, fishes, animals, men, roots, stones, trees and water, this would not be perfect joy. And if the Friar Minor were to preach so eloquently as to convert all infidels to the faith, even this would not be perfect joy.

But if when we come to Our Lady of Angels, all drenched with rain and frozen with cold, covered with mud and exhausted with hunger, we should knock at the door, and the porter coming should say angrily: 'Who are you?' and when we answer: 'We are two of your Brethren,' he should reply: 'Nay, rather you are two impostors, who go about the world stealing the alms of the poor;' and if he should not let us in, but make us stand in the snow and rain, cold and almost starved to death; then, if we should bear patiently all these insults and injuries without disturbance of mind or murmuring, and if we should think humbly and charitably that the porter knew us truly, and that God inspired him to act in this way, write that this is perfect joy. And if we persevere in knocking, and the same porter should come out and treat us as importunate beggars, striking us violently and saying: 'Depart hence, you vile poltroons! Go to the hospital. Who are you? you shall not eat here;' and if we bear this patiently, and forgive these injuries with our whole heart, write that this is perfect joy. And if we, being overpowered with hunger, frozen with cold, and finding night approaching, knock at the door, and crying and weeping implore to be admitted, and the porter enraged exclaim, 'These are most impudent and obstinate men; I will pacify them;' and coming out with a thick and knotted stick, he take us by the cowl, and throwing us on the ground, beat us so severely as to cover us with wounds: if we bear all these injuries, all these evils and blows with joy, considering that we ought to share in the sufferings of Christ the Blessed, write and note most diligently, that this is perfect joy.

And now listen to the conclusion. Of all the gifts of the Holy Spirit which Christ has ever granted or will grant to His servants, the principal is the grace to conquer self, and willingly to suffer injuries for the love of God. For in all the above-mentioned wonderful works we could not glory, because they are not ours, but God's. 'What hast thou that thou hast not received? And if thou hast received it, why dost thou glory as if thou hadst not received it?' But in the Cross of afflictions and tribulations we may glory, for this in our own. And therefore the Apostle says: 'Far be it from me to glory, save in the Cross of Our Lord Jesus Christ.'

MONASTIC CONFERENCES OF THE HOLY FATHER
ST. FRANCIS.

CONFERENCE I.
*That the little Flock will be Multiplied.**

BE consoled, my beloved Children, and rejoice in the Lord; do not be sad because of the smallness of our number, nor let my and your simplicity terrify you; for the Lord has shown me in very truth how He will make you increase to a great number, and by the grace of His blessing will cause you wonderfully to multiply. Many will be converted to God, and throughout the whole world He will increase His family. For your sakes I must needs say what I have seen, and which I would rather have kept secret, if charity did not oblige me to repeat it. I saw a great multitude of men coming to us, and wishing to take our holy habit and join in our manner of life. And even now I have the sound of them in my ears, as they come and go according to the commands of holy Obedience. I see the roads full of a great multitude of almost every nation hastening to these parts. The French are coming, the Spaniards are hastening, the English and Germans are running, and a vast number from divers other countries are approaching with all speed.

* This is called the Colloquy of Consolation, because in it the Blessed Father consoled his Brethren when, being only four or six in number, they were discouraged thereat.

CONFERENCE II.

Of the Vocation of the Friars Minor, and of Preaching the Word of God.

LET us, beloved Brethren, consider our vocation, to which by the mercy of God we have been called, not for ourselves only, but for the salvation of many; that we may go through the world, exhorting all, more by our example than by our words, to do penance for their sins, and to remember the commandments of God. Do not fear because you are insignificant and unlearned, but preach penance with courage and simplicity; confiding in our Lord, Who has overcome the world, that the Holy Spirit will speak by you and in you, exhorting all to turn to Him and observe His precepts. Let us who have relinquished all things take care that we do not lose the kingdom of heaven for trifles; and if we find money in any place, let us not value it more than the dust we tread under our feet. Let us not, however, judge or despise those who live delicately and are clothed sumptuously. God is their Lord as well as ours, and He is powerful enough to call them to His service, and having called to justify them. Let us therefore reverence them as our Brothers and masters. They are our Brethren, because formed by the same Creator; they are our masters, because they help the virtuous to do penance, by ministering to their temporal wants. Go, then, and announce peace to men, preaching penance for the remission of sins. You will find some faithful men, mild and kind, who will receive you and your words with joy; and, on the contrary, you will find others, without faith, proud blasphemers, who, insulting you, will resist all you say. Prepare your hearts, therefore, to bear all, patiently and humbly. Do not fear, however, for before long many wise and noble persons will come to you, and they will preach with you before kings and princes and great nations. Be ye therefore patient in tribulations, watchful in prayer, strenuous in labours, modest in speech, grave in manners, and grateful for benefits; because for all these things God has prepared for you an eternal kingdom, which may He Who lives and reigns one God in three Persons, grant to us; and He will grant it without doubt, if we are faithful to the vows we have willingly made to Him.

CONFERENCE III.

*Of the Religious who live as Hermits.**

LET those who wish to live religiously in hermitages be three, or at the most four, in number. Let two of them be considered as Mothers, and have two sons, or at least one. The former must lead the life of Martha, and the latter that of Mary Magdalen. Those who lead the life of Mary shall have a cloister, and each of them his own cell, so that they may not live or sleep together. Let them always say Compline when the sun is about to set. Let them endeavour to keep silence, and let them recite the Divine Office.

* In the beginning of the Order many Brethren retired to solitary places in order that they might more easily devote themselves to prayer and contemplation, living according to the rules laid down for them by their holy Founder.

They must rise to say Matins, and seek first the kingdom of God, and His justice. They must say Prime and Tierce at the proper time, and after Tierce they may break silence and go to their Mothers; and if it pleases them they may ask an alms of them for the love of God, as the poorest of the poor. Afterwards they must say Sext, None, and Vespers at the usual hours. In the cloister where they live no one may be permitted to enter or to eat. Those Brothers who act as Mothers must endeavour to avoid all persons, so that no one may speak to them. And the sons may not speak to anyone except their Mothers and the Custode, when it pleases him to visit them with the blessing of God. And when the sons in turn assume the office of Mothers, they shall interchange what has here been marked out for them. Let all that is above prescribed be carefully and faithfully observed.

CONFERENCE IV.

Of True Obedience.

BELOVED Brethren, fulfil at once the command that is given you, and do not wait for it to be repeated. Do not imagine there is anything impossible in the command, for even if I were to command anything above your power, holy Obedience would supply you with strength. You must not consider who or what he is who commands, but only that he is your Superior. Among other graces which the Divine goodness has bestowed upon me this is one, that I would as willingly obey a novice of an hour, if he were appointed my Guardian, as I would the oldest and most discreet of the Brethren. The subject should not consider his Superior as a man, but he should see in him the God for Whose love he obeys. The more contemptible the Superior may be, the more pleasing to God is the humility of him who obeys.

CONFERENCE V.

On Holy Poverty.

YOU know, my beloved Brethren, that Poverty is the queen of virtues, because it shone so brightly in the King of kings, and in the Queen, His Mother. Know, my Brethren, that Poverty is the straight road to salvation, the nurse of humility, the root of perfection; its fruits are numerous, but hidden. This is the treasure buried in the evangelical field, to purchase which all should be sold, and what cannot be sold should be despised. Whoever wishes to attain to perfect Poverty must renounce not only all worldly prudence, but also in some degree all literary acquirements, that so, stripped of all things, he may enter into the power of God, and, naked, offer himself into the arms of the Crucified. No one has perfectly renounced the world who reserves the most secret place in his heart for his self-love. Let holy Poverty, therefore, shine among you, and principally in the houses you build, remembering the words of the Gospel: 'Foxes have holes, and the birds of the air have their nests; but the Son of Man hath not where to lay His Head.' Therefore, build poor little houses as poor people should; which you must not look upon as your own, but as the property of others, and dwell therein as strangers and pilgrims. For pilgrims are accustomed to abide under strange roofs, to sigh for their country, and to proceed peacefully on their way. This evangelical Poverty is the foundation of our Order, on which the whole structure of Religion so depends, that by its solidity it is sustained, and by its weakness it is overturned. Inasmuch as the Brethren turn away from holy Poverty, so much will the world turn away from them; they shall seek for its help, but not find it. If they embrace my Lady Poverty, the world will nourish them; because they are sent for the salvation of the world. This is the treaty between the Brethren and the world: they owe good example to the world, and the world owes them their necessary subsistence; but if they cease to give good example, the world will justly refuse to support them.

CONFERENCE VI.

Of Avoiding the Sight and Conversation of Women.

WE ought, my beloved Brethren, to avoid most carefully the sight of women, and all conversation and familiarity with them, which have been the occasion of ruin to many; for on this account we often see the weak to be overcome and the strong shaken. Unless a man be most prudent, I consider it as easy to avoid harm in conversing with women as the Scripture says it is to pass through fire without burning the feet. I do not even think it safe to dwell on the thought of them, for this may rekindle concupiscence in a mortified body, or sully the purity of a chaste mind. Any intercourse with women is certainly frivolous, except for confession, and a very brief instruction, as may be necessary for their salvation, or befitting for courtesy. What affairs, I ask, can a Religious have to treat of with a woman, except when she piously asks to receive the Holy Sacrament of Penance, or counsel for the improvement of her life? From excessive security the enemy is too little avoided, and if the devil can seize a man by one hair, he will quickly make it into a rope. We must not only mortify the vices of the flesh and bridle all incentives to them, but we ought with the greatest vigilance to watch over our exterior senses, through which death often enters into the soul.

CONFERENCE VII.

Of Asking for Alms with Confidence.

MY beloved Brethren and Children, be not ashamed to beg for alms, for Our Lord made Himself poor in this world for the love of us, and after His example we have chosen to follow the way of perfect Poverty. Now, if we have chosen the way of Poverty for love of Him, we must not be ashamed to ask for alms. It does not become the heirs of the kingdom of heaven to blush at the tokens of their heavenly inheritance. For this is our inheritance, which Our Lord Jesus Christ acquired and left to us, and to all who will follow His example, and live in this most holy Poverty. I tell you in truth that many of the wisest and most noble of this world shall come to this Congregation, and shall consider it a great grace and honour to beg alms. You, therefore, who are the first-fruits of the Order, do not refuse to do willingly and joyfully what you will leave as an example to the Saints who come after you. Go then confidently and joyfully to ask alms with the blessing of God. And you should do this more gladly than if you could repay your benefactors a hundredfold, for in return for their charity you offer them the love of God, saying: 'Give us an alms for the love of God,' which is of far greater value than anything in heaven or on earth.

CONFERENCE VIII.

Of Discretion in Nourishing the Body.

MY beloved Brethren, we must provide discreetly for the wants of our brother the body, lest we become overwhelmed with sadness and weakness. The servant of God should satisfy his body with moderation in eating, drinking, sleeping, and its other necessities, so that it may not grow weary of watching and of persevering reverently in prayer. We must not give brother body cause to murmur, saying: 'I perish with hunger, therefore I cannot bear the burdens you put upon me; I cannot remain upright and in a respectful posture during your long prayers; I cannot rejoice in my tribulations, nor can I do good to others, because you do not supply me with what is necessary.' If, however, the servant of God prudently and becomingly provides his body with all that is necessary, and our brother the body, after being sufficiently nourished, still grumbles, and becomes negligent and idle, or sleepy in prayer, and watching, and other good works, know then that the lazy horse requires the spur, and the ass that will not move must expect the stick; therefore he must be punished as a lazy, good-for-nothing beast, who wishes to eat, and not to labour or to bear burdens. If, indeed, through poverty, we cannot provide our brother the body with what is necessary for him either in health or sickness, the Religious should humbly and truthfully ask his Superior for what he wants for the love of God, and if he cannot obtain it let him bear his want patiently for the sake of Our Lord, Who sought for some one to comfort Him and could find none. And this his necessity, will by God be imputed to him as a martyrdom. And if he does all that depends on him, that is, if he humbly make known his necessity, he will not be guilty of any sin, even if his body suffer grave injury therefrom.

CONFERENCE IX.

Of Indiscreet Fervour in Abstinence.

MY Brethren, let each one consider his own constitution, for although some among you may be able to support nature with very little food, I do not wish that others who require more nourishment should endeavour to imitate them in this matter; but let each one, considering the requirements of his nature, provide for the needs of his body. As, therefore, we must avoid all excess in eating, which weighs down both body and soul, so likewise, and even more, must we beware of any excess in abstinence, for the Lord loves mercy and not sacrifice.

CONFERENCE X.
Of bearing with small Discomforts.

THOSE wants, my beloved Brethren, which do not come from reason, but from mere sensuality, are manifest signs of the loss of fervour. A tepid spirit, which is becoming gradually deprived of grace, turns necessarily to the things of flesh and blood. If the soul is deprived of spiritual delights, what is there left for it but to seek carnal ones? And then the animal appetite makes the necessity appear real; then the carnal desire influences the conscience. But even if a brother has a real necessity, and at once hastens to satisfy it, what reward will he receive? An occasion of merit has been offered him, but he studiously endeavours to avoid it; thus, not to suffer these necessities patiently, is nothing else but to return to the flesh-pots of Egypt.

CONFERENCE XI.
Of Rejoicing Spiritually in the Lord.

ALWAYS, my beloved Brethren, have a holy joy in God, both interior and exterior. If the servant of God endeavours to have and to keep spiritual joy, which springs from a pure heart, and is acquired by devout prayer, then the devils cannot harm him; they are forced to say: 'Since this servant of God rejoices alike in tribulation and prosperity, we cannot find an entrance into his heart, and are unable to injure him.' But the devils rejoice exceedingly if they can extinguish or even lessen this joy and devotion, which come from prayer and good works. For if the devil can once succeed in getting anything of his own into the heart of a servant of God, unless it be at once wisely and carefully destroyed and rooted out (as it soon may be) by the virtue of holy prayer, contrition, confession, and satisfaction, then in a short time of one hair he makes a rope, by constantly adding something to it. Therefore, my beloved Brethren, as this holy joy comes from cleanness of heart, and the purity of continual prayer, we must principally endeavour to acquire these two virtues, that thus we may have this joy both exterior and interior, which I desire so greatly, and love so much to see and feel, both for myself and you, to the edification of our neighbour, and the confusion of the enemy. Sadness belongs to the devil and his children, but to us perpetual joy and jubilation in the Lord.

CONFERENCE XII.

Of the Humility and Peace to be observed towards Priests.

MY beloved Brethren, we have been sent to assist priests in the salvation of souls, that what is wanting in them may be supplied by us. Everyone will receive his reward, not according to his dignity, but according to his labour. Know, my Brethren, that the salvation of souls is most pleasing to God, and this we shall procure much better by living in concord with the clergy than by being at variance with them. If they hinder this work, God is their judge, and He will avenge it in due time. Therefore be subject to the Prelates, that, as far as you can prevent it, no envy may arise. If you are the sons of peace, you will gain both the clergy and the people, and this will be much more acceptable to God than if you gained the people only, and scandalised the clergy. Hide their faults, supply their deficiencies; and when you have done this, humble yourselves all the more.

CONFERENCE XIII.
How to Recognise a Servant of God.

OH, how good a thing it is, my Brethren, to serve God! The service of God is better than the empire of the world. But who can be sure that he is the servant of God? There is nothing better than to serve God, but yet there is nothing more difficult than for a man to know with certainty whether he is the friend and the servant of God. I own to you that I asked Our Lord that He would deign to make known to me when I am His servant, and when I am not. This most benign Lord, in His mercy, thus answered me: 'Thou mayst know thyself to be My true servant when thou thinkest holy thoughts, speakest holy words, and performest holy works.' I have told you this in order that you also may know when you are true servants of God, and pleasing to Him, and that I may be put to shame before you when you see me fail in all or any of the aforesaid things.

CONFERENCE XIV.
Whether it is more Pleasing to God to Pray or to Preach.

I HAVE a great doubt, my beloved Brethren, which I wish to propose to you, that you may solve it with the help of God. What, my Brethren, do you counsel me? Which do you think best, that I should give myself to prayer, or that I should go about preaching; inasmuch as I, poor, simple, and unskilful in speech, have received a greater grace of prayer than of eloquence? In prayer, likewise, we find profit, and an accumulation of graces; in preaching we distribute the gifts we have received from heaven. In prayer we obtain the purification of the interior affections, and union with the one true and Sovereign Good, with an increase of virtue; in preaching we suffer the soiling of our spiritual feet, distraction about many things, and relaxation of discipline. Finally, in prayer we speak to God and hear His voice, and leading a sort of angelic life, we have our conversation among the angels; while in preaching we must use much condescension with men, and living an earthly life among them, we must think, see, hear, and speak about earthly things. But there is one thing on the other side which seems to outweigh all these advantages before God, namely, that the Only-Begotten Son of God, Who is the Infinite Wisdom, descended from the Bosom of His Father for the salvation of souls, that, teaching the world by His example, He might preach the Word of life to men, whom He would redeem, cleanse, and nourish with His precious Blood; reserving nothing for Himself which He did not bountifully lavish for our salvation. And because we ought to follow the example shown us by Him, it would seem to be more pleasing to God, that interrupting our repose, we should go forth to labour. Wherefore give me your advice in this matter.

CONFERENCE XV.
Of those who Apply themselves to Learning.

THOSE Brothers who study from curiosity will find their hands empty in the day of tribulation. Therefore I would rather they should be strengthened in virtue, that when the day of trial comes, they may have the Lord with them in their anguish; for a time of tribulation will come, when their books will be thrown away as useless. I do not wish my Brothers to be too anxious for books and knowledge; but I desire them to be grounded in holy Humility and pure Simplicity, in holy Prayer, and my Lady Poverty. This is the only secure way to our own salvation, and the edification of others; for Christ, Whom the Brethren are bound to imitate, has taught us only this way, both by His Word and example. Many Brethren, under pretence of edifying others, will turn aside from their vocation, which is holy Humility, pure Simplicity, Prayer and Devotion, and our Lady holy Poverty. And it will happen to them that, while they imagine they are full of devotion, inflamed with love, and illuminated with the knowledge of God through their understanding the Holy Scriptures, they will, on this very account, remain cold and vain; and thus they will not be able to return to their first vocation, because they have lost the time of living as they ought, in vain and false study.

CONFERENCE XVI.
Of Vain and Conceited Preachers.

THERE are many, my Brethren, who devote themselves entirely to acquiring knowledge, losing their holy vocation by leaving the road of humility and prayer, and becoming dissipated in body and mind—who, if they find anyone converted and moved to penance by their sermons, become proud and puffed up by their work, and another's gains, when they have rather preached only to their own prejudice and condemnation, and have in reality worked nothing, except as the instruments of those by whom the Lord has truly acquired this fruit. For while they believe that sinners are moved and converted by their knowledge and preaching, it is really by the prayers and tears of some poor, humble and simple Brothers that God works these conversions, although these holy Brothers are generally unconscious of it. God wills it to be so, lest they should become proud thereof. These, my Brethren, are 'knights of the round table,' who hide in deserts and lonely places, that they may more diligently give themselves up to prayer and meditation, weeping for their own sins and those of others, living simply and conversing humbly, whose sanctity is known to God, but hidden from their Brethren and from all men. But when the angels present their souls to God, then the Lord will show them the fruit and reward of their labours; namely, many souls that have been saved through their prayers, tears, and example. And He will say to them: 'Behold, My beloved children, such and such souls that have been saved by your prayers, tears, and example, and, "because you have been faithful in a few things, I will place you over many things." Others have preached and laboured with words of wisdom and knowledge, and I, on account of your merits, have rendered their words fruitful; receive, therefore, the reward of their labours, and the fruit of your merits, that is, the eternal kingdom which you have taken by violence with your humility and simplicity, your prayers and tears.' These, therefore, carrying their sheaves, namely, the fruit and merit of their holy Humility and Simplicity, shall enter rejoicing and exulting into the joy of their Lord; while those, on the contrary, who have thought of nothing but knowing and pointing out the way of salvation to others, without walking therein themselves, will stand naked and empty-handed before the tribunal of Christ, bearing only the sheaves of shame, confusion, and sorrow. Thus the truth of holy Humility and Simplicity, of holy Prayer and Poverty, which is our vocation, will be exalted, glorified, and magnified; which truth those who are puffed up by the vain love of science contradict by their life and idle words, calling the truth falsehood, and persecuting those who walk in this truth. Then the errors and false opinions which they have held—which they have declared to be the truth—and by which they have plunged many into an abyss of blindness, will end in sorrow, shame, and confusion; and on account of the darkness of their minds, they will be cast into the exterior darkness, with the spirits of darkness.

CONFERENCE XVII.
Of the Marks and Praise of a Good Preacher.

I WISH, my beloved Brethren, the ministers of the Word of God to be such, that, devoting themselves to spiritual studies, they should not be hindered by undertaking any other duties. For they are chosen by the great King to proclaim to the people the laws which proceed from His mouth. The preacher ought first to imbibe in secret prayer what he afterwards brings forth in holy words; he ought to be inflamed interiorly before he speaks exteriorly. This office is certainly worthy of honour, and those who fulfil it ought to be reverenced by all, for they are the life of the body, the adversaries of the devils, the light of the world. Those preachers are to be commended who sometimes examine and try themselves; but those know badly how to act who devote themselves entirely to preaching and not at all to devotion. Others, again, are to be pitied, who often sell what they do for the oil of empty praise. The office of preaching, my Brethren, is more acceptable to the Father of mercies than any sacrifice, especially if it be undertaken with the fervour of charity, so that the preacher labours more by his example than by his words—more by tears of devotion than by loquacious speaking. Therefore that preacher is to be pitied as devoid of true piety, who in his sermons seeks not the salvation of souls, but his own praise; or who destroys by the wickedness of his life, what he builds up by the truth of his doctrine. A Brother, simple and slow of speech, who by his good example excites others to good, is much to be preferred to such an one. 'The barren has borne many children,' says the Prophet, 'and she that had many sons has become weak.' The barren is the poor little Brother who has not the office of bringing forth sons in the Church. In the day of judgment he will bear many, because those whom he now converts to Christ by his hidden prayers will then be called his, for his glory by the Judge. He who had many sons shall be made weak, because the vain and loquacious preacher, who rejoices now because he thinks he has gained many by his own strength, shall know then that they do not in anywise belong to him.

CONFERENCE XVIII.

Of Murmuring and Detraction.

THE vice of detraction, my Brethren, is an enemy to the very source of piety and grace, and is abominable to the most merciful God; because the detractor feeds on the blood of the souls he has murdered with the sword of his tongue. The impiety of the detractor is far greater than that of the thief, because the law of Christ (which is fulfilled by showing mercy) commands us to desire more ardently the salvation of the soul, than the safety of the body. The Religious who murmurs against his Brethren, or his Superiors, what does he do but drench his Mother, holy Religion, with the gall of bitterness and insults? Detractors are of the generation of Cham, who ridiculed the shame of his father instead of hiding it; thus these make known and exaggerate the faults of their Superiors and their Order, and they consequently deserve to be cursed by God. These, like swine, wallow in mire; for, after the manner of these unclean animals (being themselves far more unclean in their consciences), they feed and gorge themselves on the defects and weaknesses which they curiously seek for, and often falsely affirm they see and find in others; like mad dogs, they grumble at religious discipline and correction; they bark against their Order and their Superiors; and when they can, they bite. This is what the detractor says: 'My life is most imperfect, I have no particular grace or merit, therefore I cannot find favour either with God or man. I know what I will do. I will discover the defects of my Brethren, and thus I shall obtain favour with my Superiors. I know they are men like unto myself, and in this way I may also get into office, because, when the cedars are fallen, the branches only will remain in the way.'

Alas! miserable man, feed thyself upon human flesh, and, unable to live otherwise, gnaw the entrails of my Brethren.

Detractors wish to appear good without being so, to declaim against vice, but not to give up practising it; they praise only those in authority, whose favour they wish to gain; and they never praise anyone unless they think he will hear of it. They make themselves pale with fasting for the sake of praise, that they may be considered spiritual; they can judge all things, and may not be judged by any. They glory in the good opinion of men, not in good works; in having the name of angels, but not the virtues.

CONFERENCE XIX.

The Brethren are not to be called Masters.

Do not, my Brethren, seek to be called Master; for the name of Master belongs only to Christ, Who has created all things. I would willingly know how to do all things, but I would never willingly be looked upon as a Master, nor honoured with the title of Master, lest I should seem to act in opposition to the words of Christ in the Gospel; for it is better to be humble, with very little knowledge, than (were that possible) to know how to do all great and wonderful works, and oppose the lowly teaching of our glorious Master. For the name of Master belongs only to Our Lord Jesus Christ, Whose works are perfect, and Who has commanded that no one on earth should be called by this title; for this only befits Him, Who is the One, True, and Perfect Master in heaven, the Blessed Christ, Who is God and Man, the Life, the Creator of the world, worthy of praise and glory for ever and ever. Amen.

CONFERENCE XX.

Of the Benefits that will accrue to the Order by being subject to the Holy Church.

THE Roman Church, my Brethren, is the Mother of all Churches, and the Mistress of all Religious Orders. I am going to recommend my Brethren to the Holy Church, whose powerful rod will strike the wicked, and under whose care the children of God shall advance in perfection, and ever enjoy true liberty. Acknowledge then, my Brethren, the sweet benefits of your Mother, and always embrace her venerable traditions with special devotion. Under her protection no evil shall befall our Order, nor the son of Belial ravage the vine of the Lord with impunity.

This Holy Church will be jealous for the glory of our Poverty, and will not suffer the cloud of pride to overshadow the renown of our Humility. She will keep the bond of peace and charity unbroken among us, punishing the discontented with the most rigorous censures. The observance of evangelical purity will constantly flourish under her protection, nor will she allow the good odour of our life to perish in the least.

CONFERENCE XXI.

Of the Tribulations of the Order, and of those who follow the Rule.

THE time will come, my Brethren, when this Order, beloved by God, will be so disgraced by the evil example of evil Brethren, that it will blush to appear in public. Those who at that time shall come to join the Order will be led solely by the Spirit of God; there will be no stain of flesh and blood in them, and they will indeed be blessed by God. Although their works may be most meritorious, still charity, which causes the saints to labour so fervently, growing cold, these Religious will have to suffer immense temptations, and those who at that time are found faithful shall be better than their predecessors. Woe to those who, contenting themselves with the look and appearance of religion, and confiding in their knowledge and worldly prudence, are found idle, that is, not exercising themselves in virtuous works, in the way of the Cross and of penance, and in the pure observance of the Gospel precepts which by their profession they are bound to keep simply and entirely. These will not constantly resist the temptations which God will permit for the trial of the elect. But those who are proved and found faithful shall receive the crown of life, for which they have been prepared by the persecutions of the perfidious and reprobate.

CONFERENCE XXII.

Of Conversing with Holiness among the Faithful.

IN the Name of the Lord, go two and two in your journeys, humbly and modestly, and above all keep strict silence from the early morning until Tierce, praying to God in your hearts. Let no idle or useless words be spoken among you, but, even as you walk, let your conversation be as humble and edifying as if you were in your Convent or in your cell. For wherever we are, or wherever we go, we have always our cell with us. Our brother the body is our cell, and the soul is the hermit who dwells therein to praise God and meditate on Him, and if the soul does not remain in quiet in this cell, other cells which are built will be of little profit. Let your conversation among the people be such that whoever sees and hears you may devoutly praise the Most High God, our heavenly Father. Announce peace to all men, saying: 'The Lord give you His peace.' But since you preach peace with your lips, much more have peace in your hearts. Let no one be moved to anger or scandal on your account, but endeavour to lead all to peace, benignity and concord by the example of your meekness. For to this we are called, to heal the wounded, to bind up what is broken, and to bring back those who have gone astray. Many, in truth, may now seem to you to be members of the devil, who will yet be disciples of Christ.

CONFERENCE XXIII.

How the Brethren are to Act among Infidels.

MY Children, God has commanded me to send you into the land of the Saracens, that you may preach and confess His faith, and oppose the law of Mahomet. And I myself will go among other infidels, and I will send the other Brethren to all parts of the world. Prepare yourselves, therefore, my Sons, to accomplish the Will of the Lord. And, O beloved

Children, in order more perfectly to fulfil the command of God for the salvation of your souls, take care that there be among you peace and concord and the bond of indissoluble charity. Fly from envy, which was the beginning of our perdition. Be patient in tribulation, humble in prosperity, and thus you will be victorious in all combats. Be imitators of Christ in Poverty, Obedience, and Chastity. For Our Lord was born poor, lived poor, taught poverty, and died in poverty. And to show how much He loved chastity He chose to be born of a virgin; His first soldiers were the virgin Innocents; He always counselled and practised virginity, and He died in the company of virgins. Obedience, likewise, He observed from His birth to His death on the Cross. Place your hope in God alone, Who will guide and help you. Take with you your Rule and your Breviary, that you may recite most diligently the Divine Office, and be all obedient to Brother Vitalis, your Superior. O my Children, while I rejoice at your good will, my heart feels a kind of loving bitterness at the thought of your departure and separation from me; but we must prefer the commandment of God to our own will. I entreat you keep the Passion of Christ ever before your eyes, which will strengthen and animate you to suffer for Him.

CONFERENCE XXIV.

On the assiduous Meditation of the Passion of Christ.

ALWAYS keep before your eyes, my dearest Brethren, the way of Humility, Poverty, and the holy Cross, by which Our Lord Jesus Christ admonishes us to consider that if it behoved His Majesty to suffer, and thus to enter into His glory, much more should we, who are such great sinners, embrace the way of the Cross and of suffering. And surely if all Christians are bound to take up their cross, much more are we obliged to do so, who profess to follow the standard of the Cross; for it is the will of God that we should not only bear the cross ourselves, but that we should excite others, and lead them by our words and example to do the same, so that, together with them, we may follow Christ, our Leader. This goodwill and desire to imitate the Passion of Our Saviour is the peculiar gift which the Holy Ghost gives to those souls who really love and serve God; for those who are attached to earthly things, and love themselves only, abhor this doctrine of the Holy Spirit, and do not consider it necessary, in order to acquire perfection, to become partakers of the sufferings of Christ. On the contrary, promising themselves greater profit in other ways, which are not true ways, but hidden precipices, and flying from the bitterness of tribulation by many human and self-willed devices, they have their hearts hardened and blinded by self-love, and falsely assert that in this liberty of life they can better serve God. They do not realise the innumerable interior delights which that soul enjoys who is entirely absorbed in the contemplation and compassion of the sufferings of her Lord, nor indeed could they perfectly taste of them unless they underwent some tribulation for Christ. But the soul dead to herself, and entirely despoiled of selfish affections, humbly permits herself to be guided by the Holy Ghost, that He may work in her according to His good pleasure, as a perfect Master of the excellent doctrine which Christ has left written in the book of His humility, patience, and suffering, which is the sure road to Christian perfection. Hence this soul, which has been purified by God, desires most vehemently to be transformed into His sufferings; looking upon all other ways and consolations as earthly food which perishes, but on this as the only medicine of salvation, whose taste is bitter, but whose fruit is most sweet; for what is bitter to the taste is most sweet in its results. Wherefore, preferring her good to her pleasure, she proves how admirable is the sweetness of everlasting life; she despises momentary and earthly consolations, and fully experiences that her love cannot more perfectly rest in anything than in a loving compassion for Christ; and that the more she is transformed into Christ Crucified, the more she is transformed into the Most High and Glorious God. For the Humanity is not separated from the Divinity; and Christ Himself, praying to His Father, has said: 'I will that where I am, they also may be.' And thus the soul contemplates both these states of her Lord, so as never to be separated from Him. For if we fly from His Passion, we shall be separated from Him in His Glory, according to the words of the Apostle St. Paul: 'If we suffer with Him, we shall also be glorified with Him.' The soul therefore contemplates Christ both as mortal and immortal, for one is the state of those who still run, the other of those who have already received the prize. And as the prize is only given to those who run, so heaven will only be given to those who bear the Cross; for the servant is not greater than his Lord, nor the disciple above his Master. For this reason we see that God communicates His grace to those who follow Him in this way, but, on the contrary, withdraws it from those presumptuous ones who imagine they can be united to Him in other ways without ever going out of themselves, but who, in truth, are miserably running to a precipice.

CONFERENCE XXV.
Why, having renounced the Office of General, St. Francis bore with the Defects of the Brethren.

SOME of you, my Brethren, wonder and ask me why I do not correct the faults which are committed in the Order. May the Lord pardon such Brethren, for they are displeasing to me, because they wish to entangle me in things which do not belong to my office. As long as I was Superior over my Brethren, and they remained steadfast in their vocation and profession, I ministered to them both by words and example with much solicitude, although I was very infirm even from the beginning of my conversion. But afterwards I saw that the Lord had multiplied the number of the Brethren, and that they, through tepidity and want of courage, began to decline from the strait and secure road in which they had been walking; and entering upon the broad way which leads to death, would not consider their vocation and profession, nor leave the perilous and deadly path they were treading for the preaching, admonitions, and good example which I constantly offered them;

therefore I resigned the government and Generalship of the Order to God and the Ministers. But although, when I renounced the office of Superior, I told the Brethren in the general Chapter that, on account of my infirmities, I could no longer take care of them, nevertheless, if the Brethren would even now act according to my wishes, for their consolation and benefit, I should not desire them to have any other General but myself as long as I live. For if a good and faithful subject knows and does the will of his Superior, that Superior need have very little anxiety about him. Moreover, so much should I rejoice in the well-doing of my Brethren, both for their profit and my own, that even were I ill in bed it would not be irksome to me to serve them; for the office of Superior is spiritual only, that is to subdue vices, and spiritually to correct and amend them. But if I cannot do this by preaching, by admonitions and example, I will not become an executioner to scourge and punish, as do the rulers of this world. But I trust in the Lord that invisible enemies, who are the executioners of God to punish in this world and the next those who transgress His commandments, will take vengeance on them, causing them to be chastised by the men of the world in shame and contempt, that they may return to their profession and vocation. Nevertheless, as long as I live I will not cease by works and example to teach the Brethren to walk in the way which the Lord has shown me, and which I have hitherto taught and shown them, that they may be inexcusable before God. And henceforth I am not bound to render an account of them before God.

CONFERENCE XXVI.
Of the Qualities that should Characterise the Minister-General.

THE leader of so great an army, consisting of persons of such various dispositions, the shepherd of such a large and wide-spreading flock, can scarcely be equal to the greatness of his charge, but I will endeavour to describe to you, my Children, what the leader and shepherd of this family should be. This man ought to be of grave demeanour, of great discretion, of good fame, devoid of all particular affections, lest loving one part too much, he scandalise the whole; a man who is a friend of prayer, in such a manner, however, that he give certain hours to his own soul, and certain others to the flock committed to his care. First of all, he ought early in the morning to offer the most Holy Sacrifice of the Mass, and at that time, with great and prolonged devotion, he should earnestly recommend himself and his flock to the Divine protection. After his prayer, he must devote himself to hear everyone, to answer everyone, and to provide for everything with patience, charity, and sweetness. He should not be an accepter of persons, but should care for the simple and ignorant as much as for the wise and learned. If the gift of science has been bestowed upon him, he should strive still more to give an example of piety, simplicity, patience and humility. Let him cherish all virtues in himself and others, and constantly exercise himself in the practice of them; thus exciting others more by his example than be words. Let him be a hater of money, which is thy chief enemy of our profession and perfection; and remembering that he is the head and the model for the imitation of others, let him be careful never to retain any about him. Let him be content with his habit and a few books, and on account of his office he must have a writing-desk and a seal. Let him not be a collector of books, nor a great reader, lest he should take from his duties the time he gives to study. Let him kindly console the afflicted, so that he may be the last refuge of those in tribulation, lest the weak, if they do not find comfort from him in their troubles, should be overcome with the sadness of despair. In order to bring the froward to meekness, let him humble himself, and relax something of his authority, so that he may gain souls to Christ. Let him have compassion on those who abandon the Order, as on sheep that have gone astray; and let him never refuse to show them mercy, considering how strong that temptation must be which can lead souls to such a step, and that if God had permitted him to experience the same, he might have fallen into a deeper abyss. I wish him, as one holding the place of Christ, to be honoured by all with devotion and reverence, and to be provided for by all with great kindness, according to his necessities, and as far as our Rule allows. Nevertheless he ought not to take pleasure in honours, nor rejoice in favours more than in injuries, and he ought not to change his manners on account of honours, except to improve them. If he require better and more costly food than others, let him not take it in private, but in public, so as to prevent others from being ashamed of the same indulgence in their infirmities and weaknesses. It belongs to him especially to discover the secrets of consciences, and to draw the truth from hidden sources. Let him not at once believe any accusations, until he discover the truth by diligent examination. Let him not listen to great talkers, and let him be on his guard against those who are constantly finding fault, and not easily give credence to them. Moreover, he should be such that he will never, through the desire of retaining honour, infringe or relax the rule of justice and equity, in such a manner, however, that no soul may be destroyed through excessive rigour, nor tepidity arise from too great mildness, nor relaxation of discipline spring from weak indulgence ; let him be feared by all, but loved by those who fear him. Let him always consider the office of superiority as a burden rather than an honour. I wish him to have as assistants men of exemplary lives, rigid against self-indulgence, strong to suffer, and compassionate to those who fall ; having an equal affection for all, receiving nothing in reward for their labours except absolute necessaries, desiring nothing but the glory of God and the good of the Order, merit for their own souls, and perfection for the souls of their Brethren ; affable to all, and receiving all who come to them with a holy joy, showing forth to all purely and simply the form and example of the observance of the Gospel, according to the Rule of our holy Profession.

Such ought to be the Minister-General and his assistants.

CONFERENCE XXVII.

Of the Qualities of the Provincial Ministers.

I WISH my Brethren, the Provincial Ministers, to be so kind and affable to their inferiors that the guilty may not fear to trust themselves to their affection. I desire them to be moderate in their commands, forgiving towards offenders; bearing with sinners rather than resenting the sin, enemies to vice but physicians to the vicious. In fine, I wish them to be such that their lives may be a mirror of discipline to others. I wish them to be loved and honoured by all, as those who bear a burden of anxiety and labour. I consider that those who observe these rules and govern souls in this manner, will deserve a great reward from God.

CONFERENCE XXVIII.

What Manner of Life is to be observed at St. Mary of the Angels, and that the Brethren are never to give up that Place.

MY beloved Brethren, I wish this place to be always under the immediate government of the Minister-General, and therefore he should take great care to establish there a good and holy Community. The best and holiest clerics and the most exemplary Brothers must be chosen, and those who best know how to recite the Divine Office, so that not only seculars but even other Brothers may be glad to see and hear them. From among the lay-Brothers let there be also selected holy, discreet, humble and edifying men to serve them. I desire likewise, that no person and no Brother enter into this Monastery, except the Minister-General, and those Brothers who serve. Nor may the inmates speak with anyone except the lay-Brothers and the Minister when he visits them. I also wish that the lay-Brothers, who serve them, be bound never to speak to them idle words, or the news of the world, or anything that is not profitable for their souls. Therefore I specially command that no one should enter this place, that the Religious may the better preserve their purity and sanctity, and that nothing useless may be said or done there; but it must be kept sacred with hymns and praises of God. And when one of these Brethren goes to God, I desire that the Minister-General put another holy Brother in his place. For if the other Religious should hereafter decline from purity and sanctity of life, I desire that this holy place may be, and ever remain, a model and a good example to the whole Order, and as a candle always burning and shining before the Throne of God, and the Blessed Virgin, by which the Lord may be appeased for the defects of all the Religious, and may always preserve and protect this Order, His own little plant. Take heed, my Brethren, that you never forsake this spot. If you are cast out by one door, re-enter by the other. For this is a sacred place, and the dwelling of Christ, and of the Blessed Virgin Mary His Mother. Here, when we were few in number, the Most High multiplied us; here, by the light of His wisdom, He illuminated the minds of His poor ones; here, by the fire of His love, He inflamed our wills;

here, whoever prays devoutly shall obtain what he asks for, but he who sins shall be more grievously punished. Therefore, my Children, consider this place most worthy of all honour and reverence, as the true Tabernacle of God, singularly beloved by Him, and His holy Mother. And here with your whole hearts, and with the voice of joy and exultation, praise God the Father, and Jesus Christ His Son, in the unity of the Holy Ghost. Amen.

MAXIMS OF THE HOLY FATHER ST. FRANCIS.

I. MAN'S greatest enemy is his body. The body does not think over past evils to deplore them, nor does it look forward to future ones in order to fear them; its only care is to enjoy the present. But what is still worse, it usurps all good, transfers it all to its own glory, and impudently arrogates to itself what is given to the soul. It seizes for itself all the praise due to virtue, the esteem shown to fasts and vigils; it seeks even the reward due to tears, leaving nothing to the soul.

II. It is a noble prodigality to offer the love of God in exchange for alms, and those who think less of this love than of money are to be considered most foolish; for the love of God is of such inestimable worth that with it we may purchase the kingdom of heaven, and the love of Him Who has loved us so much should be much valued.

III. A Religious should earnestly desire the grace

Maxims of St. Francis.

of prayer, for without it he will never advance in the service of God, nor obtain anything from Him.

IV. The blessed treasure of Poverty is so excellent and divine, that we are unworthy to possess it in our vile vessels. By this virtue all earthly and transitory things are trampled under foot, all stumbling-blocks are removed from among us, and the human mind is most closely united to the Eternal Good. This it is which causes the soul on earth to converse with the Angels in heaven. This it is which unites us to Christ on the Cross, which hides us with Christ in the tomb; by it we rise with Christ from the sepulchre, and accompany Him to heaven. This it is which, when guarded by true humility and charity, gives to souls who love it, even in this world, the gift of agility, by which they fly to the highest heavens.

V. The Son of God descends from the bosom of the Father to the depths of our lowliness, that, as Our Lord and Master, He may teach us humility both by word and example. It is therefore foolish to be puffed up with human favour, or to be proud of earthly honour. For what is great before men, is abominable before God; and what a man is in the sight of God, that he is and no more.

VI. Superiors ought never to neglect holy and devout prayer, on account of the business of their office, or through solicitude in preaching. They must also sometimes go to beg for alms, work with their hands, and exercise themselves in other lowly offices like the other Friars, to give good example, and for the profit of many souls. For by this example of the Ministers and great preachers, the Brethren and the people will be edified, they will willingly give themselves to prayer, and will embrace the practice of humble and useful works. But if Superiors will not do these actions themselves, they cannot, without much shame, disadvantage and condemnation of themselves, urge others to do them. For after the example of Christ they must first do and then teach, or rather both together, do and teach.

VII. A man has as much knowledge as he shows by his works, and no more; and a Religious is a good preacher only inasmuch as he acts upon his preaching, for a tree is known by its fruits.

VIII. Our Lord and the Saints will be more honoured on their Festivals by the practice of poverty and mortification through which they entered heaven, than by superfluity and indulgence which keep souls back from heaven.

IX. Generosity is one of the attributes of God, Who causes the sun to shine, and the rain to fall upon all, whether just or unjust, and ministers to all most lovingly the necessaries of life. Generosity is the sister of charity, the destroyer of hatred, and the preserver of love.

X. It is not lawful to take the things of others to give to the poor. It is a sin worthy of punishment, not an act deserving a reward, to give away what belongs to others.

XI. It is a shame for anyone to be distracted with vain follies, when in the time of prayer he is speaking to the great King.

XII. The knowledge of himself will easily lead to the knowledge of God that man who, in studying the

Holy Scripture, searches into the mysteries despises with humility, and not with presumption.

XIII. When a servant of God is troubled in anything, he ought immediately to have recourse to prayer, and persevere in it before his Heavenly Father, until salutary joy is restored to his soul. For if he remains long in sadness, there will grow in him that confusion of heart which if not purged by tears will produce a grievous rust therein.

XIV. The price we pay for fame is the lessening of the secrets of the conscience. It is far more hurtful and dangerous to abuse virtues than to be without them; neither is it a greater virtue to seek for good, than to preserve it when acquired.

XV. What a Superior grants to an inferior through condescension, and because he has asked for it, is called a permission. But what the Superior commands without the inferior asking for it may be considered holy obedience. Therefore I consider obedience better and safer than a permission, for in the latter something of self-will is found, whereas in the former the precept of the Superior alone is accomplished. The highest obedience is when one vessel draws another, when the will of the Superior governs the will of the inferior, and flesh and blood have nothing to do with it. But it may be considered the highest and most perfect obedience, when leave is obtained to go and preach to the Infidels out of zeal for the salvation of souls and the desire of martyrdom, provided this desire comes from a Divine inspiration, for then one vessel draws another, the Divine Will draws the human will; therefore, to ask the people acceptable to God, and has all the merit of humility and of obedience.

If we endeavour to be at rest when we take food of the body, which will itself soon be the food of worms, with what peace and tranquillity should not the soul take the food of life, which is God, Who converses familiarly with us in prayer, and when we perform the duty of reciting the Divine Office!

XVII. Idleness is the sink of all bad thoughts; let all, therefore, labour and exercise themselves in work, lest through idleness their heart or their tongue should go astray.

XVIII. When the servant of God receives Divine consolations in prayer, he should say, 'O Lord, Thou hast sent this consolation to me, who am a sinner, and most unworthy, and I confide it to Thy keeping, for I feel I am one who robs Thee of Thy treasure.' And when he returns from prayer, he should think himself as poor and sinful as if he had received no such grace.

XIX. Superiors should rarely command through Obedience; they should not at first hurl the thunderbolt, which should be the last resort; nor should they too quickly lay their hand upon the sword. But if anyone does not fear the sword, if the subject delays to fulfil the precept of Obedience, then he fears not God and has no reverence for authority, unless there be some good cause for the delay. The Superior, therefore, must not be rash in commanding, for what is authority in the hands of a rash man but a sword in the hands of a madman? But what more desperate than the case of a man who neglects and despises Obedience?

XX. I consider holy Obedience so fruitful in merit, that they who submit their necks to this yoke cannot pass any time without profit, nor even spend a single hour without merit.

XXI. No one should take a foolish pride in what a sinner can do. A sinner can fast, pray, weep, and macerate his body; this only he cannot do, remain faithful to his God. In this, therefore, we may glory, in returning to God all His glory, in serving Him faithfully, and in ascribing to Him whatever He gives us.

XXII. All reverence and honour should be shown to the priests of God, who are superior to all other men in dignity. They are the spiritual Fathers of Christians, and the spirit and life of the world. As for me, if I were to meet a priest and an Angel in the road, I would immediately kiss the priest's hand, and I would say to the Angel: 'Wait for me, O Angel, for this hand has touched the Word of life, and has something supernatural about it.'

XXIII. I rejoice more over the kingdom of France than does the king of France himself, because I rejoice in the joy the king has in his kingdom. But I have this advantage over the king in the joy which I feel, for the king has all the labour and expense of his kingdom, while I rejoice without labour and without expense.

XXIV. Religious Superiors should take great care not to change the customs, except to improve them;

not to seek for favours, not to exercise power; but to fulfil their office.

XXV. The highest wisdom consists in doing good works, keeping a guard over oneself, and meditating on the judgments of God.

XXVI. True Poverty is the root of obedience, the mother of self-denial, the destroyer of self-complacency, the extirpator of vanity and avarice.

XXVII. Obedience is the work of faith, the test of true hope, the proof of charity, the mother of humility, the author of the peace of God, which exceeds all understanding.

XXVIII. In books the Brethren should seek the word of God, not value nor beauty. They should have but few books, and those in common, and let these be such as are suitable for poor Religious.

XXIX. A poor man may be more generous than a rich one; for if a rich man gives away all that he has, he will fall from his state in life, to his own confusion ; and if he does not give of the things he has, although he would be willing to do so if he would not lose his position thereby, his will is good, but it cannot be taken for the deed, because he still possesses goods. But the poor man who has nothing, who would like to give to the poor, but has nothing to give, who would like to build hospitals, but has not wherewith to do so—in him the will is taken for the deed.

XXX. To him who tastes God, all the sweetness of the world will be but bitterness. Taste, therefore, and see how sweet the Lord is, and thou wilt never weary of enjoying Him. It is quite otherwise with the love of the world, for bitterness is always hidden in it ;

the love of worldly things produces many fruits of sorrow; thus, if thou lovest wife, children, possessions, houses, or honours, when these die or perish they procure for thee as much sorrow as thou hast had affection and love for them.

FAVOURITE SENTENCES OF THE HOLY FATHER ST. FRANCIS.*

I. THESE are the weapons by which the chaste soul is overcome: looks, speeches, touches, embraces.

II. He who retires into the desert avoids three combats: seeing, hearing, and detraction.

III. Beloved, in this vale of misery may you possess nothing so fair and so delightful that your soul would be entirely occupied with it.

IV. Fly from creatures, if thou desirest to possess creatures.

V. Fly from the world, if thou wilt be pure. If thou art pure, the world does not delight thee.†

VI. Fly, keep silence, and be quiet.

VII. If thou excusest thyself, God will accuse thee; and if thou accusest thyself, God will excuse thee.

VIII. He is not perfectly good who cannot be good among the wicked.

---

* These *Sentences* were frequently used by St. Francis in instructing his Brethren. Some are his own, others are taken from the holy Fathers of the Church, or composed according to their doctrine.

† The play upon the words is lost in the translation. 'Fuge *mundum*, si vis esse *mundus*. Si tu es *mundus*, jam non delectat te *mundus*.'

IX. Temptation, when it is not consented to, is matter for the exercise of virtue.

X. Love makes all heavy things light, and all bitter things sweet.

XI. The love of God is never idle.

XII. Rich clothing and sumptuous dwellings, eating, drinking, sleep, and idleness, enervate men, and foster luxury.

XIII. When I say 'Hail Mary,' the heavens smile, the angels rejoice, the world exults, hell trembles, the devils fly.

XIV. As wax melts before the heat of the fire, and dust is scattered by the wind, so the whole army of the evil spirits is dispersed by the invocation of the holy Name of Mary.

XV. Let every creature become more despicable to the heart, that the Creator may become more sweet.

PART IV.

CANTICLES OF THE HOLY FATHER ST. FRANCIS.*

THE CANTICLE OF THE SUN.

'Altissimo, omnipotente, bon Signore.'

MOST high, Omnipotent, good Lord, to Thee,
All glory, honour, praise and blessing be :
Thou only art deserving of the same ;
No man is worthy to pronounce Thy Name.

Praised be my God for creatures, every one ;
And praised be Thou, my Lord, for Brother Sun,
Thy gift to us that he our day may light.
Most beautiful is he, and passing bright ;
Radiant in splendour—for in him we see
Displayed to us a glorious type of Thee.

Praise to my Lord for Sister Moon be given,
For all the clear and lovely stars of heaven.

Praised be my Lord for Brother Wind and Air ;
For clouds, and weather—be it dark or fair ;

---

* These three Canticles of Divine Love are found in all editions of the Works of St. Francis, although some writers think that the first only was composed by the Saint, and ascribe the other two to B. Jacopone of Todi. St. Bernardine of Siena gives them as the composition of St. Francis, and Ozanam thinks that at the most they were re-touched by B. Jacopone. The author of this beautiful translation has kindly permitted it to be reprinted here.

For by their ministry Thou e'er dost give
The sustenance whereby all creatures live.

Praise to my Lord for Sister Water be;
Most useful, humble, precious, chaste is she.

Praised be my Lord for Brother Fire, so bright;
By whom Thou dost illuminate the night;
For he is lively, and most beautiful;
And most robust withal, and powerful.

Praised be my Lord and God for Mother Earth,
Who governs and sustains us; who gives birth
To all the many fruits and herbs that be;
And coloured flowers in rich variety.

Praised be my Lord for those who pardon wrong
For love of Thee: enduring sorrow long;
Bearing their woes in peace.—Blessed are they!
By the Most High they shall be crown'd one day.

Praised be my Lord for Sister Death, from whom
No living soul escapes. She brings the doom
Of endless woe to all who pass away
In guilt of mortal sin. But blessed they
Who die in doing Thy most holy Will.
To them the Second Death can bring no ill.

O praise and bless my Lord right thankfully,
And serve ye Him with great humility.

CANTICLE II.

'In foco l' Amor mi mise.'

LOVE sets me all on fire,
Love sets me all on fire.

I.

Into Love's fire I'm cast
By my sweet Bridegroom new,
As on the ring He passed,
This loving Lamb me threw
Into a prison fast.
He pierced me through and through,
And broke my heart at last.
Love sets me all on fire.

II.

He pierced my heart; and lo!
On earth my body lay;
The shaft from Love's cross-bow
Hath rent my heart away.
He aimed a mighty blow,
Then peace to war gave way;
I die of sweetest woe.
Love sets me all on fire

III.

I die of sweetest woe,
No wonder, for the aim
That struck me such a blow,
From Love's own lances came,
A hundred arms' length,—know,
The blade that pierced my frame,
And laid my body low.
Love sets me all on fire.

IV.

He aimed His blows so fast,
I thrill'd with agony;

I took a shield at last;
'Twas no avail to me,
His darts anew He cast,
And struck so mightily,
That all my strength was past.
Love sets me all on fire.

V.

So hard His blows that I
Found all resistance vain;
Knowing that I must die,
I cried : ' O spare my pain !'
But hopeless was my cry,
For he began again,
A new device to try.
Love sets me all on fire.

VI.

And now He cast at me
So heavy stones and great,
Each one of them would be
A thousand pounds in weight.
'Twas vain to count them, He
Took aim so sure and straight,
And hurled so rapidly.
Love sets me all on fire.

VII.

He aimed His darts so well,
None ever glanced astray.
Prone on the ground I fell,
All helpless there I lay,
Spent and immovable.
Whether I'd passed away,

Or lived, I could not tell.
Love sets me all on fire.

VIII.

But lo! I did not die:
For my belovèd Lord,
To crown His victory,
My life anew restored,
So keen and fresh, that I
That moment could have soared
To join the saints on high.
Love sets me all on fire.

IX.

In life and limb restored,
And full of courage new,
Again I drew my sword,
And to the battle flew;
Once more with Him I warred,
And when I fought anew,
I conquered Christ my Lord.
Love sets me all on fire.

X.

When Christ I overthrew,
Again was peace restored,
For well I knew how true
The love of Christ my Lord.
And now, an ardour new
Within my heart is poured.
I burn with love anew
For Christ my Spouse adored.
Love sets me all on fire,
Love sets me all on fire.

CANTICLE III.

'Amor de Caritate.'

I.
Francis.

O LOVE of Charity!
Why hast Thou wounded me?
My heart is rent in twain
And burns with love of Thee.
It burns and burns again,
All restless with desire.

II.

'Tis bound, it cannot break its chain;
Consumed as wax before the fire:
Dying, it lives in sharpest pain—
Seeking with anguish and desire
To leave its furnace, but in vain.
    How do I not expire,
    In so great agony?
    I live, and yet I die,
    In this consuming fire.

III.

I asked, not knowing, when I prayed,
For love of Christ, it seemed so sweet.
Methought in peace I should have stay'd;
Then gained on high a glorious seat.
Alas! what agony instead!
My heart is rent with burning heat.
    No language can impart,
    No words of mine explain,
    How I die of sweetest pain,
    How I live without a heart.

IV.

Left without heart, without desire,
Bereft of sentiment and thought;
All beauty seems to me as mire,
Riches and happiness as nought.
A tree of Love, with fruit far higher,
Grows in my heart; and it hath wrought
    So sudden change in me,
    And so complete withal,
    That will, mind, senses, all,
    Are cast out utterly.

V.

I've given all for Love alone,
Barter'd the world and self away;
Were all created things mine own,
I'd yield them up without delay.
And yet by Love I am outdone;
Whither I'm led I cannot say.
    By Love I am outdone,
    Counted a fool withal;
    For, having sold my all,
    My worth is wholly gone.

VI.

The friends who walked not in my way,
In vain recalled me. What has he
To give, who gives himself away?
Can a slave quit his slavery?
Sooner a stone will melt, I say,
Than Love will cease to reign in me.
    This Love within my heart,
    Like fire for ever glows;
    Transform'd, united close
    To Love—no more to part.

VII.

Fire nor sword can part in twain,
Nought can dissolve so close a tie;
Sorrow nor death can e'er attain
The soul that has been raised so high;
And from that height she sees how vain
All earthly things beneath her lie.
    My soul, how hast thou soared
    Unto so high an aim?
    From Christ the favour came,
    Embrace thy sweetest Lord!

VIII.

Creatures are nothing in my sight;
My soul for its Creator yearns;
Heaven and earth yield no delight;
For love of Christ all else it spurns.
Before the splendour of that Light,
The very sun to darkness turns.
    What is the Cherub's hoard
    Of wisdom from above?
    What is the Seraph's love
    To him who sees the Lord?

IX.

Let no one chide me then, if I
Am foolish for the love of Christ.
From such a love 'tis vain to fly;
No heart can such a power resist,
This Love consumes so mightily,
Who can in such a fire exist?
    O that I could impart
    To one who'd pity me,
    The piercing agony
    That rends my very heart!

X.

Heaven and earth with one accord
Are ever crying out to me:
'With all thy heart, O love the Lord,
For He created us that we
Might draw thy spirit heavenward,
To love Him Who hath so loved thee.'
    Lo! what abundant beams
    Of goodness all benign,
    Flow from that Light Divine
    In never-failing streams!

XI.

I would love more, if that might be;
But since my very heart is gone,
Nothing of mine is left to me.
I've given all for Love alone,
That I may be entirely
Possess'd of the Belovèd One.
    O Beauty infinite!
    Ancient, yet ever new;
    'Tis given me to view
    Thy sweet, Eternal Light!

XII.

Seeing this Beauty, I am led
Out of myself, I know not where:
My heart, like molten wax, is made
The likeness of its Lord to bear.
O wonderful exchange! instead
Of self, Christ's image sweet to wear.
    My heart, transfigured quite
    By such a power of love,
    Is sweetly drawn above

XIII.

The soul, thus bound by sweetest ties,
Is yearning for her Lord's embrace;
The more His Beauty meets her eyes,
The more she longs on Him to gaze;
In Christ alone her treasure lies,
Forgetting self to seek His Face.
    She cares for nought besides,
    But to be His alone;
    For love of self is gone,
    Where only Christ abides.

XIV.

Transform'd by Christ, with Him made one;
Held in her God's Divine embrace;
She reigns a queen—for she has won
Christ Jesus, with His gifts and grace;
Sorrow and pain alike are gone
Where sin no longer holds a place.
    No guilty marks remain;
    Dead is the man of sin;
    The soul is pure within,
    And freed from every stain.

XV.

In Christ I'm newly born again:—
The old man dead, the new restored;
And whilst my heart is cleft in twain,
Transfixed by love as by a sword,
My spirit, all on fire, would fain
Behold the beauty of its Lord.
    I cry out ardently,
    While clasped in His embrace,
    Give me, O Love! the grace,
    To die for love of Thee!

XVI.

I languish for the love of Thee,
For Thy embraces sweet I pine;
Without Thee life is death to me.
With sighs and tears this heart of mine
Craves Thy return, that it may be
Transformed by Thee, made wholly Thine.
    O Love! make no delay—
    O hasten unto me!
    Unite me close to Thee,
    Consume my heart away.

XVII.

Behold my pain, sweet Love, I pray;
This burning heat I cannot bear:
I know not what I do or say,
Led on by Love, I know not where.
I go, as one who'd lost his way—
Weary, and wandering here and there.
    I know not how I may
    Endure this agony,
    Which so transfixes me,
    And rends my heart away.

XVIII.

Robb'd of my heart, I cannot see
What there remains for me to do;
If one should ask me: 'Can it be
That Christ wants idle love from you?'
I say, there is no help for me,
My heart being riven through and through.
    This Love in me hath wrought,
    With such consuming fire,
    I'm left without desire,

XIX.

Once I could speak, but now I'm dumb;
I saw—now cannot see at all;
To what a strange abyss I'm come!
Though held, I run; I rise, yet fall;
I speak, though mute I am become;
Pursue, and am pursued withal.
    O Love eternal! why
    Am I a fool for Thee?
    Wherefore hast Thou cast me
    In such a fire to die?

XX.

Christ.

Control Thy burning love for Me;
For virtue without rule is vain:
In seeking Me so ardently,
Renew thy mind and heart again;
And let well-ordered charity
Inform the heart wherein I reign.
    As by the fruit it bears,
    A tree is to be known;
    So by this test alone
    Its real worth appears.

XXI.

For I created everything,
In number and in measure too;
Each to its end is hastening,
And all are kept in order due;

How much more Charity, as being
The very soul of order true!
    Why is that heart of thine
    By Love so foolish made?
    It is that thou hast strayed
    So far beyond the line.

XXII.

Francis.

Christ! Thou hast robb'd my heart from me,
Then why dost Thou my ardour blame?
For, since I am changed into Thee,
I can no longer be the same:
As red-hot iron seems to be
All fire, and sun-lit air a flame.
    For each of these is seen
    Changed to another form;
    So doth Thy Love transform
    The heart Thou hast made clean.

XXIII.

Thus, having lost its quality,
The creature's acting-power is gone;
For, as it only lives by Thee,
Its works bear fruit through Thee alone;
Transform'd by Christ, and verily
Changed into the Belovèd One!
    Let all impute to Thee,
    Whate'er by me is wrought,
    And if it please Thee not,
    Then blame Thyself—not me.

XXIV.

Eternal Wisdom! well I know
That I'm a fool for love of Thee;
But since thy Love hath dealt the blow,
I've bartered self away to be
Chang'd into Thee anew, and so
Lead a new life, and utterly
    Casting myself aside;
    In Love's almighty power,
    I break through every door,
    And with my Love abide!

XXV.

My heart was set on fire by Thee;
Why bid me then my love restrain?
Thou gavest Thyself utterly
For me;—Can I give less again?
Thy littleness sufficed for me;
Thy greatness how can I contain?
    If any fault there be,
    'Tis Thine, O Lord, not mine;
    For 'twas Thy Love Divine
    Traced out this path for me.

XXVI.

Love was too powerful for Thee;
From Heaven to Earth it drew Thee down
So low, that Thou didst will to be
The last of men, despised, unknown,
Homeless and poor for love of me,
To make Thy riches all my own.
    So, in Thy Life and Death,
    Most surely didst Thou prove
    Thy Heart was fired with love

XXVII.
Thy Life was spent for Love indeed,
For Wisdom was by Love outdone;
Love showed in every word and deed;
Regardless of Thyself alone;
And in the Temple thou didst plead,
' Come to Me, every weary one!'
    All ye who thirst, draw nigh
    Unto the Living Well
    Of Love ineffable,
    Sweet Gift of God most High!

XXVIII.
Was that Love wise, O Saviour mine?
Which drew Thee down on earth below.
Born, not of flesh, but Love Divine;
Made Man to save us all from woe,
Thou didst embrace that Cross of Thine
For love of us, nay, more, I know,
    Thou didst not speak a word
    When Pilate judg'd Thy cause,
    In order, on the Cross,
    To die of Love, O Lord!

XXIX.
Thy wisdom, Lord, was hidden quite,
Thy power, too, Thou didst repress;
Love only was revealed to sight:
A Love all boundless in excess,
Which overflow'd with endless might,
And poured forth all its tenderness.
    This mighty Love it was
    That led Thee captive, when
    For love of sinful men,
    Thou didst embrace the Cross.

XXX.

Then, Jesus, if I overflow
With love so sweet and so intense,
Who shall reprove me, if I go
Out of myself—bereft of sense?
Since that same Love constrain'd Thee so,
As to subdue Omnipotence!
    O Love! how can I be
    Afraid of foolishness?
    If through it I possess
    And am possess'd by Thee!

XXXI.

This Love which makes me foolish, lo!
It took away Thy Wisdom quite.
This Love, which makes me languish so,
It robbed Thee of Thy very might;
Against the power of Love, I know,
'Tis useless to resist or fight.
    My sentence hath been pass'd.
    I die for love of Thee!
    There is no rest for me:
    I die of love, at last!

XXXII.

O Love, O Love, Thou hast so wounded me,
That I can cry out nothing else but 'Love!'
O Love, O Love, Thou hast so ravished me,
That all my heart is drawn to Thee above.
    I long so ardently
    My debt of love to pay,
    O grant me, Love, I pray,
    To die for love of Thee.

XXXIII.

Jesus, my Love, my Love, behold my woe!
Jesus, my Love, my Love, O comfort me!
Jesus, my Love, Thou hast inflamed me so;
Jesus, my Love, I die for love of Thee!
O make my heart with love for ever glow.
    O grant that I may be
Transform'd with Thee, in truth and charity.
    O Love, O Love, O Love!
    Everything speaks of Thee;
    O Love, so deep thou art,
    The more thou fillest the heart,
    The more it longs for Thee!

XXXIV.

O Love, O Love, Thou dost encircle close
The heart that yields to Thy Almighty power;
Thou art its vesture and its sweet repose;
And so it cries out 'Love!' for evermore:
It never can repay the debt it owes.
O Love, O Love, I love Thee more and more;
O Love, O Love, methinks that I shall die;
O Love, O Love, Thou hast so mastered me—
O make me Thine, my Love, eternally!
I languish for the love of Thee!
    O Love most amiable!
      How sweet to die for Thee!
    O Love ineffable!
      Kindle Thy love in me!

XXXV.

O Love, O Love, my heart is broken quite,
O Love, O Love, Thou hast so wounded me.

O Jesus! draw me to Thy beauty bright.
O Love, by Thee I'm rapt in ecstasy!
O Living Love! cast me not from Thy sight!
O Love, O Love, my soul is one with Thee!
    O Love, Thou art its Life;
    From Thee it ne'er can part,
    For Thou has rent my heart,
    In such a loving strife.

XXXVI.

My Love, my Love, Jesus! for Thee I pine;
    O Love! grant unto me
    To die, embracing Thee!
O my sweet Love! Jesus, my Spouse Divine!
O Love, O Love, I pray that I may die!
O Love, O Love, O Jesus so benign!
Transform me into Thee eternally!
See how I suffer from this love of Thine!
    I am no longer mine;
    Jesus, my Hope Divine!
Rest thou, my heart, for ever in His Love!

PRAYERS COMPOSED AND OFTEN SAID BY THE HOLY FATHER ST. FRANCIS.

Praises of the Most High.

THOU art holy, O Lord God; Thou art the God of Gods, Who alone workest wonders. Thou art strong, Thou art great, Thou art most High, Thou art omnipotent. Thou art the Eternal Father, King of heaven and earth. Thou art the Triune God. Thou art good, all good, the greatest good, O Lord God, true and only God. Thou art Love and Charity, Thou art Wisdom, Thou art humility, Thou art patience, Thou art Beauty, Thou art safety, Thou art rest, Thou art happiness, Thou art our hope and our joy. Thou art justice and temperance, Thou art fortitude and prudence. Thou art all riches, Thou art meekness. Thou art our protector, Thou art our guardian and defender, our strength and refuge. Thou art our faith, hope, and charity. Thou art all our sweetness, Thou art infinite Goodness, most great, most admirable, Almighty, pious, merciful Saviour,—my Lord and my God.

Prayer.

Omnipotent, Eternal, most Just, and most Merciful God, grant us miserable creatures to act always for Thee, to do always what we know Thou willest, and to will always what is pleasing to Thee; that, being purified interiorly and enlightened and inflamed by the fire of Thy Holy Spirit, we may follow closely in the footsteps of Thy Beloved Son, Our Lord Jesus Christ, and thus by Thy grace arrive at the possession of Thee, Who livest and reignest gloriously in the most perfect Trinity and simple Unity, Omnipotent God, for ever and ever. Amen.

Prayer to be said before the Divine Office.

Holy, holy, holy, Lord God Almighty, Who art and Who wert, and Who art to come.

Worthy art Thou, O Lord our God, to receive praise, glory, honour and benediction.

Let us praise and exalt Him for ever.

Worthy is the Lamb that was slain to receive power, and divinity, and wisdom, and strength, and honour, and benediction.

Let us praise and exalt Him for ever.

Let us bless the Father and the Son, with the Holy Spirit.

Let us praise and exalt Him for ever.

Praise the Lord, all ye servants of His, and all who fear Him, both small and great.

Praise and exalt Him for ever.

Let heaven and earth praise His glory,

And exalt and praise Him for ever.

And let every creature that is in heaven, on earth, and under the earth; the land and sea, and all that is in them,

Praise and exalt Him for ever.

Glory be to the Father, and to the Son, and to the Holy Ghost.

Let us praise and exalt Him for ever.

As it was in the beginning, is now, and ever shall be, world without end.

Let us praise and exalt Him for ever.

Prayer.

O most Holy, High and Omnipotent God, the great and supreme Good. Thou, Who art all Good and the only Good, to Thee do we render all praise, all honour, all blessing, and to Thee do we refer all good for ever. Amen.

Prayer used by the holy Father at the beginning of his Conversion.

O great and glorious God, and my Lord Jesus Christ, enlighten, I beseech Thee, the darkness of my mind. Give me a right faith, a certain hope, a perfect charity; grant that I may know Thee, O Lord, in order that I may always and in all things act according to Thy most holy and perfect will. Amen.

To obtain Divine Love.

Fill my heart, O Lord, I beseech Thee, with the most fiery and most sweet strength of Thy love, and remove far from it all earthly things, that I may die for love of Thy love, Who for love of my love didst deign to die. Amen.

Prayer the holy Father was accustomed to say at the Elevation of the Most Holy Body of Christ.

O Lord God, Heavenly Father, look upon the glorious Face of Thy Christ, and have mercy on me, and on all other sinners for whom Thy Blessed Son Our Lord deigned to suffer death, and for whose salvation and consolation He has chosen to remain for ever with us in the Holy Sacrament of the Altar, and Who with Thee and the Holy Spirit lives and reigns, one God for ever and ever. Amen.

Prayer in Time of Sickness.

I give Thee thanks, O Lord God, for all these pains, and I beseech Thee if it be Thy Will to increase them a hundredfold; for this is most pleasing to me, that afflicting me with suffering, Thou dost not spare me; let Thy Will be accomplished in me, and my consolation will be full.

Prayer when he resigned the Generalship.

O Lord, I commend to Thee this Thy family, which hitherto Thou hast confided to me, and which now, being no longer able to govern on account of my infirmities, as Thou, O my Lord, knowest, I am obliged to leave to Ministers, who in the day of judgment will have to render an account to Thee, if through their negligence, or bad example, or harsh correction, any of my Brethren should perish.

Prayer the holy Father said Daily.

My God and my All! Who art Thou, my sweetest Lord and God? and who am I, a poor little worm, Thy servant? Most holy Lord, I wish to love Thee! most sweet Lord, I wish to love Thee! O Lord my God, I have given Thee all my heart, and all my body, and I most earnestly desire, if I only knew how, to do still more for Thy love. Amen.

Salutation to the Blessed Virgin Mary.

Hail, holy Lady! most holy Queen, Mother of God, Mary! thou art ever-Virgin, elected by the most Holy Father of Heaven, consecrated by His most Holy and Beloved Son, and by the Holy Ghost, the Paraclete; in thee is and was the plenitude of all grace and all good! Hail, Palace of God, His Tabernacle, His Mother! Hail to you all holy virtues! infused into the hearts of the faithful by the grace and illumination of the Holy Spirit, that from unfaithful they may become faithful. Most holy Mother of Our Lord Jesus Christ, Spouse of the Holy Ghost, pray for us to thy beloved Son, Our Lord and Master, together with St. Michael the Archangel, and all the Angels and Saints of heaven. Amen.

Prayer to Our Blessed Lady.

Holy Mother of God, most sweet and most beautiful! intercede for us with the King (delivered up to death for us), thy own most sweet Son, Our Lord Jesus Christ, that through His tender mercy, and in virtue of His most holy Incarnation and bitter Death, we may obtain pardon for all our sins. Amen.

Another.

Holy Virgin Mary! there is none like unto thee among women. Thou art the daughter and handmaid of the Supreme King, the Heavenly Father; the most holy Mother of Our Lord Jesus Christ; the Spouse of the Holy Ghost! Pray for us in union with the Archangel St. Michael, and all the Angels and Saints of heaven, to thy Divine Son, our beloved Lord and Master. Glory be to the Father, and to the Son, and to the Holy Ghost. As it was in the beginning, is now and ever shall be, world without end. Amen.

Paraphrase of the Lord's Prayer.

Our Father, most Blessed and most Holy, our Creator, our Redeemer, and our Comforter.

Who art in Heaven, in the Angels and Saints, illuminating them with the knowledge of Thyself, for Thou, O Lord, art Light; inflaming them with Thy Divine love, for Thou, O Lord, art Love; dwelling in them and filling them with beatitude, for Thou, O Lord, art the Sovereign Good, the Eternal Good, from Whom proceeds all good, and without Whom nothing is good.

Hallowed be Thy Name. May Thy knowledge shine in us, that we may know the breadth of Thy benefits, the length of Thy promises, the height of Thy Majesty, and the depth of Thy judgments.

Thy Kingdom come, that Thou mayest reign in us by Thy grace, and bring us to Thy Kingdom when we shall enjoy Thy open vision, Thy perfect love, Thy blessed company and Thy eternal fruition.

Thy Will be done on earth as it is in Heaven, that we may love Thee with our whole heart by always thinking of Thee; with our whole soul by always desiring Thee; with all our mind by always directing our intention to Thee, and seeking Thy glory in all things; and with all our strength by employing all the powers and senses of our soul and body in the service of Thy love, and in nothing else; and that we may love our neighbour as ourselves, drawing all to Thy love with all our power, rejoicing in the good of others as in our own, compassionating them in their troubles, and giving offence to no one.

Give us this day, by our remembrance, understanding and reverence for the love He bore to us, and of all He did, and said and suffered for us, *our daily bread;* that is, Thy beloved Son Our Lord Jesus Christ.

And forgive us our trespasses, by Thy ineffable mercy, in virtue of the Passion of Thy beloved Son Our Lord Jesus Christ, and by the merits and intercession of the Blessed Virgin Mary and of all the Saints.

As we forgive them that trespass against us, and what we do not fully forgive, do Thou, O Lord, make us forgive; that for Thy sake we may truly love our enemies, and devoutly intercede for them with Thee; that we may never render evil for evil, but for Thy love may endeavour to serve all.

And lead us not into temptation, whether hidden or manifest, sudden or constant.

But deliver us from evil, past, present and future.

Amen. Spontaneously and out of Thy free mercy.

Prayer of the Blessed Father to obtain Poverty.

O Lord Jesus! show me the ways of Thy beloved Poverty. For I know that the Old Testament is a figure of the New. In the Old Testament it is said: 'Every place that your foot shall tread on shall be yours.' To tread under foot means to despise; Poverty tramples on all things, therefore she is the queen of all. But, O my most sweet Lord Jesus Christ, have pity on me, and on my Lady Poverty, for I burn with love of her, and without her I cannot rest. O my Lord, Who didst cause me to be enamoured of her, Thou knowest that she is sitting in sadness, rejected by all; 'the mistress of nations is become as a widow,' vile and contemptible; the queen of all virtues, seated on a dunghill, complains that all her friends have despised her, and are become her enemies;—they have proved themselves deceivers and not spouses. Behold, O Lord Jesus! how truly Poverty is the queen of all virtues; for, leaving the abode of Angels, Thou didst come down to earth that Thou mightest espouse her to Thyself with constant love, and produce from her, in her, and by her, the children of all perfection. And she clung to Thee with such fidelity that she began her service even when Thou wert in Thy Mother's womb, for Thy Body was of all the smallest; at Thy Birth she received Thee in a manger and a stable; and during Thy life she so stripped Thee of all things that she would not even allow Thee a stone whereon to rest Thy Head. As a most faithful consort she accompanied Thee when Thou didst go forth to fight for our Redemption; and in the conflict of Thy Passion she alone stood by as Thy armour-bearer; when Thy disciples fled, and denied Thy Name, she did not leave Thee, but with the whole band of her princes, she fearlessly adhered to Thee. On account of the height of Thy Cross, even Thy Mother (who so devotedly loved Thee, and shared so deeply in the bitterness of Thy Passion) could not reach Thee; but Thy Lady Poverty, with her companion Want, embraced Thee more closely than ever, and was more firmly united to Thee in

Thy sufferings. Therefore she would not allow Thy Cross to be smoothed or in any way polished; the very nails were (as is believed) too few in number, not sharpened nor ground; but she provided only three,—blunt, thick, and rough,—in order to increase Thy torments. And when Thou wast consumed with thirst, she, Thy faithful spouse, was there, and did not allow Thee to have even a drop of water; but by means of the impious executioners, she prepared for Thee a draught so bitter, that Thou couldst only taste, not drink it. In the strong embrace of this Thy spouse, Thou didst breathe forth Thy Soul. Nor did she forsake Thee at Thy burial, but she took care that Thou shouldst have neither sepulchre, nor ointments, nor winding-clothes, except what were lent Thee by others.

This Thy most holy spouse was not absent from Thy Resurrection, for rising gloriously in her embrace Thou didst leave in the Sepulchre all these borrowed things. Thou didst bear her with Thee to heaven, leaving all that is in the world. And now Thou hast given to Thy Lady Poverty the seal of Thy Kingdom, that she may sign the elect who walk in the way of perfection. Oh, who would not love the Lady Poverty above all! I beseech Thee to grant me this privilege; I beg to be enriched with this much-desired treasure. O most poor Jesus, I ask this favour for myself and my children for ever, that for love of Thee they may never possess anything of their own, that they may use the goods of others sparingly, and that they may suffer Poverty as long as they live in this miserable world. Amen.

TESTAMENT OF THE BLESSED FATHER ST. FRANCIS.

THE Lord granted to me, Brother Francis, thus to begin to do penance; for while I was in sin, it seemed to me too bitter a thing to see lepers, but the Lord Himself led me among them, and I showed mercy to them. And when I left them, that which had appeared to me bitter was changed into sweetness of body and soul; and not long after this I forsook the world. And the Lord gave me such faith in His churches that I would simply adore and say: 'We adore Thee, most holy Lord Jesus Christ, here, and in all Thy churches throughout the world, and we bless Thee because by Thy holy Cross Thou hast redeemed the world.'

After that Our Lord gave me, and still gives me, such faith in priests who live according to the Rule of the holy Roman Church, on account of their Orders, that even if they were to persecute me, I would still have recourse to them. And if I had the wisdom of Solomon, and found priests the poorest according to this world, I would not preach in the churches where they dwell, against their will. And these and all others I will fear, love and honour as my masters; and I will see no sin in them, because in them I behold the Son of God, and they are my lords. This I do, because in this world I see nothing corporally of the Most High Son of God, but His most holy Body and Blood, which they consecrate and receive, and which they alone administer to others. And these most holy Mysteries I wish above all things should be honoured and reverenced, and kept in becoming places. Wherever I find His most holy Names or written Words in unseemly places, I will collect them, and I wish that they may be gathered up and honourably kept. All theologians and those who minister to us the Divine Word, we must honour and reverence, as those who minister to us spirit and life.

Since the Lord gave me Brethren to take care of, no one showed me what I ought to do ; but the Most High Himself revealed to me that I should live according to the Rule of the Holy Gospel. This I caused to be written in few and simple words, and our Lord the Pope confirmed it for me. Those who came to adopt this Form of life gave all they possessed to the poor. And they were contented with one tunic, which those who wished, patched inside and out ; and with a girdle and drawers, and we would have nothing more. We, who were clerics, said the Office like other clerics, and the lay-Brothers said *Pater nosters.* And we most willingly dwelt in poor little abandoned churches, and we were simple,* and subject to all. I laboured also with my hands, and desire always to labour, and I earnestly wish all the other Brethren to work at all honest employments. Let those who do not know how to work learn, not through cupidity, that they may receive the price of their labours, but in order to give good example, and to avoid idleness. When men do not give us the price of our work, let us have recourse to the table of the Lord, begging alms from door to door.

The Lord revealed to me this salutation, that we should say : 'The Lord give thee His peace.' Let

* *Idiota*, fools for Christ's sake.

the Brethren take care not on any account to accept the churches, dwellings, or anything else that may be built for them, unless they are in accordance with the holy Poverty which we have promised in the Rule; always dwelling here below as strangers and pilgrims.

I strictly command all the Brothers, under obedience, that in whatever place they may be, they never presume to ask any letter from the Roman Court, either themselves, or by any person interposed, either for a church, or for any other place, under pretence of preaching, or on account of bodily persecutions; but wherever they are not received, let them fly to another country, and there do penance with the blessing of God. As for me, I will strictly obey the Minister-General of this Fraternity, and the Guardian whom it may please him to give me; and I will be as a slave in his hands, so that I may neither move nor act contrary to his will, because he is my master. And although I am simple and infirm, nevertheless I always wish to have a cleric who may say the Office with me according to the Rule. All the other Brethren are bound thus strictly to obey their Guardians, and to perform the Office according to the Rule. And if any should be found who will not perform the Office according to the Rule, or who wish to change it in any manner, or who are not Catholics, all the Brethren, wherever they may be, are bound, under Obedience, to present such an one to the Custode nearest to the place where he is. And the Custode is bound, under Obedience, to keep him strictly as a prisoner, day and night, until he can personally deliver him into the hands of his Minister. The Minister is likewise

Brothers who shall keep him night and day as a prisoner until they can present him to the Lord Cardinal of Ostia, who is the Lord Protector and Corrector of this Fraternity.

Let not the Brethren say : 'This is another Rule ;' for this is the record, admonition, exhortation, and my Testament, which I, your poor little Brother Francis, make for you, my blessed Brethren, to the end that we may observe in a more Catholic manner the Rule which we have promised to God. The Minister-General, the other Ministers and the Custodes, are bound under Obedience, not to add to these words, nor to take anything from them. And they shall always have this writing with them, together with the Rule ; and in all the Chapters they hold, when they read the Rule, they shall also read these words. I strictly command all my Brethren, both the clerics and lay-brothers under Obedience, not to put any gloss upon the Rule, or on these words ; saying : 'Thus are they to be understood ;' but as the Lord gave me to speak and write the Rule and these words purely and simply, so shall you understand them purely and simply and without gloss, and observe them to the end in holiness of life. And whosoever shall observe these things, may he be filled in heaven with the blessing of the Most High and Heavenly Father, and on earth with the blessing of His beloved Son, together with the Holy Ghost the Paraclete, and all the Angels and Saints of heaven. And I, Brother Francis, your poor little servant in the Lord, confirm to you as much as I am able, both within and without, this holy Benediction. Amen.

PART V.

SAYINGS OF THE HOLY FATHER ST. FRANCIS.

1. *He Announces himself as the Herald of a great King.*

A LITTLE after his conversion, as the man of God was walking through a wood, thieves fell upon him and demanded who he was. He answered boldly and prophetically, 'I am the herald of the great King.'

2. *God will Reward our Labours more generously and more faithfully than Man.*

The holy Father's brother was constantly mocking at his poverty and misery, and once, in a time of great cold, he sent a companion to ask if he would sell some of his sweat. 'No,' answered the servant of God, 'I shall sell my sweat at a much higher price to God.'

3. *How the Passion of Christ should be Wept over.*

Not long after his conversion, the Saint was weeping and groaning loudly near Our Lady of Angels, and being asked by a certain spiritual man why he wept so bitterly and so loudly, he answered: 'I weep over the Passion of Christ, and far from being ashamed thereof, I would that my cries could be heard all over the world.'

---

4. *How the Love of God in the Interior dispels all Exterior Cold.*

Being asked how he could bear the extreme cold of winter when so thinly clad, the holy Father answered: 'If our hearts were inflamed with the love of our heavenly country, we should easily bear this external cold.'

---

5. *The Soldier of Christ should not Reserve for himself any Earthly Riches.*

On account of the complaints of his father, the holy man was advised by the Bishop of Assisi to give back the money he had taken secretly in order to repair the ruinous Church of St. Damian, and which, utterly despising, he had thrown out of a window of the said church. He answered boldly, and as one entirely detached from earthly things: 'I will restore to my father not only the money which is his by right, but also even the very clothes I wear.'

---

6. *That Parents and all Earthly Things are to be Despised for the Love of God.*

The Saint not only renounced, before the same Bishop in the presence of his father, all his rights of inheritance, but even stripped himself of his clothes, exclaiming: 'Hitherto I have called thee my father on earth, but henceforth I can with all confidence say: "Our Father Who art in heaven;" for all my riches and all my hopes are placed in Him.'

---

7. *That the Poor of God are not to become Accustomed to well-prepared Meals.*

While the man of God was endeavouring with all his might and with great labour to repair the Church of St. Damian, the priest carefully prepared his repasts for him; but the blessed man and new soldier of Jesus Christ began, after some days, to think within himself, and thus to take himself to task: 'Thou who art a pilgrim in the world, wilt thou find wherever thou goest this priest who shows thee so much kindness? This is not the life of poverty which thou hast chosen. Therefore go now, as a poor man ought, with a dish in thy hand, and collect in it from door to door the food which the faithful will bestow on thee for the love of God. Thus must thou willingly live, for the sake of Him Who was born poor, Who lived most poorly in this world, Who hung naked and poor upon the Cross, and who was buried in another man's sepulchre.'

---

8. *That in the Service of God, the Maledictions of the World are to be lightly Esteemed.*

After the conversion of this holy man, his father was accustomed to curse him whenever he met him. St. Francis therefore adopted a poor and wretched old man for his father, and kept him with him as a companion; so that whenever his own father cursed him, he on the contrary might bless him, and fortify him by the sign of the Cross. As, therefore, when he was cursed by his father, he was blessed by this poor man, he said once to the former: 'I believe, father, that God can give, and has given me another father, who bestows on me blessings for your curses.'

9. *All Goods are to be Restored to their Owners.*

Brother Bernard of Quintavalle, who was not the last among the citizens of Assisi, and who was the first among the companions of the blessed man, being moved by his admirable sanctity to relinquish the world and follow him, once asked him, 'Father, if anyone had received for many years from his Lord money, or even only a few gifts, and no longer wished to make use of them, what do you think would be the best thing to do with them?' St. Francis answered: 'They should be restored to him who had given them.' By these words the Saint intimated that Bernard ought to leave the world, and distribute to the poor all the goods he had received from God.

10. *How much the Simplicity of the Saints is to be Esteemed.*

The holy Father admired greatly the sanctity and holy simplicity of Brother Juniper, and alluding to his name he said once to those who were near him: 'I would, my Brethren, that we had a large forest of such Junipers, and I tell you that he who attains to the simplicity of Brother Juniper, is a true Friar Minor.

11. *Sensuality is to be Repressed by the Rigour of Abstinence.*

St. Francis being asked why he subdued his sensual appetite with such severity of discipline that he scarcely took enough food to support nature, answered: 'It is difficult to satisfy the necessity of the body without indulging the inclination of the senses.'

12. *Temptations of the Flesh must be promptly Resisted by the Spiritual Man.*

Soon after his conversion, the Saint threw himself repeatedly during the winter-time into a ditch full of ice, in order that he might perfectly subdue his domestic enemy, and preserve the white robe of purity from the fire of sensuality. Giving an account of this to his Brothers, he said: 'It is incomparably more tolerable to the spiritual man to endure cold in his body, than to feel the least movement of sensuality in his soul.'

13. *The Rebellion of the Flesh is to be Overcome by Treating it with great Severity.*

The holy man, once feeling, through the arts of the devil and his perfidious suggestions, a strong temptation of the flesh, instantly took off his habit and scourged himself severely with his cord, saying to his body: 'Ah, Brother Ass, thus must thou remain, thus shalt thou be scourged. The habit belongs to Religion; it is the sign of sanctity, and may not be stolen by a sensual man. If thou wishest to go anywhere as thou art, go.'

14. *Holy Poverty is to be Considered the Honour and Inheritance of his Religious.*

When invited by others to dinner, the Saint would say : ' I do not wish to give up my royal dignity, the inheritance and possessions of myself and my Brethren, which is that we should beg from door to door.'

15. *Idle Religious are like Flies.*

If the holy Father found any Brother idle, wandering about and living on the labours of others, he expelled him from the company of the Brethren, saying: ' Go thy way, Brother Fly, since thou desirest to eat of thy Brothers' labours, and to be lazy in the service of God, like a drone, an idle and useless insect which neither works nor toils, but lives on the spoils and earnings of the good bees.'

16. *The Religious must Cultivate Silence.*

Finding a certain Religious had a habit of speaking idle words, the holy Father sharply rebuked him, saying : ' Modest silence is the sure guardian of a pure heart, and is not the least among the great virtues; for life and death are in the power of the tongue, not so much on account of the taste as of speech.'

17. *The Vice of Detraction is Pernicious to Religious, and Abominable to All.*

Hearing a certain Religious speaking ill of his Brother, St. Francis said to his Vicar: 'Arise, arise, inquire diligently, and if thou findest the accused Brother innocent, thou shalt inflict on the accuser a punishment striking to all. Great evils will befall the Order unless it is delivered from detractors; the sweet odour of many will be corrupted unless stinking mouths are closed. I desire thee to take the greatest care that this pestilent evil spread no farther. The Brother who despoils another of the glory of his reputation shall be despoiled of the habit; nor can he raise his eyes to God until he first restore what he has taken away.

---

18. *The Servant of God, even if he is Grieved interiorly for his sins, must show Spiritual Joy exteriorly.*

If St. Francis saw any of his companions with a sad or downcast countenance, he reproved him, saying: 'If thou art grieving over thy sins, my Brother, why dost thou show thy sorrow exteriorly? Let this sadness be between thee and God, and pray to Him that through His mercy He may spare thee, and restore to thy soul the joy of His salvation, which thou hast lost through thy sins. But before me and others, show thyself always joyful, for it does not become the servant of God to manifest sadness exteriorly, nor to have a troubled countenance.'

19. *Man owes to the Grace of God his Preservation from any Sin.*

The holy man obliged his chosen companion, Brother Leo, much against his will, to overwhelm him with many reproaches, calling him a thief, a blasphemer, an adulterer, a murderer, and such like. The blessed Father heard him most patiently, and wept over all these sins as if they were his own. Brother Leo having asked him why he compelled him to say so many and such great untruths against an innocent man, the Saint replied: 'They are no lies, for I am in truth the greatest of sinners, and all these sins, and even worse, I should have committed, if God in His mercy and by His grace had not preserved me from them. For if a great robber had received the grace that I have, he would have made a much better use of it, and would be much holier than I am.'

20. *Religious should Rejoice in Holy Poverty, and not in Worldly Riches.*

Once when the holy Father was travelling in France with Brother Masseo, they found in a solitary place a sparkling fountain, and by it a large flat stone like a table. Upon this the Saint placed a crust of bread, which they had received as an alms, and being filled with joy, and exulting in his poverty, he said to his companion: 'We are not worthy of such great treasures.' As he repeated these words several times, his companion said: 'How can you talk of riches when we are in such extreme poverty?

Where are our servants and our maids? our cups and goblets? where our costly wine and dainty viands? where the tablecloth to cover this stone?' 'This,' said the Saint, 'do I consider the greatest treasure, this do I look upon as the most delicious food, where there is nothing worked out by human industry, nothing prepared by worldly ingenuity, but whatever we have is given to us by the direct Providence of God.

21. *Worldly Possessions cause Disturbance and Trouble.*

When the Bishop of Assisi told St. Francis that it appeared to him too hard and difficult not to allow his Order to have or receive any possessions, the holy man replied: 'Nay, rather it appears to me too hard and troublesome to have them; for to preserve and defend them requires much solicitude, and in order to quell the quarrels and disturbances which arise from them we should need to have arms always in readiness.'

22. *The Soldier of Christ ought to Divest himself of all Worldly Things.*

St. Francis once told a person who asked admission into the Order to go and distribute all his goods to the poor; but instead of this he gave all away among his friends and relations. When he returned and told the Saint what he had done the holy Father rejected him, saying: 'Go, Brother Fly! thou hast not left thy kindred and thy father's house. He is not worthy to join the poor of Christ who has defrauded the poor. Thou hast begun in the flesh, thou hast laid an insecure foundation for a spiritual life. Go thy way.'

---

23. *Superiors ought to be an Example to Inferiors by their Labours and Virtues.*

When St. Francis was on his way to preach in France he was asked by the Cardinal of Ostia, Ugolino (who was afterwards Sovereign Pontiff), why he would not remain with him at the Roman Court, as he so much desired. 'My lord,' replied the holy man, 'I should feel great shame and confusion if I were to remain with you here, while my Brethren and Children are living in poverty and misery in different parts of the world; for surely I ought to share with them the tribulations which they must endure for the love of God.'

---

24. *Carnal Men cannot understand Spiritual Things.*

The holy Father taught his Brethren to use this short but holy salutation: 'May the Lord give thee His peace.' Some persons, however, were displeased at this, and the Brethren feared to use it. The Saint, however, said: 'Let them say what they choose about these holy words, for they do not understand the things of God; but do not you be ashamed of them, for before long many heroes and princes will show you great reverence on account of this salutation.'

---

25. God will never refuse Food and Clothing to the Poor of Christ.

Pope Honorius III. tried to persuade St. Francis to accept some revenues, predicting that his Friars would suffer many miseries if they lived entirely on alms. The Saint replied: 'I confide in the Lord Jesus, that as He has promised, and will give us, life and eternal glory in heaven, He will not refuse us the small amount of food and clothing which are necessary for the body on earth.'

---

26. God alone is to be Feared, and all things are to be referred to His will.

The man of God endured many horrible conflicts with the demons in time of prayer, but the more vehemently he was beset by the enemy, the stronger in virtue and the more fervent in prayer did he become. Then he would say to Christ: 'Protect me under the shadow of Thy wings from the face of those who afflict me.' But to the devils he would say: 'Do with me what you will, wicked and deceitful spirits; for you have no power except what is given you from on High, and I am ready joyfully to bear all that God will permit you to do.'

---

27. Man's Body is his greatest Enemy.

The holy man being in the Church of St. Peter de Bonario, near Treves, wished, after having finished his prayer, to repose a little, but he could not do so, his mind being disturbed by carnal suggestions. Being somewhat troubled by this dangerous combat he went out of the church, and began to cry aloud : In the Name of Almighty God, I call on you, O devils, to exercise on my body all that may be given and permitted you by Our Lord Jesus Christ, for thus you will avenge me of my cruel enemy and worst adversary; than which I know no greater.

28. *The Secrets of God are not to be Divulged.*

St. Francis thought it not right to show forth exteriorly the secrets of the Divine Wisdom which were revealed to him, unless he were urged thereto by the charity of Christ, or the good of his neighbour. He used to say: 'For the small reward of vainglory and human honour, we should lose our priceless treasure, and provoke God not to give us any more of His gifts.'

29. *The Canonical Hours are to be Recited with great Devotion.*

The holy Father, that he might not lose any moments of time, had made a little vessel of wood ; but as this work came into his mind once, when he was reciting the Canonical Hours, and caused him a slight distraction, in fervour of spirit he threw the vessel into the fire, saying : 'I will sacrifice to the Lord that which has hindered my sacrifice.'

30. *The Religous ought not to have Cells of their own.*

Seeing a Brother once coming from the cell he himself occupied, the Saint asked him whence he came. He answered: 'From your cell, Father.' To which the holy man immediately replied: Thou callest mine that which I do not consider mine. Henceforth I must dwell elsewhere, for I have promised to have nothing of my own.'

31. *The Light of the Soul is to be Preferred to that of the Body.*

The doctor tried to persuade the holy Father to restrain his tears, if he wished to preserve his bodily sight. To which he replied: 'Brother Doctor, it is not right to lose even the least spiritual light, for the sake of that light which we have in common with the flies; for the soul does not receive light for the sake of the body, but the body for the sake of the soul.'

32. *Contemplation is to be Preferred to Study.*

Being asked by a certain Brother what book he considered the most useful and profitable for him to read, the Saint replied: 'Read the book of the Cross, and do not indulge in vain and curious studies. Blessed is he who abstains from these for the love of God.'

33. *The Sight of Women is to be Avoided.*

The companion of the Saint once asked him why he did not look at a certain noble virgin who charitably and humbly visited the sick and ministered to them, to which St. Francis replied: 'Who ought not to fear the Spouse of Christ? if we preach to her by the modesty of our eyes, she will be the more confirmed in her chastity. Let her look at me, but I will not look at her.'

34. *Religious ought not to Desire Privileges which are Contrary to the Perfection of their State.*

Being urged and entreated by certain Religious to ask privileges of the Sovereign Pontiff for the greater liberty and credit of the Order, the holy Father said: 'The greatest privilege of myself and my brethren, is to have no privileges in this world, but to obey all, and to consider ourselves inferior to all.'

35. *Religious ought not to Relax their Abstinence without Necessity ; and that the Vice of Hypocrisy is to be Avoided.*

On account of a serious illness the holy Father once relaxed a little the rigour of his abstinence and ate some meat, for which afterwards he reproached himself, saying: 'It is not right that people should believe I abstain, while I eat meat in secret.' Therefore, animated with a courage and fervour more admirable than imitable, he went almost naked with a cord round his neck to the public square, where, a crowd being assembled, he cried out: 'I have eaten meat in secret ; do not, therefore, my Brethren, henceforth call me a spiritual man, but despise me as a glutton and wine-bibber.'

36. *No one is to be Praised in this Life.*

When people praised the holy Father as a Saint, and called him Blessed, he would say: 'I may yet have sons and daughters; do not praise one who is not yet safe. No one ought to be praised whose end is uncertain. If at any moment God should withdraw from me the treasures of His grace, which He now grants to me, what else would remain to me but a soul and body which sinners possess in common with the faithful?'

37. *Superiors ought to give an Example of Virtue to their Inferiors.*

Although the Saint's innocent flesh, which by long and severe penance he had brought into subjection to the spirit, needed no punishment on account of any offences, nevertheless he daily renewed its pains and labours. When some blamed him for this, he said: 'On account of others I keep these hard ways, for I am given as an example to many. If I should speak with the tongues of men and Angels, and have not charity in myself, and do not give good example to my neighbour, I shall profit others little, and myself nothing.'

38. *The Servants of God ought not to Desire Money.*

When the man of God was travelling in Apulia, and was near Bari, his companion was displeased because the blessed Father advised him to despise and leave where it was, a bag or purse apparently full of gold, which was lying on the ground. Contrary to his advice, however, the Brother lifted up the purse, when a large serpent sprang out, and vanished together with it. The diabolical deception had been revealed to St. Francis, and that his companion might truly realise this, he said to him: 'Brother, money is to the servants of God nothing else but a poisonous serpent, or devil.'

39. Religious should be Ashamed of Superfluous Dress or Furniture.

St. Francis once met a poor man in the road, and being pierced to the heart at his destitute condition, he exclaimed in a sorrowful voice to his companion: 'Oh, how the indigence of this poor man puts us to shame, for we have chosen Poverty for our richest inheritance, and yet he is poorer than we are!'

40. The Poor of Christ should Relieve those who are Poorer than themselves.

Returning once from Siena, St. Francis met a poor man half-naked, and turning to his companion he said: 'Brother, we must give back to this poor man the cloak I wear over my habit, for it is his. I only agreed to keep it until I should meet some one poorer than myself.' His companion not consenting to this on account of the holy Father's infirmities, the Saint insisted, saying: 'I should expect to be looked upon as a thief by the Supreme Almsgiver, if I did not bestow what I have on those whose need is greater than my own.

---

41. *Mendicant Religious ought only to Beg for Necessaries.*

St. Francis often exhorted his Brethren to avoid all useless discourses, and too great solicitude in collecting alms; as also to shun begging for superfluities, saying: 'My Brethren, ask only for necessary food and clothing. I thank God and I rejoice that I have never been a thief by stealing alms, for I have always taken less than was offered me, for fear of defrauding other poor, and whoever acts otherwise I consider a thief.'

---

42. *Almsgiving is sometimes more Meritorious than Prayer.*

The holy Father besought Brother Peter of Catania, one of his first disciples, to give something to the mother of two Friars Minor, who asked an alms. Brother Peter answered that there was nothing in the house to give, except the New Testament in the church, out of which the Brothers recited the lessons at Matins. 'Give it,' he said, 'to our mother' (for thus he called the mother of his Brethren), 'and let her sell it to relieve her poverty; for I believe firmly it will be more pleasing to God and the Blessed Virgin to give this book to the poor, than to keep it ourselves to read.

43. *We must do Good to please God, and not Man.*

In the beginning of his conversion, and before he had put off the secular habit, the holy man used often to lament and accuse himself that, for the love of worldly glory, he had been most liberal towards men; and, firmly purposing to employ all that remained to him in the service of the poor, he would say: 'Since I spared neither expense nor trouble to please my friends for the sake of the vain and transitory glory of the world, it is but just that henceforth I should be equally bountiful towards the poor, for the sake of God, Who is so liberal a rewarder.'

---

44. *The Festivals of the Saints ought to be Kept, not by Feasting, but by Imitating their Example.*

A certain Provincial having come to the Convent of Reatino, the Brethren laid the tables on Christmas Day with more care, and provided a better meal than usual. St. Francis, however, severely reproved them, saying: 'On the day of Christ's Poverty, do you offend against poverty? Remember that on this day the Blessed Virgin had hardly bread to eat, and that the Sovereign of the world had for His cradle the manger of the beasts. Imitate the poverty of the Mother, and be mindful of the cries of her little Infant.'

45. *How great is the Power of the Saints—and that Religious should carefully Avoid all popular Demonstrations.*

After the death of Blessed Peter of Catania, great crowds used to visit his tomb in the Church of St. Mary of the Angels, on account of his eminent sanctity and many miracles. This caused much inconvenience to the Friars, and detriment to religious silence and recollection. The blessed Father therefore went to the tomb, and thus spoke: 'Brother Peter, thou wast always most promptly obedient to me during life, and thou wilt not refuse me thy humble submission after death.. On thy account, the religious quiet of thy Brethren is disturbed, because so many people come to show due honour to thy body. I command thee, in virtue of holy Obedience, to work no more miracles, lest what is intended to honour God and the Saints, should turn to the manifest injury of this religious house.' Wonderful to relate, the deceased Friar worked no more miracles, and the people no longer came to his sepulchre!

---

46. *Of the Insupportable Hideousness of the Demons.*

Blessed Brother Egidius, the third companion of the holy Father St. Francis, once asked him if there were any sight in the world so terrible that he could not bear to look upon it during the space of a *Paternoster*. The Saint replied: 'The sight of the devil is so intolerable that nothing in the world can be imagined more horrible and fearful, and no one could endure it even for a moment unless he were supported by the Divine power.

47. *We should Trust in God's Goodness rather than in Money.*

When St. Francis was ill with his last sickness at Nocera, the citizens of Assisi sent a solemn embassy to bring him thence to their city, lest he should die in any other place; and they, stopping to dine on their way back at the town of Sarthiano, complained to the holy man that they could not procure any provisions for money. Whereupon he reproved them, saying: 'You can find nothing to eat because you trust more in your flies' (thus he was accustomed to call money) 'than in God. But go back to the houses where you have been, and humbly beg an alms, offering in payment the love of God.' They obeyed the command of the Saint, and found that the want which could not be supplied by their money was abundantly relieved by the poverty of St. Francis.

48. *The Saints do not Fear to Die, but Rejoice equally in Life or Death.*

A few days before his death, the holy Father asked the doctor what he thought of his illness. He answered cautiously: 'By the mercy of God all will be well with thee.' But the Saint exclaimed, with a joyful and intrepid soul: 'Tell me, I say, truthfully, what thou thinkest. Fear not; by the grace of God I am not a coward to fear death, for I am so closely united to my Lord by the grace of the Holy Spirit that I am not sad at the thought of death; nor do I rejoice more at the prospect of a long life, for I am equally happy to live or to die.'

49. *How Conformed to the Will of God the Saints are in Suffering.*

As towards the end of his life St. Francis was overwhelmed with many infirmities, a simple and devout Brother, compassionating his sufferings, said to him: 'Pray to God, my Father, that He may deal more mercifully with thee, for He seems to be laying His hand on thee more heavily than is just.' When the Saint heard him speak thus, he exclaimed with tears: 'If I did not know thy great simplicity, and the purity of thy soul, I should, for the future, hold thee in abhorrence, because thou hast dared to question the justice of the Divine judgments in my regard. I deserve far greater torments, and most willingly will I bear heavier chastisements if God wills to inflict them on me.'

50. *How great is the Consolation of the Perfect, in Meditating on the Passion of Christ.*

At a time when the Saint was oppressed with constant suffering, he was asked why he did not have something read to him to recreate his mind, wearied by such constant suffering. 'Nothing,' he replied, 'is so delightful to me as the remembrance of the life and Passion of my Lord, on which I meditate daily and constantly; and were I to live till the end of the world, I should never want any other book.'

---

51. *There is more Profit in bearing Insults than in receiving Honour.*

When, in a certain town, many people showed the Saint great honour, he said to his companion: 'Let us leave this place, for we shall gain no profit here where we are honoured; our merit is to be gained when we are despised and insulted.'

---

52. *Temptations make the Servants of God stronger.*

One of the Brothers once told the Saint that a possessed girl had revealed to him, although against her will, that great troops of devils had conspired against him to overthrow his virtue and his Order, because he was their greatest enemy. He answered fearlessly: 'Now I shall be stronger.'

---

53. *It is not easy to Dispute about the Faith with Infidels.*

When the holy man was preaching in Egypt, the Sultan invited him to hold a disputation with his priests. The Saint answered that he could not argue about the faith by the force of natural reason, because it was above reason ; nor through the authority of the Holy Scriptures, because the priests did not acknowledge them. 'Make therefore,' he said, 'a great fire, and I, in testimony of our faith, will enter the flames ; and if I escape unhurt, the truth of my religion will be apparent.'

54. *Hypocrisy is to be Avoided.*

Once, when the holy Father was suffering from a weakness of the stomach, the Guardian persuaded him to allow a fox-skin to be sewn under his worn-out habit. He replied that he would consent, on condition that another piece of fur of the same size should be sewn outside his garments, that all might see the luxury he allowed himself, and that they might know he wore soft furs under a penitential habit.

55. *That Just Requests are sometimes to be Refused, in order to Repress Unjust Desires.*

A young and inexperienced novice having asked permission to keep a Psalter, the holy Father refused him several times, and at length said to him : 'My son, when thou hast got a Psalter, thou wilt desire to have a Breviary, and other books to study ; and when thou hast learned something thou wilt desire to have a Chair as a great theologian or prelate, and thou wilt command thy Brother to bring thee thy Breviary.' Having said this, he uncovered his head in great fervour of spirit and sprinkled ashes on it saying, 'Shall I have a Breviary—shall I have a Breviary?'

---

56. *That we must bear patiently the Punishment of our sins in this world.*

The holy Father being sometimes scourged, and otherwise tormented by the devil, would exclaim with great fervour of spirit, and without being in the least cast down: 'O God, I give Thee thanks for Thy immense love and charity towards me, which Thou now clearly showest; for Thou dost punish my sins in this life, that Thou mayest pardon them in the next. I, as far as is in my power, joyfully consent to bear every suffering and tribulation which it may please Thy Divine Majesty to inflict upon me for my sins.'

---

57. *The hope of future glory, renders the endurance of Sufferings sweet.*

Being asked how he could bear such great sufferings in his eyes and his whole body so joyously and courageously, the Saint replied: 'So great is the glory which I expect, that all pains, all sickness, all humiliations, all persecutions, all mortifications are pleasant to me.'

FAMILIAR COLLOQUIES OF THE BLESSED FATHER ST. FRANCIS.

COLLOQUY I.

That Meekness and Patience will Soften the hardest Hearts.

WHEN the blessed Father came once to the city of Imola, he went to the Bishop and humbly asked him to allow him to assemble the people to hear the Word of God; but the Bishop answered him harshly: 'It is sufficient, Brother, that I preach to my people myself.' The truly humble man bowed his head and went away; but after a short time he again presented himself before the Bishop, who demanded rather angrily what more he had to ask him. The Saint replied with a humble heart and manner: 'My lord, if a father turns away his son by one door, he must return by another.' The Bishop, overcome by this humility, embraced him joyfully, saying: 'Henceforth I give thee and thy Brothers a general leave to preach in my diocese, for thy humility deserves this reward.'

COLLOQUY II.

The Friars Minor ought not to Reserve for themselves any of the Goods of the Novices.

WHEN there was such great poverty at St. Mary of the Angels that they could not provide for the necessities of the guests who came, the Vicar went to the man of God, and representing to him the extreme want of the Brethren, begged him to allow them to reserve some of the goods of novices who entered, as a fund to which they might have recourse in time of need. To which the Saint, enlightened from above, replied : 'Far be it from us, dearest Brother, to act contrary to our Rule for the sake of any man. I would rather strip the altar of the glorious Virgin if necessity required it, than allow the least thing against our vow of Poverty, and the regular observance of our evangelical profession. For it would be more pleasing to the Blessed Virgin that we should observe the holy Gospel perfectly, and leave her altar unadorned, than that we should decorate her altar, and fail in fulfilling the evangelical counsel which we have promised to her Son.'

COLLOQUY III.

That the Friars Minor should not Erect superfluous Buildings.

THE same Vicar of the holy Father, Brother Peter of Catania, caused a small building to be erected for the greater convenience of performing the Divine Office, and to procure for the Friars who came as guests every day in great numbers more quiet and tranquillity. At this the blessed Father was a little displeased, and said : 'Brother, this place is the model and example for the whole Order. I would rather that the Religious of this house should suffer some troubles and inconveniences for the love of God, so that others who come here should see a good example of poverty, than that they should have more buildings, lest the guests when they return to their own Monasteries should begin to build spacious houses, saying: "At St. Mary of the Angels, which is the first and principal house of the Order, they have many buildings; there cannot therefore be any fault against holy Poverty if we construct the same."'

COLLOQUY IV.
That the Praise of all that is Good is to be Referred to God.

THE holy Father once preached to the people at Terni in presence of the Bishop, who, surprised at the eloquence and learning of the humble preacher, when he had come down from the pulpit, rose, and said to his flock: 'Give great praise to God, Who by the mouth of this insignificant poor man has taught you so much good, has revealed to you His mysteries, and has placed before you the reward of virtue and the punishment of vice. Therefore avoid sin, doing what God has taught you to-day through this poor man.' On this the blessed Francis threw himself at the Bishop's feet, exclaiming: 'I tell you truly, my Lord Bishop, no one has ever shown me so much honour as you have done to-day. Others call me holy and blessed for my works, giving the praise and glory to me, and not to God; but you in your wisdom have truly honoured me, giving to the Lord the praise and honour which are His, separating the precious from the vile, and attributing to God wisdom and power, and to me foolishness and weakness.'

COLLOQUY V.

Those who are Fools for God's Sake are stronger than the Wise of this World.

MOVED by the suggestions of some lax Brethren who desired an easier life, the Cardinal Ugolino of Ostia begged the holy Father to follow the counsels of the most prudent and learned men of the Order, and consent to mitigate the severity of his Rule, or to choose one of the old Rules of St. Augustine, St. Basil, or St. Benedict, to be observed by himself and his Brethren. The zealous lover of evangelical perfection did not answer the suggestion at once, but having called the Brethren to Chapter, he thus spoke to them before the Cardinal with great fervour of spirit: 'My Brethren, my Brethren, God has called me to walk in the way of simplicity and humility, and He has shown me that this is His will both for myself and for those who will follow and adhere to me. I will not therefore have the Rule of St. Benedict, or St. Basil, or any other proposed to me, except that which has been given and shown me by the Divine Mercy. Our Lord has Himself told me that He wishes me to be His poor little fool in this world, and I will not follow, nor allow those who belong to me to follow, any other road to heaven than this one, which although it may appear folly to the world, is true wisdom in the sight of God. I fear that your wisdom and your knowledge will end for you in ignorance and confusion.' These words filled the Cardinal and the Brethren with great fear, and throwing themselves at the feet of the Saint they humbly implored his pardon.

COLLOQUY VI.

The Poor of Christ should Prefer Living on Alms to Feasting with the Rich.

ST. FRANCIS once consented to dine with the same Cardinal Ugolino, but while the tables were being prepared, he went out secretly and begged some crusts of bread in the street. When he returned and was seated at table with the Cardinal, he produced these, and divided them among the guests and attendants, as if he were presenting them with some dainty morsel, while he himself eat of them more willingly than of the richest dishes. The noble Cardinal was confused and ashamed at this conduct, but remained silent on account of his guests. But after dinner, taking the holy man aside, he gently reproved him in private, not having ventured to do so in public. 'Why,' said he, 'O beloved friend, hast thou done this? Thou hast offered me a great insult by bringing these morsels of bread to the feast to which I invited thee, and covered me with shame before all present.' The blessed Father answered him: 'Nay, rather, my lord, I did thee a great honour, while I was honouring a still greater Lord. I must be a model and example to my Brethren, and the more so because I know for certain that in the Order there are and will be many true Friars Minor both in name and deed, who for the love of the Lord our God, and by the grace of the Holy Spirit Who will teach them, will humble themselves in all things, and serve their Brethren in all lowliness and subjection. But on the contrary, there are and will be others who, out of human respect or evil custom, will disdain to humble themselves, and will refuse to beg alms and to do such like servile works. Therefore I must teach all who shall enter this Order, so that both in this world and the next they may be without excuse before God. When, then, I am invited by you, or by any other great lord, I will never blush to go and seek alms; but on the contrary, I consider it a true nobility, and a royal dignity and honour to imitate Him Who, although He was the Lord of all, and possessed all things in His glorious Majesty, was despised and in want of all things when He took upon Him our humanity. I desire, therefore, that all the Brethren, both present and future, should understand clearly that I feel the greatest consolation, both for soul and body, when I am seated at the table of the poor, and I rejoice much more when I see before me the poor food received in alms for the love of God, than when, either at your or others' tables, I sit down to rich and dainty dishes, of which I eat unwillingly. The bread of alms is holy and blessed bread, sanctified by the praise and love of the Omnipotent. For when a Brother begs, he first says: "Praised and blessed be the Lord our God!" and then he adds: "Give me an alms for the love of God." Thus praise sanctifies the bread, and the love of God blesses it.' When he heard these words, the Cardinal shed tears of devotion, and exclaimed: 'My Son, do what is good in thine eyes, for I see that God is with thee, and thou art with Him.'

COLLOQUY VII.
The Friars Minor should remain in their Humble Vocation.

THE same Cardinal once asked the blessed Father whether or not he was willing that the Friars Minor should be promoted to ecclesiastical dignities, asserting that the universal Church would derive great benefit from being governed by men of such sanctity and virtue. 'My lord,' replied the man of God; my Brethren are called less than others,* in order that they may not presume to become greater. If you wish them to bear fruit in the Church of God, keep them in the state to which they are called, and do not make them ascend to ecclesiastical dignities.'

COLLOQUY VIII.
That it is not becoming for Superiors to indulge their Appetite, or make use of Delicate Meats.

ONE of his companions asked St. Francis why he did not deal more mildly with himself, and why he afflicted his tender body, half dead with penance, with such rigorous abstinence; begging him that

* Minores—majores.

for the future he would allow better food to be prepared for him. This true model of penitents and Superiors replied : 'I know well, Brother, that many things are necessary for my body, and that I do not always give it what it really requires; but I remember that I am placed by God as a model and example to many, and therefore I will not use more delicate nor better dressed food, but poor food, poorly cooked ; and in all things that are needful for this life, I rejoice and delight only in those which savour of holy Poverty, and all that are sumptuous and delicate I utterly abhor.'

COLLOQUY IX.

The Rule of the Friars Minor was not Composed by St. Francis, but given him by God.

THE Sovereign Pontiff Honorius III., who solemnly confirmed the Rule of the Friars Minor in the eighth year of his pontificate, considered some precepts of the said Institute too hard and difficult for human weakness. He therefore exhorted St. Francis to mitigate some points, to change others, and to do away with some altogether. But the holy lawgiver replied : 'Most Blessed Father, it was not I who put those words and precepts into the Rule, but Christ, Who knows better than any what is useful and necessary for the salvation of the Brethren and the well-being and preservation of this Order; for all things that are to happen in the Church and in this

Order are present and known to Him. I therefore must not and cannot change or efface the words of Christ.'

COLLOQUY X.

It is a great Advantage to the Church that various Religious Orders should Flourish therein.

THE Seraphic Father when in Rome, met there the blessed Father St. Dominic, the glorious Patriarch and Founder of the Order of Friars Preachers. When they were consulting together about the salvation of souls, and how they could best procure the welfare of the Catholic Church, that great glory of the Preachers said to his friend and Brother, Francis: 'Beloved Brother, on account of the great spiritual friendship I feel for thee, and the heartfelt love I have for thy children, as also for the consolidation of the fraternal peace and charity which exist between my Brethren and thine, I should rejoice to have them formed into one Order, that those whom the strong love of the Fathers has thus united, may not be separated by the difference of Rule and manner of life.' But Francis with exceeding humility replied: 'It is the will of God, my most dear Brother, that we should each found a different religious Order, that by the variety and diversity of precepts, by the greater severity of some, and the greater mildness of others, human weakness may be assisted; for what pleases some would displease others, what would seem hard to some will appear easy to others, and thus souls who might be lost to God in the rigour of one Order, may make great profit in the other.

COLLOQUY XI.

The more Humble the Servants of God are, the more Holy they are.

BLESSED BROTHER PACIFICUS when he was in the company of the Saint, entered with him the Church of St. Peter de Bonario, near Treves, and praying very fervently was rapt in ecstasy, during which he saw many thrones prepared in heaven, and one among them higher than the rest, adorned with precious stones and refulgent with glory. Admiring the exceeding splendour of this throne, Brother Pacificus began to wonder and consider within himself for whom it was prepared. While thus pondering he heard a voice saying to him: 'This throne belonged to one of the fallen angels, and is now reserved for the humble Francis.' The Brother then coming out of his rapture, followed as usual his blessed Father who was leaving the church. As they were travelling, and conversing together on the things of God, the Brother, remembering his vision, asked the man of God what he thought of himself. 'I think,' replied the humble servant of Christ, 'that I am the greatest of sinners.' But the Brother answered: 'You cannot, my Father, say or think that with an upright conscience.' The Saint exclaimed: 'If the greatest sinner had received all the graces Christ has lavished on me, I believe truly that he would be far more pleasing to God than I am.'

COLLOQUY XII.

All the Virtues of the Saints come from God, and are to be Referred to Him.

BLESSED MASSEO, one of the disciples of the holy Father, wondered within himself, and was anxious to know, whether the man of God was not a little puffed up with all the honour shown him both by princes and people. In order to try his humility once, when the Saint came forth from a wood in which he had been praying for several days, and was surrounded. by a great crowd, he cried out to him in a loud voice, as if astonished, 'Why is this to thee? why is this to thee?' The blessed Father asked, 'What?' 'Why,' replied Brother Masseo, 'does every one honour thee, seek thee, follow thee, and imitate thee? All desire to hear thee, wish to see thee, and hasten to obey thee. Why is this? Thou art not handsome nor elegant; thou hast very little wisdom or science; thou art not of noble birth. Why then does all the world come to thee, and run after thee?' When the most humble servant of God heard these words, he remained some time with his eyes raised to heaven, and his mind fixed on God. Then coming to himself he knelt down, and again looking up to heaven, he gave thanks to the most liberal Giver of all good, and with great fervour and impetuosity of spirit he said to his disciple: 'Dost thou wish to know why this is to me? Dost thou wish to know why this is to me? This happens to me through the will of the Omnipotent God, who sees alike the good and the bad. The most holy eyes of God saw that there was no greater sinner on earth than myself, no one more foolish among men, no one viler among creatures, and therefore He chose me above others as His instrument to undertake and accomplish His wonderful work upon earth. For God always chooses the foolish things of the world to confound the wise, and the vilest, weakest, and most contemptible things of the world, to destroy the strongest, and to confound the greatest and most noble; that all may know that the sublimity of virtue comes from God, and not from creatures, so that he who glories may glory in the Lord, and that God alone may be glorified for ever.' When he heard these words, the disciple threw himself at the feet of his master, and from the humility of his words he understood the lowliness of his soul.

COLLOQUY XIII.

The Saint Complains that certain Superiors of his Order Follow other Ways instead of his.

AFTER the blessed Father had renounced the office of General, a simple and devout Brother, grieving to think that he and the other Brethren were deprived of the care and protection of such a Father, complained to him very sorrowfully, saying: 'What grief and sadness I and my Brethren feel thou mayest judge, O good Father, if indeed we can call thee Father, who rejectest the care of thy children. Why is it, I beseech thee, that having brought us to God with such care and love, thou dost now abandon us to be nourished by others? Take upon thyself once more the care of thy children, and lead them to the perfection of holy Religion, lest those who were so fervent under thy guidance should become tepid through the negligence of others.' The blessed Father replied: 'My son, I love my Brethren with all possible love, and I would love them still more as my own children if they would follow in the footsteps of their Father, instead of imitating the example of others; nor did I relinquish the care of them as long as it pleased them to treat me as their Father. But there are some Superiors who propose to the Brethren other examples, they counsel them other things, and lead them astray, setting light by my precepts, and despising my salutary admonitions. Whether they do ill or well, the consequences will show in the course of time. Yet woe to those Superiors who thus contradict me, for I see clearly they are opposing the will of God, although I reluctantly condescend to them. It is a great grief and affliction to me, my Brother, to see that the Rule which I obtained with great labour and prayer from the mercy of God, and which would prove of the greatest utility to the Order and to the Brethren both present and to come, is overturned by the worldly wisdom of certain Superiors, who by their authority command some things to be kept which I have declared unimportant, and neglect and despise as foolish those which I have commanded to be observed.'

COLLOQUY XIV.

The Religious should Win the Minds of the People more by their own Humility than by the Sufferance of the Bishops, and that by Examples of Holiness they will Profit the Church more than by Privileges and Exemptions.

AFTER the general Chapter of Assisi, at which more than five thousand Brethren were assembled from every Province, the holy Father sent them two and two to preach the Word of God in all countries. Many of them returned to him complaining sorrowfully that some Bishops were opposed to them, and would not allow them to preach in their dioceses. 'Father,' said they, 'we went to the places thou didst assign to us, we obeyed thy commands, but we could not fulfil our desires, nor those of the people; for many Bishops expelled us from their dioceses, and, as often happens to the poor, being unknown and suspected, we had to endure many insults. We beg of you, therefore, Father, to obtain for us from the Sovereign Pontiff permission and privilege to preach all over the world, without the consent of the Bishops.' At which the blessed Father, filled with holy indignation, exclaimed: 'O my Brethren, you know not the will of God, and you seek by your foolishness to rob me of the conquest of the world. For our Lord Jesus Christ wishes that I should overcome the world by the most profound subjection and humility, and that I should perform the great work of drawing souls to Him by the example of my lowliness. My Brethren, you will convert all by your words if you humble yourselves before all by your actions. Those who cruelly persecute you will be converted to Christ by the example of your patience, and will desire to kiss the very ground on which you walk. I ought not so much to wish for liberty under pretence of the salvation of others, as I should wish to have that profound humility which becomes my state, and by which I shall both advance in virtue myself, and shall strengthen others in virtue. You must first by holy humility, and the reverence the people have for you, gain over the Bishops, that they may see and love your holy lives, and be satisfied with the respect you show to them. Then they will themselves ask you to preach to their people, and will command all to be present at your sermons. Humility will obtain more for you than privileges. If the Prelates of the Church see you truly humble, and entirely free from avarice, and that you exhort the people to pay what is due to their own Churches, they will beg of you to labour for the salvation of their flocks, and to hear the confessions of all, although I do not desire you to burden yourselves much with this ministry; for those who are converted to God, and deplore their sins, will find many priests to hear their confessions. In this way you will easily conciliate Bishops and Prelates.'

COLLOQUY XV.

What they ought to be who Devote themselves to Study.

SOME of his companions, hearing that many doctors in Paris, and others in Germany, Italy and France had joined his Order, asked the blessed Father if he were willing that his children should devote themselves to the study of the Holy Scriptures. He replied : 'I am willing, provided that, after the example of Christ, of Whom we read that He prayed more than He read, they never omit the practice of prayer. And let them not study only that they may know how to speak, but that they may practise what they learn, and that when they have done this they may propose it for the practice of others. I wish my Brethren to be disciples of the Gospel, and so to advance in the knowledge of truth, as at the same time to increase in holy simplicity, that thus they may not separate the prudence of the serpent from the simplicity of the dove, which the greatest of Masters with His blessed lips has commanded us to unite.'

COLLOQUY XVI.

How the Convents of the Friars Minor should be Founded.

WHEN the blessed Father was staying at Siena on account of the weakness of his eyes, a certain gentleman of the city, named Bonaventure, gave the Friars a piece of land on which to build a Monastery. He consulted St. Francis as to how he wished it built, saying: Father, what thinkest thou of this place? What kind of a house or Monastery will it please thee to have built here in which thy Brethren may dwell, for I believe their prayers and good works will be of no small profit to my soul, if they will give me a share in them.' The blessed Father replied: 'I give thee many thanks, most honourable brother, for this field, which I find very suitable for the site of a Monastery, and now, in a few words, I will explain to thee how it should be built. The Brethren must consider how many acres of this land they require, always remembering the claims of holy Poverty which they have vowed to God, and the good example they owe to their neighbour. When they have well weighed the matter, they must go to the Bishop of the diocese, and say to him: "My Lord, a gentleman, for the love of God and the good of his soul, has given us land on which to build a Monastery; but first of all we come to thee who art the Father and Lord of all the souls committed to thy care, and the patron and most kind protector of all the Brethren who now, or hereafter, shall dwell here, that, with God's blessing and thine, we may construct here a poor little Convent." For God has called us to help the Prelates and priests of His Church to spread the faith, and we are therefore bound, as much as possible, to love, honour and venerate them. For this reason we are called Friars Minor, because we are bound by our name, as well as by our works and example, to be the most lowly of all men. And because at the beginning of my conversion, the Lord, by means of the Bishop of Assisi, consoled and strengthened me wonderfully in my vocation, for this and many other most excellent things which I see in Superiors, I will love, and venerate, and honour as my masters, not only the Bishops, but even the poorest priests. Having then received the permission and benediction of the Bishop, let the Brethren go and mark the boundary of the land they have accepted with a piece of charcoal, and let them surround it with a good wooden fence instead of a wall, as a sign of poverty and humility. Let them then erect some poor little buildings of wood and clay, and a few cells in which the Brothers may pray and labour, in order to give edification, and to avoid idleness. Let them build small churches, and never under pretext of preaching, nor for any other reason, erect large or magnificent ones; for they will show their humility and give a good example to the people more by preaching in other churches. And if Bishops or clerics, either secular or regular, come to this place, the poor cells and small house will preach to them, and profit their souls, more than the most eloquent words.'

COLLOQUY XVII.

Some Things must be Borne with on account of Circumstances.

BROTHER LEO, the companion and confessor of the blessed Father, seeing that in some places grand and spacious Monasteries were erected, not becoming the poverty of the Friars Minor, wished very much to know what St. Francis thought of the matter, and spoke to him about it in presence of the other Brethren. The holy Father thus answered him: 'My Brethren, listen. Some of our Order even now build many and large Monasteries, and after our time others will erect such grand houses that they would be quite suitable for the great ones of the world, and they will wear habits of fine cloth. But at that time it will be a great thing if my Brethren keep themselves from mortal sin.'

COLLOQUY XVIII.

He who Enters Religion from a wrong Motive Lies to the Holy Ghost.

IN the city of Lucca there was a certain youth, illustrious by the nobility of his birth, but full of levity and inconstancy. He was much given to weeping, but his tears flowed from human causes, and not from the Spirit of God. This man came to the Brethren and expressed a most ardent desire to be received into the Order. They therefore brought him to the holy Father, when shedding abundant tears, and putting on a show of great fervour, he again humbly begged to be admitted among his disciples. But the Saint, who knew the external deceit and the internal tepidity, looking on him sternly, rebuked him, saying: 'Miserable and worldly man, why dost thou lie to the Holy Ghost, and seek to deceive me? Thy tears are human, and the Spirit of God is not with thee. Return to thy carnal things, thou art not worthy of spiritual ones, because thou dost not understand anything spiritual.'

COLLOQUY XIX.

Favours and Graces will be Granted to those who are Zealous for the Rule.

THE holy Father having predicted to a certain priest, who was a master in theology, that the Brethren would, after a short time, decline from the strict observance of the Rule, he asked of the man of God permission to seek a safe and strict retreat if this relaxation should occur in his time. The benevolent Father answered him: 'Know that what thou hast asked of me has been granted thee by Christ;' and placing his hand on his head, he blessed him, saying: 'Thou art a priest for ever, according to the Order of Melchisedech.'

COLLOQUY XX.

The Afflicted and Tempted are to be Consoled, and that it is a great Benefit for the Saints to be Tried by Temptation.

GOD permitted that Brother Roger, one of the disciples of the holy Father, should, for the increase of his merit, be frequently tormented by many and grievous temptations, so that sometimes he was in danger of falling into despair. Once, when these temptations were more violent and obstinate than usual, he said to himself: 'I will arise and go to my Father, and if he receive me kindly and affectionately, I shall know that God will yet have mercy upon me; if not, I shall be convinced that I am totally abandoned.' Having thus resolved, he left Ancona for Assisi, where the holy Father was staying in the Bishop's palace, having been attacked by a great and mortal sickness. But the loving Father knew by inspiration the trouble of his child, and the cause of his journey; he therefore sent two of his companions, Brothers Masseo and Leo, to meet him, and welcome him warmly. 'Go,' he said, 'to meet Brother Roger, who is coming here to see me. Embrace him for me, and lovingly kiss and salute him, telling him on my part that I love him with all my heart, and more than all the Brothers that are in the world.' The two Friars obediently fulfilled this command, and the sinking soul of Brother Roger was at once strengthened in faith, and his whole soul replenished with exceeding joy. He thanked God for giving him this prosperous journey to the place where his suffering Father lay. When he arrived, St. Francis, animated by the fervour of his charity more than by any natural strength, rose to meet him, and throwing himself on his neck, exclaimed with paternal affection: 'My beloved Brother Roger, amongst all the Brethren in the world, thou art the dearest to me;' and making the sign of the Cross on his forehead, he kissed the place, saying: 'Beloved son, this temptation has been sent thee for thy greater profit. But if thou dost not wish to have this merit any longer, may no affliction or temptation henceforth assail thee.' Wonderful to relate, the temptation immediately vanished, and the Brother never suffered any trouble from that time.

COLLOQUY XXI.

How great should be the Patience of the Friars Minor under Afflictions.

ONE of his companions once asked the Saint how much the Friars Minor should suffer with patience, and praised him as a perfect model of this virtue. The holy Father replied: 'I should not consider myself a Friar Minor unless I acted in the manner I will describe to thee. Supposing that in virtue of my office, and according to the custom of Superiors, I go to the Chapter, I assemble the Brethren, I propose to them the Word of God, and I admonish them of their faults. This being done, the Brethren rise up against me, and say: "Thou dost not suit us; thou art not fit for the office of General, or Superior; how canst thou guide us rightly, how canst thou govern us, since thou art only a poor foolish, ignorant, and illiterate man? Therefore in future presume not to call thyself our Superior." Thus I am rejected with insults and derision, and turned out by all the Brethren. I tell thee that unless I could hear these words with the same serenity of countenance, the same joy of soul, and the same desire of perfection, as I should hear others pleasing and honourable to me, I should by no means consider myself to be a true Friar Minor. For if I rejoice and exult when they honour me for their own profit, virtue, and devotion, in which nevertheless there is danger for my own soul, how much more ought I to rejoice and be delighted when they abuse me to my own profit and welfare, for this is certainly most advantageous to me. For in governing others there is danger, in praise there is a snare, in humble submission of the soul there is profit.'

COLLOQUY XXII.

A Religious should never Shake off the Yoke of holy Obedience.

WHEN St. Francis gave up the office of General, he went humbly to Brother Peter of Catania, who had been appointed in his stead, and besought him, saying: 'My Father and beloved Brother, I acknowledge thee as my Father and lord. I confide my soul to thy care and keeping, and I humbly promise thee obedience and reverence as my lawful Superior. I beseech and entreat thee by the living and true God to appoint one of my Brethren in thy place, to command me and take care of me; and him I will always strictly obey in thy stead; for, on account of the great merit and profit of holy Obedience, I desire to have thee, my Superior, always with me and before me.' Having obtained this favour, he remained faithful to the practice of what he had promised until death; for whether at home or abroad, in the church or in the street, he did nothing without the consent and permission of his companion.

COLLOQUY XXIII.

That we should gratefully Remember the Benefits of God.

IN the holy Convent of Mount Alvernia, in the Cardinal's Chapel, (so called because there repose the ashes of the most illustrious Cardinal Galleotti de Ubertini, Count of Aretini,) there is still seen a square stone, covered with an iron grating, on which the blessed Father often took his meals, and on which he was wont to pray with great earnestness. On this account it is greatly honoured and venerated with religious care, and, lest it should be destroyed by the devout visitors, both ecclesiastic and secular, who desired to carry away some fragments of it as relics and who could not be restrained by the Religious, it was protected by this grate. Once, when Brother Leo was going to cover this stone with a cloth as he usually did at the hour of dinner, the holy Father forbade him, saying: 'Dearest Brother, do not cover this stone, but carefully wash it, first with water, then with wine, then with oil, and lastly with balm, for Christ Himself has been sitting on this stone, and from it has deigned to reveal to me what I am now going to tell thee. Thou must wash and bless this table four times, because from it Our Lord has promised me these four graces for the Order: 1. That this Order shall last unto the end of the world; 2. That those who love the Order and its members, even if they are sinners, shall obtain the grace of contrition and mercy from God, either during their life or at the hour of their death; 3. That enemies and persecutors of this Order, unless they repent, shall not live long; 4. That none of its members shall remain in it if they live wickedly, or, forgetting their profession, persevere obstinately in mortal sin; for either they shall confess their sin and become penitent, or their wickedness being discovered they shall be expelled. The Lord also added other things which I will reserve for thee until the hour of my death.' Having said this, he rose, and pouring oil on the stone, he exclaimed: 'This is the Altar of God.'

Besides the irrefragable testimony of the first Fathers of the Order and many writings, the stone itself bears witness of this circumstance, having on it a memorial of the reverence due to it, and that it is truly the altar of God. For soon after the death of St. Francis, the Brethren of the Convent of Alvernia removed the stone from the side of the mountain where it was, and where the Lord manifested His wonders, and placed it with great reverence near the high Altar, and by the care of the afore-mentioned Brother Leo, these words were indelibly engraved on it: 'This is the table of Blessed Francis, on which he had marvellous apparitions, and which he sanctified by pouring oil thereon and saying: "This is the Altar of God."' O true Jacob, worthy of so many favours and never forgetful of any! His humility procured them for him, and he was grateful for all.

COLLOQUY XXIV.

Religious should not Frequent the Palaces of the Great.

BEING asked by Leo, Cardinal of the Holy Cross, to stay with him a short time in Rome, the holy Father humbly consented, on account of the reverence and love he bore to this Prelate. But the first night of his abode there, when after prayer he wished to take a little repose, a troop of demons came and cruelly assaulted the man of God, and when they had beaten him long and severely, left him half dead. Then his companion came to him, and the holy Father related to him what had happened, adding : 'I believe, Brother, that the devils, who can do nothing but what Divine Providence permits, have thus ferociously assaulted me, because my sojourning in the palaces of the great is not good. My Brethren who are dwelling in poor houses when they hear that I am dwelling with Cardinals, will suspect me of mixing in worldly affairs, of being advanced to honours, and of enjoying pleasures. I think, therefore, it is better for one who is called to be an example to others, to fly from the Court, and remain in lowly dwellings with the humble, that he may animate those who are suffering from poverty by bearing the same.' Very early, therefore, the next morning he arose, and, excusing himself to the Cardinal, departed.

COLLOQUY XXV.

In the Poor we are to Consider the Poverty of Christ and His Mother.

IT happened once that a Brother harshly repulsed a beggar who was importuning him for an alms. When the tender lover of the poor heard this, he commanded the Brother to strip himself of his habit, and prostrate himself at the feet of the beggar, humbly acknowledging his fault, and begging pardon and prayers. When he had done this, the holy Father said to him sweetly: 'Brother, whenever thou seest a poor man, thou shouldest consider the poverty of Our Lord, and His Mother. And in like manner when thou beholdest the sick, thou shouldest remember the infirmities Christ took upon Himself.'

COLLOQUY XXVI.

In Religion we must Follow not our own Judgment, but that of Our Superior.

TWO youths once earnestly begged to be admitted into the Order, and St. Francis, wishing to try their obedience, and their readiness to renounce their own will, took them with him into the garden, saying: 'Come with me and plant some cabbages for the use of the Religious in the same manner that you will see me do.' Then taking the plants, he put them into the ground with their roots upwards. One of the youths, who was truly obedient, did exactly the same;

but the other, who was wise in his own eyes, began to argue against this novel method of gardening, asserting that cabbages should be planted the other way up. The blessed Father said to him : ' My son, imitate me, and do as I do.' But he refused, repeating that what he was doing was folly. Then our holy Father said : ' Brother, I see that thou art a great master, go thy way. A simple and humble Order is not fit for such masters, but for simple and foolish persons, such as this thy companion. He shall remain with us, but we cannot receive thee. Go thy way.'

COLLOQUY XXVII.

The Demons are Grieved when we are Joyful.

SOME one asked the holy Father how it was that he always had a serene and joyful countenance, even when he was assailed with temptations, and the fear of sin or hell. St. Francis replied : ' Sometimes the thought of my sins causes me great sorrow ; sometimes Satan desires to make me sad on account of my tepidity and heaviness of soul; for my joy torments him, and he envies me the graces I have received from God. I know also and see that if the devils cannot hurt me in myself, they try to hurt me through my Brethren, by endeavouring to extinguish holy joy in their hearts. But if they cannot injure me or my Brethren, they retire in great confusion. When, therefore, I am tempted to sadness and bitterness, I consider the joy of my Brethren, and the sight of their happiness and cheerfulness drives away my heaviness and sadness, so that I am excited to interior rejoicing and exterior cheerfulness.

COLLOQUY XXVIII.
Temptations are Allowed for our Greater Profit.

ONE of the Brethren was assailed by a grievous and obstinate temptation, which drove him almost to despair; and he dreaded the holy Father discovering the state of his soul, lest if he knew him to be thus assaulted by the devil, he should love him less. But the kind Father sent for his afflicted child, and consoled him lovingly, saying: 'Be not afflicted or dismayed, my son. Believe me, I now consider thee a greater servant of God than before, and be assured that the more thou art tempted, the dearer dost thou become to me. No one, my son, can repute himself to be the servant of God, until he has passed through temptation and tribulation. A temptation overcome, is like the ring by which God espouses a soul to Himself. Many flatter themselves upon their numerous good works, and rejoice never to have suffered tribulations and temptations. But, because they are frightened even before they begin to fight, God, knowing their weakness, does not try them with temptations; for hard combats are reserved for great virtue. It is a sign of His special favour when God leaves nothing unpunished in His servants in this world.'

COLLOQUY XXIX.

The Lord's Prayer is the most Salutary of all Prayers.

BEING asked by the Brethren to teach them how to pray, the holy man answered : 'When you pray, say, "Our Father, Who art in Heaven," etc., and " We adore Thee, O Christ, in all Thy churches throughout the whole world, and we bless Thee, because by Thy holy Cross Thou hast redeemed the world." '

COLLOQUY XXX.

The Devils are easily Put to Flight.

A CERTAIN Brother named Angelo, had a great fear of the devils, on account of the terrible combat he heard St. Francis had had with them. Being called by the holy Father he confessed this weakness to him, and even begged to be allowed a companion at night to sleep in his cell with him, for his fears were greater and more distressing by night than by day. The Saint replied : 'O timid soul ! why dost thou fear such weak and insignificant enemies, whose strength and power thou knowest well are in the Hands of God. In order that thou mayest experience this, I command thee to ascend this night, alone, the highest point of the neighbouring mountain, and there to cry out in a loud voice : ' Proud devils, come to me now all of you, and exercise your fury on me, and do to me what you are able.' The Brother humbly obeyed this order, but no devils appeared, and he was delivered for ever from his great fear.

COLLOQUY XXXI.

How the Devil Hardens the Hearts of Men.

BROTHER RUFINUS was attacked with such a grievous temptation concerning the Divine predestination, that he had never experienced a greater. The devil persuaded him that all his works were vain and useless, and appeared to him once in the form of Christ crucified, saying to him: 'Why, poor miserable man, dost thou torment thyself to no avail? Why so many prayers and fasts? All the world cannot change what God has once decreed. Thou art not of the number of the elect, but of the damned. Moved by compassion, I have come to warn thee, and to exhort thee not to inflict such suffering on thyself; remember thou art damned, together with the son of Peter Bernardone, and all who follow him.' Terrified by these words, Brother Rufinus was seized with that profound sadness which usually comes from the prince of darkness, and almost lost his faith in God, and in the blessed Father Francis. The holy man knowing this, and seeing the great danger in which his disciple was, sent Brother Masseo to Mount Subasio, where Brother Rufinus was dwelling in great fear and anguish. When Brother Masseo saluted him in the name of their blessed Father, Rufinus, like one out of himself, replied that he would have nothing more to do with that Francis, and that he no more belonged to him. Brother Masseo exclaimed: 'Alas! Brother Rufinus, what dost thou say? Who has bewildered thee, that thou dost no longer obey the truth? What means this? Dost thou not know that our blessed

Father is as an angel from heaven? How many souls have been saved, and will be saved, through his preaching! Come with me at once to our holy Father, who desires to see thee, and has sent for thee.' Brother Rufinus unwillingly consented, and when St. Francis saw him coming he said to him: 'Alas! Brother, how has the devil so miserably deceived thee? Dost thou not know that he sometimes transforms himself into an angel of light? The devil hardens men's hearts, God softens them, as He says: "I will take away from you your stony heart, and will give you a heart of flesh." Visions from God bring joy, those from the devil produce sadness. Try this vision, I beseech thee, in this manner; when it appears to thee again, receive it with contempt and insults. The pride of the devil will not suffer him to bear this, he will fly from thee, and betray his deception; meanwhile rejoice in the Lord, and trust in His mercy.' Brother Rufinus began to shed tears at these burning words, and went sorrowfully back to the mountain, where, shut up in his cell, he wept without ceasing, until the devil again appeared to him in the form of a crucifix, and said to him: 'Did I not forbid thee to speak to Francis?' Then Brother Rufinus exclaimed: 'Go, Satan, go to the place that belongs to thee; open thy lying mouth, and I will fill it with dirt.' Hearing this the devil departed with great speed and noise, and as he left he detached fragments of rock from the mountain, which were hurled violently into the valley beneath.

COLLOQUY XXXII.

Idleness is to be Shunned, and Labour Encouraged.

THE holy Father would reprove, before all the Brethren, those who were idle, or who worked negligently, saying: 'The tepid who will not apply themselves humbly and earnestly to labour, will soon be vomited from God's mouth. Therefore I wish all my Brethren to labour, and to apply themselves diligently to good works, that so we may be less burdensome to the people, and may avoid many evils both of the heart and tongue, lest by evil thoughts and words we injure the reputation of others. Those who do not know how to work must learn, but the profit or reward of the labour is not to be at the disposal of him who earns it, but at that of the Superiors or Guardians.

COLLOQUY XXXIII.

We must Bear a little in this World, to Enjoy the Glory of the next.

WHEN exhorting his Brethren to the observance of the Rule and profession, St. Francis was accustomed to say: 'O beloved Brethren, and Children eternally blessed, listen to me, listen to the voice of your Father. We have promised great things, but greater are promised to us. Let us observe the former, and sigh after the latter. Pleasures are short, the punishment is eternal. Sufferings are light, the glory infinite. Many are called, few are chosen; there will be retribution for all.'

COLLOQUY XXXIV.
Murmuring and Discontent are to be Conquered by Meekness.

WHEN the seraphic Father was returning to Assisi, from preaching the Word of God in Egypt and trying to convert the Soldan, he had for his companion Brother Leonard of Assisi, who was born of noble parents. Now St. Francis was compelled by weakness and fatigue to ride upon an ass, and his companion, who followed him on foot, feeling quite worn out, gave way to a little human infirmity, and began to say within himself: 'His parents were not equal in rank to mine, and yet he rides on an ass, and I must follow him on foot.' While he was thus thinking, the holy man suddenly dismounted, saying: 'It is not right, Brother, that I should ride, and thou shouldst go on foot, for thou wert nobler and more powerful in the world than I was.' The Brother, surprised and covered with shame at finding his thoughts discovered, threw himself in tears at his holy Father's feet, confessing his fault, and asking pardon.

COLLOQUY XXXV.
Disobedience comes from the Devil.

AT one time while his Vicar was holding Chapter, the Saint was alone in his cell, praying for the Brethren.

One of them, excusing himself for his faults, refused to submit to discipline. The holy man saw this in spirit, and calling one of the Friars, said to him : 'I see, on the back of that disobedient Brother, a devil, who is holding him tightly round the neck, and he, having spurned the yoke of Obedience, allows himself to be driven about by such a rider. But when I prayed for this Brother, the devil left him in confusion. Go, therefore, and tell him to submit immediately to the orders of holy Obedience.' The Friar, thus admonished, entered into himself, and at once humbly cast himself at the feet of the Vicar, asking pardon.

COLLOQUY XXXVI.

Against Lying and Giving Scandal to the Brethren.

Two of the Brethren came once from Lavora to see the holy Father, and the elder of the two gave some scandal to the younger. St. Francis asked the latter how his companion had behaved on the journey, and he replied: 'Well enough.' 'Take care,' said the Saint, 'that thou lie not under pretence of humility. I know very well—I know what has passed; but wait a little and thou wilt see.' The young Friar marvelled that the man of God should know his companion's fault; but the elder one being hardened in sin and impenitent, after a few days left the Order.

COLLOQUY XXXVII.

Those who Cherish the Friars Minor are Pleasing to God, and how the Order was Foretold in the Gospel.

MANY times when the holy Patriarch was exhorting his Brethren to beg for alms, he would use these words: 'Go,' he would say, 'for the Friars Minor have been given to the world in these last times, that the faithful may fulfil towards them the command of Christ, and that they may be commended by the Judge with these sweet words: "Inasmuch as ye did it to one of My least brethren, ye did it unto Me." But the impious and the cruel shall be rejected, and shall hear these terrible words: "Inasmuch as ye did it not to these My least brethren, ye did it not to Me." It is therefore a great privilege to beg under the title of a Friar Minor, since the Lord of truth has promised with His own mouth so signal a reward to the just for assisting them.'

COLLOQUY XXXVIII.

The Bread Obtained by Begging for the Love of God is the Bread of Angels.

ST. FRANCIS was accustomed to beg on Feast-days whenever he could, saying that in the poor of Christ this prophecy was fulfilled: 'Men shall eat the bread of angels.' 'For this,' he said, 'is the bread of angels which is begged for the love of God, which is given out of charity at the suggestion of the good angels, and collected by holy Poverty from door to door.'

COLLOQUY XXXIX.

Religious and Learned Men ought to Preach to the People by the Example of a Holy Life.

BEING once asked by a Doctor of Theology of the Order of Friars Preachers how these words of the Prophet Ezechiel were to be understood: 'If thou dost not warn the wicked man, that he may be converted from his wicked way and live, the same wicked man shall die in his iniquity, but I will require his blood at thy hand,' the Saint replied: 'If these words are to be understood in a general way, I believe them to mean that the servant of God ought so to burn and shine by his life and conduct, that by the light of his example, and the tongue of his holy conversation, he may reprove all the wicked, and make known to them their iniquity. But if, on the contrary, he becomes a cause of scandal to the people or his neighbour, he will not escape the vengeance of God.'

COLLOQUY XL.

True Obedience is like Death.

THE holy Father once commanded a disobedient Religious to be stripped of his garments, placed in a deep pit, and covered with earth. When the Brethren were fulfilling this order, and only the head of the offender remained uncovered, the compassionate Father drew near, and said: 'Art thou dead, Brother? art thou dead?' The disobedient Friar, now penitent, replied: 'Yes, Father, I am now indeed dead.' 'Rise, then,' said the Saint, 'if thou art truly dead, and henceforth obey the command of thy Superior, as thou oughtest, and show no repugnance to anything he enjoins, any more than a corpse would do. I wish my followers to be dead, not living.'

COLLOQUY XLI.
What a precious Treasure is Poverty.

THE holy man once entered a certain church with Brother Masseo, and began to beseech God to inspire him and his followers with the love of holy Poverty, and he prayed with such fervour that his face shone like fire. Then, all inflamed with this divine ardour, he approached Brother Masseo with open arms, and called him to him. The Brother, filled with wonder and admiration, threw himself into the arms of his blessed Father, and so great was the fire which burnt in the heart of Francis, that solely by the breath which came from his mouth, Masseo was raised many cubits above the earth. The Brother afterwards said, that while he was thus lifted up, he was filled with such sweetness that he had never in his life experienced anything like it. Then Francis said: 'Let us go to Rome, to beseech the holy Apostles Peter and Paul, that they would teach us how we may rightly and fruitfully possess this precious treasure of holy Poverty, for it is so divine and glorious, and we are so vile and abject, that we are unworthy to contain it in such vessels. It is indeed a heavenly grace, which so teaches and penetrates us, that henceforth we may trample under foot all earthly things, and may cast away from us all impediments which could hinder the soul from being most freely and speedily united to its God.'

SOME PROPHECIES OF THE HOLY FATHER ST. FRANCIS.*

I.

He Prophesies that he will found a Religious Order, and take it for his Spouse.

WHILE St. Francis was still living in the world, he was invited by his friends to a sumptuous banquet. But he withdrew into a corner, and appeared as if rapt in thought. His companions asked him of what he was thinking, and whether he were considering about taking a wife. 'Yes,' he replied, 'and one so beautiful that you have never seen her equal;' meaning the holy Order, which by the inspiration of God he was about to found.

II.

He Asserts that he will be a great Prince.

ALTHOUGH St. Francis was at one time given to the vanities and pomps of the world, he always had in his

---

* 'The spirit of prophecy,' says St. Bonaventure, 'was so resplendent in St. Francis that he foresaw the future, and penetrated the secrets of hearts, beholding things absent as if they were present.' Those given above are but a few out of the many prophecies uttered by the Saint.

heart a little flame of Divine love, which disposed him by degrees for greater things, and which was shown principally by his great charity for the poor. Once when he had bestowed abundant alms on them, he met a poor soldier, and immediately gave him the new clothes he was wearing. The following night he saw in his sleep a vast and magnificent palace, full of arms all marked with the sign of the Cross, and he was told that all he saw was for himself and his future soldiers. This filled him with extreme joy; and when asked the cause of his gladness, he replied: 'I know that I shall one day be a great Prince.'

III.

He Foretells his Love for the Poor, and that he will be their Father.

ONCE at the beginning of his conversion, his mother, Pica, was preparing the table for his dinner, when Francis placed on it a great many loaves. His mother, being astonished, asked him why he placed so much bread on the table, when there were so few guests. Francis replied that it was for the poor. 'But where,' said Pica, 'are the poor?' He answered: 'They are in my heart.'

IV.

That he would be Renowned throughout the World.

WHEN the citizens of Perugia were at war with those of Assisi, Francis was taken prisoner, together with others of his fellow-townsmen. In his captivity he was so filled with Divine consolations, that the interior sweetness overflowed to the exterior, and caused him to show outwardly his intense joy. One of his fellow-captives said to him : 'Why, I pray thee, when we are weeping and overwhelmed with sadness, dost thou alone rejoice in this manner? If, on account of the levity of youth, thou dost not feel thy imprisonment, at least out of compassion condole with us in our misery.' Francis replied : 'The captivity of my body does not afflict me, because my soul enjoys a great liberty. I truly feel for your afflictions, yet I must rejoice still more at my own happiness. Do you not now think very little of me? Believe me, him whom you now behold a prisoner in fetters, you will see hereafter renowned throughout the whole world.'

V.

He Prophesies the Foundation of a Convent of Poor Clares at St. Damian's.

WHEN St. Francis, in obedience to the voice and command he had heard from the Crucifix, that he should repair the house of God, had begun the restoration of the little Church of St. Damian, near Assisi, before he had yet entirely given up the world, he used to beg alms of those who passed by, to help him in his work, saying, or singing in French : 'Come and help me to rebuild this church, for there will be here a Monastery of poor ladies, who by the fame of their life and sanctity will glorify our heavenly Father throughout the whole world.'

VI.

The Friars Minor are sent by God for the Salvation of the whole World.

THE Cardinal Hugolino once asked the holy Father why he sent his Children and Brethren into such remote parts of the world, where they had to endure so many sufferings from hunger, thirst, and fatigue. The Saint replied: 'My lord, you think that the Lord has sent the Friars Minor only for the good of this country, but I tell you in truth that God has chosen and sent them for the profit and salvation of souls throughout the whole world. And they will be well received, not only by the faithful, but also by pagans and infidels, and will win many souls to God.'

VII.

That Hospitality to the Poor is very Pleasing to God.

WHEN the holy Father was preaching at Celano, a certain soldier out of devotion humbly invited him to dinner. He consented, and his family rejoiced much at the coming of their poor guest. Whilst the meal was being prepared, the man of God, according to his wont, retired into a secret place, and there, with his eyes and hands lifted up to heaven, offered his prayers and praises to the Lord. Having finished his prayer, he called his kind host aside, and said to him: 'I have, my friend, entered into this house to dine with thee, according to thy desire. But listen now, and attend at once to my advice, for thou wilt not eat here, but elsewhere. Confess thy sins quickly with true contrition and penitent sorrow; do not allow anything to remain which thou dost not truly confess. God will give thee this day thy reward for the charity with which thou hast received His poor ones.' The soldier followed his advice, and at once confessed to the companion of the Saint, arranged the affairs of his house, and prepared himself for death as well as he could. They then sat down to table, and the rest indeed began to eat, but the host, as the man of God had predicted, expired. Thus he received the reward of his hospitality, according to the words of truth. 'He who receives a prophet, shall receive the reward of a prophet;' for by means of the Saint's warning, he escaped eternal death, and entered into everlasting life.

VIII.

The Punishment for Relapse into Sin is most Severe.

THE holy Father was once ill in the city of Rieti, when a certain worldly and immoral priest, named Gideon, who was afflicted with a grievous malady, was brought to him, and besought him with many tears to make over him the sign of the Cross. St. Francis said to him: 'O Gideon, strong by name, but weak in thy soul, thou livest entirely according to the desires of the flesh, not fearing the judgments of God. How, then, can I sign thee with the Cross? However, on account of the devout prayers of the bystanders, I will sign thee in the Name of the Lord. But know that thou wilt suffer much greater evils, if, being delivered from thy infirmity, thou returnest to thy vomit; for on account of the sin of ingratitude, worse things than the first shall come upon thee.' The Saint therefore made the sign of the Cross over the priest as he lay paralysed, and he was at once restored to perfect health; and rising up, he began to praise God, saying, 'I am cured.' But after a few days, forgetting God, he returned to his sins; and one evening, being at supper in the house of a certain canon, and intending to sleep there that night, the roof suddenly fell in. All in the house escaped death except the wretched man, who was killed. This was the just judgment of God, according to the prophetic words of St. Francis: 'the last things of that man shall be worse than the first,' on account of his ingratitude, which is a vice most odious to God; for he ought to have been grateful for the pardon received, and doubly careful not to displease Him in future.

IX.

The Saint Prophesies the Reconciliation of a certain Man with his Wife, and that now is the Time of Mercy, but hereafter of Justice.

A CERTAIN noble lady, who had a great devotion to the man of God, came to him in deep sorrow on account of the cruelty and hard-heartedness of her husband, who contradicted her in all her good works; and she begged him, as her father and friend, to obtain of God that her husband's heart might be softened. The Saint, touched by the grief and devotion of the lady, said to her: 'Go in peace, and believe me, that very shortly thou shalt receive consolation from thy husband.' And he added: 'Tell him from me on the part of God, that now is the time for mercy, but later for justice.' Having received his blessing, the lady returned home, and repeated these words to her husband. Then the Holy Ghost fell upon him, and being completely changed into a new man, he gently replied: 'Lady, let us serve God, and save our souls.' Having from that time led a holy life together, they both on the same day happily departed to Our Lord.

X.

That Singularity and Hypocrisy are Bad and Pernicious in a Religious.

THERE was a certain Brother who appeared exteriorly to be a great Saint and of most holy conversation, but who was very singular. He was wholly intent on prayer, and observed silence so strictly, that he was accustomed to confess by signs instead of words. It happened that the holy Father came to the Convent where this Friar was, saw him, and spoke of him to the others. The Brethren all commended and praised him very highly; but the Saint said: 'Be silent, my

Brethren, and do not praise to me what is a temptation of the devil, and a fraudulent deception.' The Brethren were vexed at this, thinking it impossible that so many signs of perfection could be a deception. But before long the Brother left the Order, thus plainly showing how clear was the insight of the man of God into the secrets of the heart.

XI.

He Foretells that the Cardinal of Ostia will be Pope.

ST. FRANCIS predicted many times to the Cardinal of Ostia, Hugolino, whose intimate friend he was, that he would be made Pope, and he always addressed the little notes he used to send him in these words: 'To the future Father of nations, and most venerable Bishop of the whole world.' The event proved the truth of this prediction, for the Cardinal succeeded Honorius III., under the title of Gregory IX.

XII.

Apostates from the Order will Perish miserably.

WHEN St. Francis was passing through Apulia, a certain man who had apostatized from the Order met him, and throwing himself at the feet of the holy Father, earnestly begged pardon for his apostasy. The man of God, pointing to a gallows that was erected on a hill close by, said to him : ' I will forgive thee this offence, and thou mayest return to the

Order; but take care, if thou shouldst again cast off the habit and forsake the religious life, thou wilt be hanged on these gallows.' The apostate returned to the Order, but he did not remain long in it. A few days after he had left it the second time he committed some crime, on account of which he was hanged on that very gibbet, according to the Saint's prediction, and thus miserably and infamously ended his life.

XIII.

The Saint Prophesies great Schisms and Tribulations in the Church.

A SHORT time before the holy Father's death, he called together his Children and warned them of the coming troubles, saying: 'Act bravely, my Brethren; take courage, and trust in the Lord. The time is fast approaching in which there will be great trials and afflictions; perplexities and dissensions, both spiritual and temporal, will abound; the charity of many will grow cold, and the malice of the wicked will increase. The devils will have unusual power, the immaculate purity of our Order, and of others, will be so much obscured that there will be very few Christians who will obey the true Sovereign Pontiff and the Roman Church with loyal hearts and perfect charity. At the time of this tribulation a man, not canonically elected, will be raised to the Pontificate, who, by his cunning, will endeavour to draw many into error and death. Then scandals will be multiplied, our Order will be divided, and many others will be entirely destroyed, because they will consent to error instead of opposing it. There will be such diversity of opinions and schisms among the people, the religious and the clergy, that, except those days were shortened, according to the words of the Gospel, even the elect would be led into error, were they not specially guided, amid such great confusion, by the immense mercy of God. Then our Rule and manner of life will be violently opposed by some, and terrible trials will come upon us. Those who are found faithful will receive the crown of life ; but woe to those who, trusting solely in their Order, shall fall into tepidity, for they will not be able to support the temptations permitted for the proving of the elect. Those who preserve their fervour and adhere to virtue with love and zeal for the truth, will suffer injuries and persecutions as rebels and schismatics; for their persecutors, urged on by the evil spirits, will say they are rendering a great service to God by destroying such pestilent men from the face of the earth. But the Lord will be the refuge of the afflicted, and will save all who trust in Him. And in order to be like their Head, these, the elect, will act with confidence, and by their death will purchase for themselves eternal life ; choosing to obey God rather than man, they will fear nothing, and they will prefer to perish rather than consent to falsehood and perfidy. Some preachers will keep silence about the truth, and others will trample it under foot and deny it. Sanctity of life will be held in derision even by those who outwardly profess it, for in those days Our Lord Jesus Christ will send them not a true Pastor, but a destroyer.*

XIV.

That Pride and Ostentation are Pernicious to Religious, and that Brother Elias will Die out of the Order.

BROTHER ELIAS of Cortona, or as some say of Piedmont, who was appointed Vicar-General on the death of Blessed Peter of Catania, and who was afterwards elected fourth General of the Order, was a man of such great worldly prudence, that he seemed made for important enterprises, and there was no one in Italy equal to him in such matters; therefore he was much esteemed and honoured by princes and nobles. When he saw St. Francis inviting some simple and humble Brothers to sit by him at table, and leaving him and other wise and learned men at a distance, he took it very ill, and could not refrain from saying within himself: 'Alas! Francis, thou simple and illiterate man, why art thou so foolish and indiscreet? Thou puttest to shame the great men who are the pillars of thy Order, and through this foolish conduct thou wilt ruin us.' But the blessed Father, knowing the secret murmurs of his heart, said to him: 'Indeed, Brother Elias, thou wilt ruin thyself and the Order through thy pompous ostentation and worldly

---

* Mark of Lisbon and others think that this prophecy received its accomplishment in the great schism which desolated the Church after the election of Urban VI. in the year 1378. But it may also partially refer to other calamities which have befallen the Church in the latter ages.

prudence. Thou, and those like thee, will bring the Order to nothing; but alas! miserable man, thou wilt not be allowed to die in it.' This indeed came to pass; for Brother Elias, swelling with human pride when he was elected General, caused the Order to become relaxed, and attempted to introduce many things contrary to the purity of the Rule; in consequence of which he was deposed from his office by Pope Innocent IV., excommunicated, and deprived of his habit: thereupon he became so enraged, that he attached himself to the Emperor Frederick. But when he was ill at Cortona he sent his brother to the Pope, beseeching him to absolve him from the sentence of excommunication, which favour Innocent, moved by his prayers and tears, granted.

XV.

That frequently, on account of the Merits of the Saints, God refrains from Punishing Sinners.

ST. FRANCIS, when dying, predicted to Brother Leo a great famine which should desolate the whole of Italy, saying: 'Alas! my Brother, because of the sins of the people, God will send a great famine in the world; but on account of the merits of a certain poor man (I know not whom), now living, God delays sending this chastisement; yet after his death the famine will be so severe that innumerable men will miserably perish with hunger.' He told Brother Leo he had heard this on Mount Alvernia (as mentioned in the 23rd Colloquy), together with other things which he was not to reveal until the hour of his death. Immediately after his departure this prophecy was fulfilled; for such a famine prevailed throughout the whole of Italy that the wretched people eat not only roots, but even the bark of trees, and the mortality was so great that nothing but death was seen everywhere. The holy Father, St. Francis, appeared during this time to Brother Leo, and told him that he was the poor man on whose account God had delayed this scourge.

PARABLES AND SIMILITUDES OF THE HOLY FATHER ST. FRANCIS.

PARABLE I.

The Providence of God will never Fail the Poor in Spirit.

THE holy Father proposed the following parable to Pope Innocent III., who considered the Rule of the Friars Minor too hard and impracticable on account of the great poverty it enjoined:

'A poor but most beautiful virgin lived in a solitary and desert place, when the king of that country, captivated by her loveliness, took her for his spouse. He dwelt with her some years in that desert, and she bore him children who had the beauty of their mother, and the features of the king their father. The monarch having returned to his court and royal throne, the tender mother brought up her children carefully; and when they were grown up, she sent them to the king, saying : " You are the children of a great king who dwells in his royal palace. I cannot, and will not, leave this desert ; but do you go to your father and declare to him who you are. He will give you all that is necessary and becoming your high rank." The children obeyed ; and when the king saw them, he recognised in them his own likeness, and the wondrous beauty of their mother. He therefore said graciously to them : " I acknowledge you to be my children, and I will treat you as princes ; for if I feed and clothe my servants and strangers, how much more shall I cherish my own offspring, in whom I see the beauty and grace of their mother, whom I so ardently love ? All the children she has borne me shall sit at my table, and dwell at my court." Most Holy Father, this King is Christ Our Lord, the Monarch of heaven and earth ; and this beautiful virgin is Poverty, who dwelt alone in the desert of this world, scorned and rejected by men. The King of kings, Christ the Lord, was enamoured of her beauty ; and as soon as He entered into this world, He espoused her to Himself in the Crib. She, in this desert, has borne Him many children—apostles, anchorets, monks, and others who have embraced voluntary Poverty ; and these, who bear the royal marks of Christ—namely, poverty, humility, and obedience—she has sent to the heavenly King, who receives them lovingly, and promises to nourish them, saying : " I, Who make my sun to rise upon the just and the unjust—I, Who feed, clothe, and preserve the infidel Moors and Pagans, who are strangers to the faith—will much more willingly give to you, my beloved children, and to all who are born of my beloved spouse, Poverty, all that is necessary for you." Most holy Father, this Lady and Queen, holy Poverty, has sent us, her children, to the heavenly King; we are not worse than those who went before us; we have not degenerated from the beauty of our Father and Mother, since we profess the most high and perfect poverty. Do not fear, therefore, lest the children and heirs of the Eternal King should perish with hunger, for we are born in the likeness of the Lord Christ, and by the virtue of the Holy Spirit, of a poor Mother, and by the spirit of poverty, we shall be abundantly nourished in the Order of Poverty. For if the King of Heaven has promised His eternal kingdom to those who imitate Him, how much more will He give us those things which He bestows indifferently on the good and bad!'

When the Vicar of Christ had attentively considered this parable, he marvelled greatly; and seeing evidently that God spoke by the mouth of the holy man, he approved the Rule.

PARABLE II.

Of the Custody and Mortification of the Eyes.

THE holy Father used frequently to exhort his Brethren to guard and mortify their senses with the utmost care. He especially taught them the custody of the eyes, proposing to them the following parable:

'A certain pious king sent two messengers successively to the queen with a communication from himself. The first messenger returned and brought an answer from the queen, which he delivered exactly; but of the queen herself he said nothing, because he always kept his eyes modestly cast down, and had not raised them to look at her. The second messenger also returned; but after delivering in a few words the answer of the queen, he began to speak warmly of her beauty. "Truly, my lord," he said, "the queen is the most fair and lovely woman, and thou art indeed happy and blessed to have her for thy spouse." At this the king was angry, and said: "Thou wicked servant, didst thou dare to cast thine eyes upon my royal spouse? I believe thou dost covet what thou hast so curiously gazed upon." Then he commanded the other messenger to be recalled, and said to him: "What dost thou think of the queen?" He replied: "She listened very willingly and humbly to the message of the king, and replied most prudently." But the monarch again asked him: "What dost thou think of her countenance? Did she not seem to thee very fair and beautiful, more so than any other woman?" The servant replied: "My lord, I know nothing of the queen's beauty. Whether she be fair or not, it is for thee alone to know and judge. My duty was only to convey thy message to her." "Thou hast answered well and wisely," rejoined the king; "thou who hast such chaste and modest eyes shall be my chamberlain. From the purity of thine eyes I see the chastity of thy soul; thou art worthy to have the care of the royal apartments confided to thee. But thou, who hast such immortified eyes, depart from the palace; thou shalt not remain in my house, for I have no confidence in thy virtue."

'My Brethren, you have heard this parable, and you understand the meaning of it. If you have gazed on any female, do penance, and guard your eyes in future. Death lurks in such glances, and enters by the windows of the eyes. The heavenly King forbids you to look upon His spouses. Now, every Christian woman is His spouse, and who would not fear to look upon the spouse of Christ? Beware of the jealous anger of the King!'

SIMILITUDE I.

Of true and perfect Obedience.

A CERTAIN person once inquired of St. Francis whom he considered to be truly obedient, and the holy man proposed to him as an example a dead body. 'Take,' he said, 'a dead body, and place it where thou wilt. It will not refuse to be moved; it will not complain of its position; it will not expostulate if it be abandoned. If it be placed in an elevated seat, it still looks down, not up; if it be clothed in purple, it appears paler. This is like a truly obedient man, who does not inquire why he is moved, does not care where he is placed, does not beg to be changed; being raised to dignities, he preserves his wonted humility, and the more he is honoured, the more unworthy does he consider himself to be.'

SIMILITUDE II.
Of the same.

'I HAVE often,' said the holy Father on another occasion, 'seen a blind man, who had no one to guide him on his way but a little dog. Wherever the dog led him, he followed. He did not ask his guide why he conducted him this way or that; if he led him over rough stones, he still followed; if through the streets and squares, it was the same; if he took him to a church, he prayed; if he entered a house, the blind man asked an alms. Thus he followed wherever the dog chose to lead him, and never went anywhere without him. Such ought to be the truly and perfectly obedient man. He should be blind in obeying: having his eyes, as it were, closed before the commands of his Superiors, and neither wish nor seek to understand them, except that he may promptly and humbly fulfil them. Wherever the wish or command of his Superior leads him, he must follow; if it be through rough and stony paths, he must cheerfully bear it; if through smooth ways, he must proceed in virtue of holy Obedience. The truly obedient man should in all things consider, not the difficulty of the command, but the authority of the one who commands, and the merit of Obedience.

SIMILITUDE III.
Of the Cares and Solicitudes of Married Persons.

ST. FRANCIS being once assailed by a violent temptation of the flesh, and the enemy suggesting to him that he should take a wife, he first chastised his body by a severe discipline, and then going half-naked into the garden, which was covered with snow, he proposed to himself the following lively and apposite example of the cares and anxieties of married persons about their families, so different from the quietude of monastic life. Plunging into the snow, he made seven heaps of it, and thus spoke to himself: 'Behold, the largest of these is thy wife, the other four are thy two sons and two daughters, and the remaining two are a manservant and a maidservant whom thou must have to serve thee. Make haste, therefore, to clothe them all, for they are perishing with cold. But if thou findest so many anxieties too troublesome for thee, be careful to serve God alone with much earnestness.' By this example the tempter, being overcome, left him, and the holy man remained the conqueror in this perilous conflict.

SIMILITUDE IV.

Of the great Multitude who should Join the Order.

WHEN the Saint had as yet only four companions, he foretold the increase of his family to Blessed Egidius, his companion, under this similitude :

'Our Order is like a fisherman who lets down his nets into the sea, and taking a great multitude of fishes, he picks out the largest and keeps them, but lets the small ones go. Our net is let down into the sea of the world, and gathers into itself men of great sanctity and religious virtue; but those who have little fervour, and are tepid in the service of God, it lets go ; or having received them, casts them out again. So great will be the multitude of fishes, that I fear lest the net should be broken by their number.'

SIMILITUDE V.

That the Servant of God should Refer all Praise and Honour to Him.

THE holy Father was daily much honoured by the people, who, out of devotion and reverence for his sanctity, would kiss his hands, his habit, his feet, and even his footprints as he passed. As he never forbade their doing this, one of his disciples, doubting his humility, and somewhat scandalised at his allowing so much honour to be paid him, said to him: 'Brother, dost thou not see and remark what these people are doing ? How canst thou permit it ? Men honour thee, and reverence thee exceedingly as a Saint, and thou dost not prevent nor repulse them ; on the contrary, it seems as if thou didst take pleasure in this homage. How is this ?' The blessed Father replied : 'So far am I, Brother, from refusing these honours, that they seem to me very little. On the contrary, the people certainly should reverence me much more.' His companion, still more troubled, replied : 'I do not understand, Brother, how thou canst be considered a Saint, when thou desirest the praise and honour of men.' Then the blessed Father replied : 'Listen, Brother, and understand. I do not ascribe or appropriate any of this honour to myself ;

I give it all to God, and I keep myself in the depths of my lowliness. I know my own vileness, and I acknowledge the Majesty of God. But these men gain no little merit by these signs of respect, for they recognise and honour God, and reverence Him in His creatures. They who acknowledge the graces of God in His creatures, cannot be ignorant of God Himself. Creatures do not lose their humility because the Majesty of God is honoured in them. Just as statues of Our Lord or His Mother are honoured, and yet the statue of wood or stone does not become puffed up or exalted, so the servant of God, who is His true and living image, and in whom God is venerated and worshipped on account of the many graces which shine forth in him, does not think more of himself, but becomes the more firmly established in his humility; he attributes all to God, nothing to himself; he looks upon himself as wood or stone, or rather as pure nothingness in respect to God, to Whom he refers all honour and glory, but to himself misery, shame, and confusion.'

BLESSINGS OF THE HOLY FATHER ST. FRANCIS.

I.

Blessing of Brother Leo.

ONCE, when Brother Leo was strongly tempted on Mount Alvernia, the holy Father sent him the following benediction, written with his own hand, and marked with his special mysterious sign, the letter

Tau,* which he always held in high esteem, and by virtue of this benediction the Brother was entirely delivered from his temptation. 'T. May the Lord bless thee and keep thee, may He show His face to thee and have mercy on thee! May He turn His countenance to thee, and give thee His peace! May the Lord bless thee, Brother Leo!'

II.

Blessing of the Sacred Convent of Alenquerque.

THE five martyrs who suffered death in Morocco, spent some time with their Brethren at Alenquerque, a town of Portugal on the Tagus, whence they were sent, provided with all necessaries, by Queen Sanchia to Lisbon, which was distant about eight leagues from the first-named city, and whence they might proceed to Africa. When the blessed Father heard that they had obtained the much-desired crown of martyrdom from the Moors, and received the account of their constancy in the faith, their courage in torments, their perseverance in holiness; with great joy of spirit he blessed the little Convent of Alenquerque, which had sent them forth to such glory, in these words: 'O holy house, sacred temple, thou hast given to God by this martyrdom beautiful flowers of purple hue and most delicious fragrance. These are the first-fruits and most glorious flowers of the Friars Minor, the happy possessors of the heavenly king-

---

* See Ezech. ix. 4—6. This letter *Tau* of the Hebrew alphabet is in the form of a cross, thus prefiguring the sacred sign in which all benedictions are given.

dom. May perfect Brethren, who will observe most devoutly the holy Gospel, never be wanting to thee, O house of God!'

III.

Blessing of the zealous Observers of the Rule.

WHEN the holy Father heard how his Brethren, who were dispersed all over the world, were drawing many into the paths of virtue by the odour of their sanctity, he rejoiced in spirit, and called down the choicest blessings on them, saying: 'Blessed be you of the Lord, who bring back wandering sinners to God, who show them the way of truth, and keep yourselves in the pure and sincere observance of the Gospel rule! May he who blesses you be blessed of God, may he who provides for you or cherishes you receive an eternal reward! May Satan exercise no power over you, nor tempt you beyond your strength! May you have power over him and his, to destroy his strongholds, and snatch his prey from him! May the power of the Father assist you, the wisdom of the Son direct you, and the love of the Holy Ghost console you! Amen.'

On the other hand, St. Francis uttered the following terrible curse from God and from himself on those who, by their spirit of propriety, the reception of money, or any other sin, should injure the purity of the Rule, or should defile with the dust of earthly things the Order whose great glory is the profession of Poverty, or who by their bad example should scandalise others, or relax the observance of the Rule: 'By thee, O most holy God, and by the whole court of heaven, and by me, poor little man, may they be cursed, who by their bad example impede or destroy the good which Thou workest, and wilt ever work by means of the holy Brethren of this Order!'

IV.
Blessing of the City of Assisi.

WHEN the Seraphic Father was being carried, during his last sickness, from the palace of the Bishop of Assisi to the little sanctuary of Portiuncula, he caused the litter on which he was borne to be set down on the top of a hill, from whence he could conveniently see the city. When he saw it he wept, and then pronounced over it this benediction: 'Blessed be thou of the Lord, O city faithful to God, for in thee, and by thee, many souls will be saved, many servants of the Most High will dwell in thee, and not a few of thy inhabitants will inherit the kingdom of heaven!'

V.
Blessing of all the Friars Minor.

THE holy Father was once attacked with so painful and dangerous a disorder, that he seemed on the point of death, and all the Brethren despaired of his recovery. Then one of them, fearing lest he should die suddenly through exhaustion, said to him: 'Bless us, O Father, and the other Brethren whom thou hast engendered in Christ, and leave us some memorial of thy wishes, which thy children may have always in remembrance for their greater increase in perfection.' Then the blessed Father, turning his eyes full of tenderness upon his Brethren, said : 'Call to me Brother Benedict, of Piratro' (who always attended him in sickness, and said Mass before him), 'that I may bless you.' When the Brother came, the Saint said : 'Write, O priest of God, the blessing with which I bless all my children, both those who are now in the Order, and those who shall belong to it to the end of the world. But as I cannot well speak, on account of my weakness, I briefly declare my will and intention to all my Brethren present and to come, as a sign of my love and blessing. May all the Brethren love one another, as I have loved them, and do love them! May they always love and honour my lady Poverty! And may they always be faithful and obedient to the Bishops and priests of our holy Mother the Church! May the Father, Son, and Holy Ghost bless and keep them always! Amen.'

VI.

Blessing of Brother Bernard of Quintavalle.

WHEN all the Brethren were assembled round the deathbed of the Saint, weeping for the loss of such a loving Father and watchful pastor, he said to them : 'Where is my first-born son, Brother Bernard ?' And when the Friar came, he said : 'Come near, my son, that my soul may bless thee before I die.' But

Bernard in his humility (fearing to assume a privilege which, on account of his dignity and office, seemed rather to belong to Brother Elias, who was then Vicar-General, and the supposed successor of the holy Father), suggested to Elias that he should go to the right hand of the dying Saint, and obtain the offered benediction. The Vicar-General therefore prostrated himself before the man of God, who, although he was almost blind from excessive weeping, was full of a prophetic light. When he placed his hand on the head of Brother Elias, he exclaimed : 'This is not the head of my first-born, Brother Bernard.' Then, crossing his arms, like another Patriarch Jacob, and placing his right hand on the head of Brother Bernard, who was kneeling on his left side, he said : ' May the Father of our Lord Jesus Christ bless thee with all spiritual blessings in heavenly places in Christ! As thou hast been chosen to be the first in this Order, to give good example, and to imitate Christ in evangelical Poverty; as thou didst offer to Him not only all that thou hadst, but thyself also, as an odour of sweetness, so mayest thou be blessed by the Lord Jesus Christ, and by me, His poor little servant, with everlasting blessings, coming in and going out, waking and sleeping, living and dying ! May he who blesses thee be filled with blessings ; may he who curses thee not go unpunished ! Be thou lord over thy brethren, and let them all be subject to thy command. Whomsoever thou desirest should be received into this Order, let him be received ; and whomsoever thou desirest should be rejected, let him be dismissed. Let no one have any authority over thee, and mayest thou be free to go and remain wheresoever thou willest!'

VII.

Blessing of the Friars Minor.

WHEN the hour of his death approached, St. Francis caused all the Brethren, who were then at Our Lady of Angels, to be summoned; and consoling them for his death with sweet words, he, with paternal affection, exhorted them to Divine love, to patience, to poverty, and to constancy in the faith of the holy Roman Church. Then he added: 'Farewell, my children, in the fear of the Lord, and abide always in it. And since the time of tribulation and temptation is approaching, blessed shall they be who shall persevere in what they have begun. I, indeed, go to God, to whose grace I commend you. I have done what I had to do; may Christ teach you what you ought to do!'

APPENDIX.

DOUBTFUL WORKS OF ST. FRANCIS.[*]

SHORT SERMONS.

I.

Of Humility and Patience.

IN this short discourse we will not separate humility and patience, which were the inseparable companions of Christ on the Cross, and which are united together with the strong love of sisters. The servant of God ought to suffer much for Christ, since he hopes to enjoy with Him eternal happiness. The Apostle says that 'the sufferings of the present time are not worthy to be compared to the eternal weight of glory which shall be revealed in us.' We cannot have, nor find, two perfect delights (earthly and heavenly), nor can this double joy be in all things complete. Christ began His teaching with humility in the Crib; and, as a good Master, He completed it by patience on the Cross. He says: 'Blessed are

[*] Wadding gives the above Short Sermons, etc., as *doubtful* works of St. Francis. If not written by the holy Father himself, they are full of the unction of his spirit, and are therefore retained here.

they who suffer persecution for justice' sake.' He well knew that the suffering would be changed into glory; persecution and fear into joy. A silversmith makes a cup or vase out of the metal he has, but he cannot make a silver chalice out of a mass of lead; it is God alone Who can draw rest out of labour, and eternal joy out of torments. Loving, humble, and patient ought those servants to be who expect from their Lord His unspeakable reward.

II.

Against Mortal Sin.

MY Brethren, let us above all things avoid mortal sin. Consider how foul and horrible a dead body appears, deprived of the spirit of life; and understand how much more foul and unclean is a soul without God, Who is its life, when it is plunged in mortal sin. If creatures have so much need of each other, how much more has the creature need of his Creator! Grace is further removed from sin than glory is from grace; for the distance is infinite between grace and sin, whereas death alone stands between grace in holy souls and glory. He, therefore, who sins mortally, withdraws from God and draws near to hell, between which and the sinner life only is interposed, and this is often extinguished by an unforeseen and instantaneous death. How many have we not seen retire to bed at night in perfect health, and the next day carried to their grave! Let us humbly beg of God to preserve holily in His grace those who are now refreshed with it, and mercifully to restore it to unhappy sinners. O most strong and loving God, how ready Thou art to pardon the penitent—how powerful and severe in punishing the obstinate!

III.
On the Value of Almsgiving.

O MAN! give alms to the poor, through whom thou givest it to thy Creator. He makes Himself thy debtor in the poor man, and will give thee a full and abundant payment, and an overflowing reward. We can give our goods to God only through the poor, and He can stand in need of our goods only in the poor. See, therefore, my Brethren, how great is the happiness of the almsgiver, who can give to Him Who gives and repays to all most abundantly; to Whom not only the rich man who has much, gives much, but he gives most of all who gives whatever he has to the poor. The widow in the Gospel gave more than all the money that was in the treasury, when she gave willingly only the two mites she had. Hence Christ praised her hidden offering when He publicly declared it to be not a trifling, but a rich gift. Then let us distribute to the poor and needy our earthly and perishable goods, by which we may acquire immense and endless happiness with God in heaven. Alms are the patrimony of the poor, which our Divine Brother, Jesus Christ, purchased for them. When, therefore, we bestow alms upon them, we do not give them what belongs to another, but we restore to them what is their own. I beseech my Brothers, the Friars Minor, in Our Lord Jesus Christ, since they have chosen to make themselves poor after His example, and to ask alms in His Name, not to be ashamed of begging from door to door. Our Lord Himself lived on alms. If, therefore, a vile creature does what he has first seen the Omnipotent Creator do, all will consider it to be not a dishonour, but an honour—not an ignominy, but a glory; especially when the poor mendicant procures for the rich man, of whom he begs, far more abundant wealth, and provides him with an unseen occasion of gain and interest. Moreover, on the part of God, he teaches the rich not to despise nor think lightly of the poor, whose confusion (if they suffer any from the rich) the severe Judge will avenge on those who inflict it, but the Father of Mercies will reward in those who suffer it. Whatever men leave behind them on earth withers, only the alms they have bestowed will bloom for ever; what they have given away in this world, they will find in heaven; they dispense earthly goods, and they will receive eternal riches. Let him who asks alms give God equal thanks, whether he is mercifully relieved or cruelly denied; when he is relieved, because God sends him wherewith to clothe and feed his body—when he is denied, because he has an occasion offered him of merit and patience.

IV.

Of the Love of our Enemies.

LISTEN, my Brethren, to the message which the Most High sends you from heaven, by means of the least of His servants. Love all, both your neighbours and those from whom you suffer anything. The former are manifestly your friends, the latter are by no means your enemies. Those who love you, who serve you, who give you food and clothing, do good indeed to your bodies; but those who persecute you, who are angry with you, who injure you, do much more good to your souls. All men are therefore your friends, and no one is to be called an enemy; all are your benefactors, and no one does you harm. You have no enemy except yourselves. If therefore you desire to hate your enemies, begin by hating your body and your sensual appetite. If you wish to be avenged of your adversary, scourge your body, and bring it into subjection to the spirit. May God Who created you, and Christ Who redeemed you, be with you, and keep you from all adversity!

V.

Of Perfect Obedience.

WE are all, my Brethren, creatures of God, on whom the Most High has mercifully bestowed many more gifts than on others. If we do not serve Him, nor fulfil His commandments as we promised in baptism, He will deprive us of the inheritance of glory, and cast us into hell; we shall lose the liberty of children, and undergo the slavery of captives. Let us not desire to have authority over anyone, but to be subject to all creatures for the love of the Creator. Upon those who act thus and persevere, the Spirit of God will rest, and He will make His abode in them. They will be children of the heavenly Father, brethren of Our Lord Jesus Christ, and spouses of the Holy Ghost. These nuptials are celebrated when the Divine Spirit and our souls are united to each other by charity. We are the brethren of Jesus Christ when we participate in His possessions, and we are called the children of God when we become like Him in our actions. Oh, how glorious it is to have a Father in heaven! how sweet and happy to cling to such a Spouse! how great and glorious to have for our Brother the Heir of the kingdom of heaven! St. Paul calls Him the First-born; St. John, the Only-Begotten Son. He is called the First-born in that nature which He took from us; He is the Only-Begotten in the Godhead which He received from His co-equal Father from all eternity. Our Lord says in the Gospel: 'Unless a man renounce all that he hath, he cannot be My disciple;' and, 'He who wishes to save his soul, must lose it;' as though He said, that he relinquishes all who renounces his own will, and he saves his soul by losing it who abdicates all dominion over himself, and subjects all that he is to the authority of his Superior. There are some subjects who are deceived by their own sense, and whenever the command of the Superior is repugnant to their unconquered self-will, they immediately say it is contrary to the Rule, and to the good of their souls. Perfect obedience is that which makes a Religious omit what seems to him the best and wisest, that he may fulfil, at the sole command of his Superior, what he himself considers less right and fitting. In this he acquires great merit by renouncing his own opinion and yielding his own will to that of another. He who truly obeys his Superior obeys God, and gives an excellent example to his neighbour. The highest obedience is that in which flesh and blood have no share. The perfectly obedient man ought not to wait until a command is given a second or a third time; for he who does not execute the orders of the Superior at once, obeys not with his free will, but only by compulsion. He who does not obey promptly, has no fear of God nor reverence for man, if he has no good reason for delay. Most fruitful is holy Obedience, for the truly obedient man passes no time without merit.

VI.

Of the Value and Dignity of the Soul.

THE greatest care ought to be taken of the soul, for man has not many, but only one. If God had given us two souls, as He has given us two eyes, or two feet, then should one be lost or taken away, we might guard and save the other. But as we have received only one, very weak and languishing, assailed by three most powerful enemies, and exposed to the fiery darts of the world, the flesh, and the devil, it is not lawful for it to repose securely for one single day, but it must always be striving and fighting. The Apostle gives us to understand how continual this warfare must be, when he says : 'Our wrestling is not against flesh and blood, but against principalities and powers.' In war, or in a battle, some time is granted to the soldiers to refresh their bodies, to lay aside their arms, to rest from their labours, and to recruit their strength; nor are they, during severe cold, compelled to rest at night exposed to the inclemency of the season, but are allowed to pass the winter in the city. But it is different with wrestlers; for then only can they be permitted to breathe, when one being overcome and thrown to the earth, the other goes away in triumph. The strife with our enemies can never cease, the time of fighting is the whole time of our life, the end of our life will be the beginning of rest; and only after death will the demon-wrestler retire, after having endeavoured most strenuously to conquer us in death. Let us, therefore, most earnestly beseech Our Lord to protect us by His grace, and, in the midst of so many dangers, mercifully to defend us from our enemies. Nothing, alas! is more vile than the price for which we sell our precious souls. On the slightest occasion we cast it into hell, and for the smallest and most insignificant reward we deprive it of the inestimable treasure of Divine grace.

VII.
Of the Obligation of Priests.

REVEREND FATHERS, you are the intimate friends and servants of God, and eat at His table; understand well, then, your dignity. Esteem devotion highly; be constant in contemplation. Let the Holy Spirit be the light of your intellect, and the fire of your will. Persevere in the observance of those things which you have promised to God, and never return in deed or in affection to the things you have abandoned. Fly from ambition; avoid superiority among your Brethren. Remember that He Who is infinitely above angels and men, when He entered this world made Himself inferior, not only to angels, but even to men, and calls Himself the least of all, saying: 'I came not to be ministered unto, but to minister.' Let those who are chosen for Superiors not command their subjects haughtily, as if they were masters, but correct them humbly, as becomes those who are called Ministers. Let them provide carefully for the necessities of all, taking great care about their temporal welfare, and greater still of their spiritual good. Let them remember that they are pastors over the souls of their subjects, of whom, according to the Apostle, they will have to give a strict account. When a sheep is lost, or perishes of cold, the shepherds try cunningly to satisfy their masters by showing the skin of the dead animal. The pastors of souls will be obliged to pay most strictly before the judgment-seat of God; not a skin for a sheep, but skin for skin, soul for soul. Let them treat their subjects with the same care as they treat themselves, and minister to them as if they were themselves. God commands sinners to do penance for their sins, and to make a true confession of them to the Priests, who ought to reprove them for their sins, and lead them back through penance to virtue. They should exhort their penitents to frequent confession and Communion; for if the holy Eucharist is the food of the soul, without which it languishes and dries up, why should not all desire to approach daily the holy Banquet in which it is offered to all? He who is fatigued by the difficulties of a journey, has most need of the refreshment of food. If, then, we are all pilgrims travelling to our own country, why do we not desire to be supported by this precious and most delicious Food? Elias partook of this Food in figure, and walked in the strength of it to the mount of God. If we often eat this Bread as we ought, we shall profit much in the way of virtue, and we shall more vigorously proceed towards our destined country.

SIX PRINCIPAL REASONS WHY ALMIGHTY GOD GRANTED THE ORDER OF FRIARS MINOR TO HIS CHURCH.

THE Friars Minor have been given and called by God, principally that they may represent Our Lord Jesus Christ, and may bring back to the minds of Christians His so great benefits, which are, as it were, forgotten, or despised, or neglected by the world. And for this reason have they been asked of God by His Son, Our Lord Jesus Christ.

First, they are given that both in word and deed they may be the witnesses and imitators of His most high Poverty, by the most perfect renunciation of all property and unlawful attachment to earthly goods, and by the poor and humble use of them; because the virtue and love of holy Poverty were, so to speak, deserted, rejected, and despised everywhere and by all, so that she could no longer find any place where she could perfectly and securely rest her foot.

Secondly, that in word and deed they may be witnesses and imitators of His most high and perfect Obedience, by which He was not only made obedient to God, His Father, even unto the death of the Cross for our sakes, and would even be subject to His parents—that is, to the most holy Virgin, His Mother, and to St. Joseph, His reputed Father, who were so far inferior to Him—but what is far more, would obey even the rulers and the priests, and taught this Obedience to others when he commanded the tribute to be paid to Cæsar, and when he said of the Scribes and Pharisees who governed the people ill : 'Whatsoever they say to you do, but according to their works do not.' For the more unworthy is he who governs, the more pleasing is the submission of the subject, and the more meritorious is his obedience ; especially if he has had nothing to do with the appointment, or continuance in office, of such a bad and incompetent Superior. The most perfect and evangelical kind and degree of Obedience is to obey, for God's sake, such Superiors and others, not only in those things which a Religious has promised to observe according to the Rule, but also in everything which is not contrary to the Rule and the salvation of his soul, without any other limitation or curtailing of the power and jurisdiction of his lawful Superiors.

Thirdly, that they may be the witnesses and imitators of the abjection and humility of Jesus Christ, by despising all honours and promotion, and the vanities of the world, and by a true contempt and mortification of themselves for the love of God.

Fourthly, that they may be witnesses and followers, both in word and deed, of Our Lord in His charity and love for the salvation of all mankind, by going throughout the world to preach by word and example, and to bring back to their Creator, their Shepherd and their Redeemer, the souls purchased by the Precious Blood of Christ.

Fifthly, that they may be witnesses and imitators of Our Lord's sobriety, penance, meekness, condescension, mercy and purity, by abstinence, fasting, and labour, by a loving and charitable condescension and kindness towards the afflicted, by receiving and healing sinners, and by purity of soul and body.

Sixthly, that they may be the witnesses and the special contemplators, imitators, and preachers of His Passion, and of the many benefits bestowed on us by His blessed Incarnation, Life, and Death, and our so great Redemption; and this not only by frequent and assiduous meditation on the bitter sufferings both interior and exterior of Himself and His Blessed Mother, but by truly and willingly bearing, for His holy Name's sake, all contradictions, tribulations, contempt and sorrow.

Blessed, then, are those Brethren who as much as possible follow in these respects' Our Lord Jesus Christ, and His most holy Mother, in this life; because in death and judgment they will appear with their Divine Leader in the ranks and company of His true soldiers and special followers, and will sit with the Apostles, judging all the nations of the earth—that is, approving the sentence of the Sovereign Judge, according to His own words: 'Amen, I say unto you, that you who have left all and followed Me, in the regeneration when the Son of Man shall sit on the throne of His glory, you shall also sit on twelve thrones, judging the twelve tribes of Israel.'

Therefore, most dear and well-beloved Brethren in Christ, for the love of God, see and understand well your vocation, and why you are called Minors; because for His sake you must endeavour now not to be greater, but to be more humble, abject, and lowly than all, in order that you may be great now in grace, and hereafter in glory. Be grateful to the Lord our God Who so lovingly, and without any merit on your part, has deigned to choose and call you to such great and sublime things, and strive to walk worthily of the vocation wherewith you are called, never looking back, but proceeding from virtue to virtue, being most certain that, if here below you follow Christ, and are made partakers of His sufferings, you will partake likewise of His consolations; and for the momentary labours of this present life, you will receive a sure and inestimable reward with Christ in the next. Which may the sweet Lord mercifully grant you, by the merits of His most holy Passion,

Death, and Resurrection, and by the intercession of His Blessed Mother, and of all the Saints. Amen.

THE TEN PERFECTIONS OF A TRUE RELIGIOUS AND PERFECT CHRISTIAN.

THE first perfection of a good Religious is, that he strives with all his mind and strength to weep for his sins, confesses them willingly and without delay, and takes care as much as possible not to fall again into the same or other disorders.

The second is, that he puts every creature above him, and himself below all. If he acted otherwise he would offend that great Lord, Who made all creatures, and Who has so honoured us as for our love to assume human nature, which, having assumed, He shares with all creatures.* On this account, therefore, a fervent Religious, or perfect Christian, ought, with a good heart and a good will, to obey all, not only his companion who is above him, or his equal, or inferior, but also every creature, as far as is lawful.†

The third is, that he tears aways his heart from every earthly and human affection, and neither seeks

---

* St. Augustine says that man is the compendium of all creatures, and contains in himself all that is below him. This is literally true, for man has mere inanimate existence, animal life, and spiritual life.

† St. Francis's meaning seems to be that man is to be subject to 'all creatures,' to submit, for example, to heat and cold, etc., because Our Lord in His human nature participates in the nature of all creatures.

nor finds any support or stay except in Him Who made his heart for Himself, but accustoms his mind to cast itself upon God, and frequently to elevate itself above the mire of the earth, so that he can without difficulty and whenever he pleases return to Christ, thinking of Him, and uniting himself to the Creator of the heart, and being intent at all times and in all places on his heavenly Benefactor. In prayer he either bewails the evil he has done, or asks and desires the virtues in which he is wanting, or he gives thanks for the blessings bestowed upon him, or for the evils and misfortunes which befall him, and he believes that the merciful God permits these things to happen to him on account of his sins, or for the chastisement of his body.

The fourth is, that he has such patience as to endeavour to love the most heartily, and to serve the most willingly, without any bitterness of soul, whoever says or does anything against him; for as God in His infinite liberality has granted him all good, so he believes that He secretly permits these evils to assail him, in order that He may make known to him his sins, so that knowing them he may be lightly chastised for them in this world, and not eternally punished for them in the next. Therefore, he loves much the man who does him any wrong or speaks evil of him, because God makes use of this person as a messenger to confer on him great benefits; as an arm or a cord by which He mercifully holds him back lest he should fall into the eternal abyss, and lest the world should defile or the devil deceive him; as a cloth wherewith He cleanses him; and as an instrument or chisel with which he carves and perfects him.

The fifth is, that he loves all the good, and compassionates all the wicked, that he honours all, and reputes himself the vilest of all, esteeming himself worse than even the most sinful. And this because he does not know whether the good that he does is pleasing to God, or whether he will persevere in it, nor does he know the end which another may reach. For this reason he never judges evil of another in his heart, and never speaks evil of him with his tongue. And when he hears evil said of anyone, he excuses him, or at least he takes no pleasure in the detraction, but shows that he is grieved, or skilfully turns the conversation to another subject.

The sixth perfection is, that he loves much to be reprehended, and also the one who reprehends him : if anyone blames him, he entirely agrees with him; but if he be commended for his virtue, he declines the praise, and says he has done no good, always bearing in mind that God alone does all good, and gives the will to do it.

The seventh is, that he willingly serves all, and accepts service from others with great reluctance, considering himself unworthy of any service, because he remembers that Christ came, not to be served, but to serve. If, then, anyone ministers to him in his wants, he returns thanks in his heart to God, Who gives this person the power and the will to serve him.

The eighth perfection is, that he endeavours to bear in mind all the blessings which he and all other creatures have received, and gives thanks to God for them all; after which he humbles himself, saying: 'Who am I, that I should give thanks for others, when I cannot sufficiently give thanks for the least of the benefits that God has bestowed on me, especially as I am such a miserable creature?' And thus he annihilates himself.

The ninth perfection is, that he keeps a strict guard over his tongue, which is the consummation of all virtue, and without which he would lose all grace; and he guards his tongue not only from evil and hurtful, false and unbecoming words, but also from those that are vain and superfluous, and which destroy the devotion of the heart.

The tenth and last perfection is, that he takes care above all things that in all his words there should appear truth, goodness, and humility; for the speech of a man should begin in truth, proceed in goodness, and terminate in humility and brevity of words; because Our Lord while on earth used brevity of speech. Thanks be to God!

THE END.

Extract from the NEW YORK CATHOLIC BOOK NEWS, May, 1879:

"*No publisher does more than Mr. Washbourne to produce a variety of excellent books, and to spread Catholic literature far and wide.*"

ROBERT WASHBOURNE'S
CATALOGUE OF BOOKS,
18 PATERNOSTER ROW, LONDON

PRAYER BOOKS   982   **SEE PAGE 30.**

Works of St. Francis of Assisi. Translated by a Religious of the Order. 4s.

Treatise on the Way of Sorrows, followed by a Practical Method of Blessing, Erecting, and Solemnly Performing the Stations of the Way of the Cross. By F. Alexis Bulens, O.S.F., of the Monastery, West Gorton, Manchester. Cloth, 1s. 6d., red edges, 2s.

Killed at Sedan. A Novel. By Samuel Richardson, A.B., B.L., of the Middle Temple, author of "Noel d'Auvergne," &c. 7s. 6d.

Zeal in the Work of the Ministry. By Abbé Dubois. Translated. 10s.

"Everything in it breathes wisdom and prudence, and not less Christian faith, piety, and love."

Agnes Wilmott's History and the Lessons it Taught. By Mary Agatha Pennell, author of "Bertram Eldon" (1s.), "Nellie Gordon" (6d.), &c. Fcap. 8vo., 1s. 6d. [*In the press.*

For Better, Not for Worse. By Rev. Langton George Vere.

Bobbie and Birdie; or, Our Lady's Picture. A story for the very little ones. By Frances J. M. Kershaw. 2s. 6d.

Solid Virtue. By Father Bellécius, S.J. New edition, revised and corrected by a Religious of the Ursuline Community at Thurles. 7s. 6d. With a Preface by Dr. Croke, Archbishop of Cashel and Emly.

Catholic Hymn Book. By Rev. Langton George Vere. 204 pages, price 2d.; in cloth, 4d. This is the best and cheapest Hymn book printed. *An Abridged Edition is now ready.* Price 1d.

My Lady at Last. A new Tale by the author of "The Last of the Catholic O'Malleys." Crown 8vo., 5s.

"In the simple style in which it is narrated lies its charm."—*Athenæum.*

Out in the Cold World. By M. F. S., Author of "Fluffy," "Tom's Crucifix," "Catherine Hamilton," "Legends of the Saints." 3s. 6d.

The Office of Holy Week, according to the Roman Rite. This edition gives (including the Ordinary of the Mass, and the Services generally included in Holy Week Books) the Vespers and Complin for every day of Holy Week; the Blessing of the Holy Oils on Maundy Thursday; and the Matins, Lauds, Mass, Vespers, and Complins of Easter Sunday. Price 1s.

⁎ *All other Books not mentioned in this Catalogue supplied.*

School Books, *with the usual reduction*, Copy Books, and other Stationery, Rosaries, Medals, Crucifixes, Scapulars, Incense, Candlesticks, Vases, &c., &c., supplied.
FOREIGN BOOKS supplied. Catalogue containing very reduced prices, post free.

R. Washbourne, 18 Paternoster Row, London.

The Rose of Venice. A tale of persecution by the Council of Ten in the old Venetian Republic. By S. Christopher. Crown 8vo., 5s.

Kainer ; or, the Usurer's Doom. By the Author of "Industry and Laziness." 1s. ; gilt edges, 1s. 6d.

Child's Picture Prayer Book. Sixteen tinted Illustrations, cloth, 1s. and 1s. 6d. ; with coloured Illustrations, 1s. 6d., 2s., 2s. 6d., 3s., and 3s. 6d. French morocco, 3s. 6d. and 4s. Calf, 5s. and 6s.

True Wayside Tales. By Lady Herbert. Foolscap 8vo., 3s. ; or cheap edition, in 5 vols., in pretty binding, price 6d. each.
  1. The Brigand Chief, and other Tales.
  2. Now is the Accepted Time, and other Tales.
  3. What a Child can do, and other Tales.
  4. Sowing Wild Oats, and other Tales.
  5. The Two Hosts, and other Tales.

Chats about the Commandments. By Miss Plues, Author of "Chats about the Rosary." 3s.

The Golden Thought of Queen Beryl, and other Stories. By Marie Cameron. 1s. 6d. ; gilt edges, 2s. ; or in pretty binding, cheap edition, in 2 vols., price 6d. each.
  1. The Golden Thought, and The Brother's Grave.
  2. The Rod that bore Blossoms, and Patience and Impatience.

Little Books of St. Nicholas. By Rev. F. Drew. Fcap. 8vo., 1s.
  Ave Maria ; or Catesby's Story. [each.
  Credo ; or, Justin's Martyrdom.
  Veni Creator ; or, Ulrich's Money.
  Per Jesum Christum ; or, Two Good Fridays.
  Pater Noster ; or, an Orphan Boy.
  Dominus Vobiscum ; or, The Sailor Boy.
  Oremus ; or, Little Mildred.

The Mission Cross. A Temperance Tale. By Mrs. Bartle Teeling, Author of "The Violet Sellers." 1s. 6d. ; cloth, 2s.

CATHOLIC PROGRESS. A Monthly Magazine. New and enlarged series, 3d., post free, 4d. ; yearly subscription, 4s.

Indulgences, Sacramental Absolutions, and the Tax Tables of the Roman Chancery and Penitentiary considered. By the Rev. T. L. Green, D.D. New Edition, with Index., 2s. 6d.

The Jesuits. By Paul Feval. English Translation. 12mo., 3s. 6d.

The Catholic Pilgrim's Progress—Sophia and Eulalie. Translated from the French by George Ambrose Bradbury, O.C., Permissu Superiorum. 3s. 6d. ; cheaper edition, 1s. 6d.

Walter Ferrers' School Days ; or, Bellevue and its Owners. A Tale for Boys. By C. Pilley. 2s. ; cheap edition, 1s.

OREMUS, A Liturgical Prayer Book : with the Imprimatur of the Cardinal Archbishop of Westminster. 32mo., 452 pages, paper cover, 2s. ; cloth, 2s. 6d. ; embossed, red edges, 3s. 6d. ; French morocco, 4s. 6d. ; calf or morocco, 6s. ; Russia, 8s. 6d. Also in superior and more expensive bindings.

A Smaller Oremus ; an abridgment of the above. Cloth, 9d. ; with red edges, 1s. ; roan or French morocco, 2s. ; calf or morocco, 3s. ; russia, 6s. Also in superior and more expensive bindings.

*** Specimen copy sent free on receipt of 1d. stamp.

The Child of Mary's Manual. Compiled from the French.

Bluebeard; or, the Key of the Cellar. A Drama in 3 Acts. 6d.
The Violet Sellers; or, Kindness costs Little and is worth Much. Drama in 3 Acts for Children. 6d.
The Enchanted Violin. A Comedy in 2 Acts for Boys. 6d.
Nellie Gordon, the Factory Girl; or, Lost and Saved. 6d.
Bertram Eldon, and how he found a Home. By the author of "Nellie Gordon." 1s.
Gathered Gems from Spanish Authors. By Mariana Monteiro, author of "The Monk of the Monastery of Yuste." 3s.

ADELSTAN'S (COUNTESS), Life and Letters. From the French of the Rev. Père Marquigny, S.J., 2s. 6d.; cheap edition, 1s.
Adolphus; or, the Good Son. 18mo., 6d.
Adventures of a Protestant in Search of a Religion. By Iota. 12mo., 2s. and 3s. 6d.
Agnes Wilmott's History, and the Lessons it Taught. By M. A. Pennell, author of "Bertram Eldon," "Nellie Gordon," &c. 1s. 6d.
AGNEW (E.), Geraldine; a Tale of Conscience. 3s. 6d.
Aikenhead (Mary), Life of. Giving a History of the Foundation of the Congregation of the Irish Sisters of Charity. 7s. 6d.
A'KEMPIS—Following of Christ. Dr. Challoner's Edition, 32mo., 1s.; embossed red edges, 1s. 6d.; roan, 2s.; French morocco. 2s. 6d.; calf or morocco, 4s. 6d.; gilt, 5s. 6d.; russia, 7s. 6d., 9s. and 12s.; ivory, with rims and clasp, 15s., 16s., 18s.; mor. antique, with corners and clasps, 17s. 6d.; russia, ditto, ditto, 16s. 20s.,
———— with Reflections. 32mo., 1s.; Persian, 3s. 6d.; 12mo., 3s. 6d.; Persian, 7s. 6d.; mor., 9s.; mor. ant. 15s.; Russia, 25s.
———— The Three Tabernacles. 16mo., 2s. 6d.
Albertus Magnus. By Rev. Fr. Dixon. 10s. 6d.; cheap ed., 5s.
Allah Akbar—God is Great. An Arab Legend of the Siege and Conquest of Granada. From the Spanish. By Mariana Monteiro. 12mo., 3s. 6d.
ALLIES (T. W.), St. Peter; his Name and his Office. 5s.
Alphabet of Scripture Subjects. On a large sheet, 6d.; coloured, 1s., mounted to fold as a book, 2s. 6d.
ALZOG'S Church History. 8vo. 4 Vols. 7s. 6d. each.
AMHERST (Rt. Rev. Dr.), Lenten Thoughts. 1s.; stronger bound, 2s., with red edges, 2s. 6d.
ANDERDON (Rev. W. H., S.J.), To Rome and Back. Fly-Leaves from a Flying Tour. 12mo., 2s.
ANDERSEN (Carl), Three Sketches of Life in Iceland. Translated by Myfanwy Fenton. 2s., cheap edition, 1s. 6d.
Angela Merici (S.) Her Life, her Virtues, and her Institute. From the French of the Abbé G. Beetemé. 12mo., 3s.
Angela's (S.) Manual: a Book of Devout Prayers and Exercises for Female Youth. Cloth, 2s.; Persian, 3s. 6d.; morocco, 4s.
Angels (The) and the Sacraments. Fcap 8vo., 1s.; gilt, 1s. 6d.
———— Month of the Holy Angels. By Abbé Ricard. 1s.
Anglican Orders. By Canon Williams. 12mo., 3s. 6d.
Anglicanism, Harmony of. By T. W. M. Marshall. 2s. 6d.
Are You Safe in the Church of England? A Question for Anxious Ritualists. By Charles Walker, of Brighton. 8vo., 6d.

ARNOLD (Miss M. J.), Personal Recollections of Cardinal Wiseman, with other Memories. 12mo., 2s. 6d.

ARRAS (Madame d') The Two Friends; or Marie's Self-Denial. 12mo., 1s.; gilt edges, 1s. 6d.

Artist of Collingwood. 12mo., 2s.

Association of Prayers. By Rev. C. Tondini. 3d.

Aunt Margaret's Little Neighbours; or, Chats about the Rosary. By Miss Plues. 12mo., 3s.

Ave Maria; or Catesby's Story. By Rev. F. Drew. 1s.

BAGSHAWE (Rev. J. B.), The Credentials of the Catholic Church. 12mo., 4s.

———— Threshold of the Catholic Church. A Course of Plain Instructions for those entering her Communion. 12mo., 4s.

BAGSHAWE (Rt. Rev. Dr.), The Life of Our Lord, commemorated in the Mass. 18mo., 1s.

BAKER (Fr., O.S.B.), The Rule of S. Benedict. From the old English edition of 1638. 12mo., 4s. 6d.

Baker (Fr. Augustine, O.S.B.), Life and Spirit of. 2s. 6d.

Baker's Boy; or, Life of General Drouot. 18mo., 6d.

BALDESCHI. Ceremonial according to the Roman Rite. Translated by Rev. J. D. Hilarius Dale. 12mo., 6s. 6d.

BALMES (J.L.), Letters to a Sceptic. 12mo., 3s. 6d.

BAMPFIELD (Rev. G.), Sir Ælfric and other Tales. 18mo., 6d.; cloth, 1s.; gilt, 1s. 6d.

BARGE (Rev. T.), Occasional Prayers for Festivals. 32mo., 4d. and 6d.; gilt, 1s.

Battista Varani (B.), *see* Veronica (S.). 12mo., 5s.

Battle of Connemara. By Kathleen O'Meara. 12mo., 3s

BAUGHAN (Rosa), Shakespeare's Tragedies and Comedies. Expurgated edition. 8vo., 6s. The Comedies only, 3s. 6d.

Before the Altar. 32mo., 6d.

Beleaguered Hearth (The). A Novel. 12mo., 2s. 6d.

BELL'S Modern Reader and Speaker. 12mo., 3s. 6d.

———— Theory of Elocution. 3s. 6d.

BELLECIUS (Fr.), Spiritual Exercises of S. Ignatius. 2s.

———— Solid Virtue. New edition. 12mo., 7s. 6d.

Bellevue and its Owners. A Tale for Boys. By C. Pilley. 2s. and 1s.

BELLINGHAM (Lady Constance) The Duties of Christian Parents. Conferences by Père Matignon. Translated with a Preface by the Rt. Rev. Mgr. Capel, D.D. 12mo., 5s.

Bells of the Sanctuary,—A Daughter of St. Dominick. By Grace Ramsay. 12mo., 1s. and 1s. 6d.; stronger bound, 2s.

BENEDICT (S.), The Rule of our most Holy Father S. Benedict, Patriarch of Monks. From the old English edition of 1638, Edited in Latin and English by one of the Benedictine Fathers of St. Michael's, near Hereford. 12mo., 4s. 6d.

Benedict's (S.) Manual. 18mo., 3s.

———— Life and Miracles. By S. Gregory the Great. From an old English version. By P. W. (Paris, 1608). Edited by Dom E. J. Luck, O.S.B. 4to. cloth, extra gilt, with 52 large Photographs, 31s. 6d.; or without the Photos., 10s. 6d. A small edition in fcap. 8vo. 2s.; or in stronger binding, 2s. 6d.

BENNI (Most Rev. C. B.), Tradition of the Syriac Church, concerning the Primacy and Prerogatives of S. Peter. 8vo., 7s. 6d.

Benvenuto Bambozzi (Fr., O.M.C.), of the Conventual Friars Minor, Life of, from the Italian (2nd edition) of Fr. Nicholas Treggiari, D.D. 12mo., 5s.

Berchmans (Bl. John), New Miracle at Rome, through the intercession of Bl. John Berchmans. 12mo., 2d.

Bernardine (St.) of Siena, Life of. With Portrait. 12mo., 5s.

Bertram Eldon, and how he found a Home. By M. A. Pennell, author of "Nellie Gordon" (6d), "Agnes Wilmott's History" (1s. 6d.). 12mo., 1s.

Bessy; or, the Fatal Consequence of Telling Lies. By Miss K. M. Weld. 12mo., 1s.; stronger bound, 1s. 6d.; gilt, 2s.

BESTE (J. R. Digby), Catholic Hours. 2s. 6d.; morocco, 6s.
——— **Holy Readings.** 2s. and 2s. 6d.; roan, 3s.; mor., 6s.

BESTE (Rev. Fr.), Victories of Rome. 8vo., 1s.

BETHELL (Rev. A.), Our Lady's Month; or, Short Lessons for the Month of May, and the Feasts of Our Lady. 18mo., 1s., stronger bound, 1s. 6d.

Bible. Douay Version. 12mo., 3s.; Persian, 8s.; morocco, 10s. 6d. 18mo., 2s. 6d.; Persian, 5s.; calf or morocco, 7s.; gilt, 8s. 6d. Large 18mo., cloth, 6s; Persian, 8s. and 9s.; morocco, 11s. 6d. With borders round pages, 8vo., cloth, 8s.; Persian calf, 21s.; morocco, 25s. 4to., cloth, 21s.; leather extra, 31s. 6d. Illustrated, morocco, £5 5s.; superior, £6 6s.

Bible History for the use of Schools. By Abp. Gilmour. 2s.

Bible History, Catholic Child's. 9d. O. T., 3d.; N. T., 3d.

Blessed Lord. *See* Ribadeneira, 1s.; Rutter (Rev. H.)., 5s.

Blessed Virgin, Devotions to. From Ancient Sources. *See* Regina Sæculorum. 12mo., 3s.; cheap edition, 1s.

——— **History of.** By Orsini. Translated by Provost Husenbeth. Illustrated, 12mo., 3s. 6d.

——— **Life of.** In verse. By C. E. Tame, Esq. 16mo., 2s.

——— **Life of.** Proposed as a model to Christian women. 12mo., 1s.

——— **in North America, Devotion to.** By Fr. Macleod. 5s.

——— **Veneration of.** By Mrs. Stuart Laidlaw. 16mo., 4d.

——— *See* Our Lady, p. 22; Leaflets, p. 16; May, p. 19.

Blindness, Cure of, through the Intercession of Our Lady and S. Ignatius. 12mo., 2d.

BLOSIUS, Spiritual Works of:—The Rule of the Spiritual Life; The Spiritual Mirror; String of Spiritual Jewels. Edited by Rev. Fr. John Bowden. 12mo., 3s. 6d.; red edges, 4s.

Blue Scapular, Origin of. 18mo., 1d.

Bluebeard; or, the Key of the Cellar. A Drama in 3 Acts. 6d.

BLYTH (Rev. Fr.), Devout Paraphrase on the Seven Penitential Psalms. To which is added "Necessity of Purifying the Soul," by S. Francis de Sales. 18mo., 1s. stronger bound, 1s. 6d.; red edges, 2s.

Bobbie and Birdie; or, Our Lady's Picture. A Story for the very little ones. By Frances J. M. Kershaw. 2s. 6d.

BONA (Cardinal), Easy Way to God. Translated by Father Collins. 12mo., 3s.

BONAVENTURE (S.), Life of St. Francis of Assisi. Translated from the Italian by the author of "The Life of St. Teresa." (Miss Lockhart). 3s. 6d.

Boniface (S.), Life of. By Mrs. Hope. 12mo., 6s.

BOUDON (Mgr.), Book of Perpetual Adoration. Translated by Rev. Dr. Redman. 12mo., 3s.; red edges, 3s. 6d.

BOUDREAUX (Rev. J., S.J.), God our Father. 12mo., 4s.

BOWDEN (Rev. Fr. John), Spiritual Works of Louis of Blois. 12mo., 3s. 6d.; red edges, 4s.

—————Oratorian Lives of the Saints. (Page 22).

BOWDEN (Mrs.), Lives of the First Religious of the Visitation of Holy Mary. 2 vols., 12mo., 10s.

BOWLES (Emily), Eagle and Dove. Translated from the French of Mdlle. Zénaïde Fleuriot. 12mo., 2s. 6d. and 5s.

BRADBURY (Rev. Fr.), Sophia and Eulalie. (The Catholic Pilgrim's Progress). 12mo., 1s. 6d.; better bound, 3s. 6d.

BRICKLEY'S Standard Table Book. 32mo., ½d.

BRIDGES (Miss), Sir Thomas Maxwell and his Ward. 1s.

Bridget (S.), Life of, and other Saints of Ireland. 12mo., 1s.

Brigit (S.) Life of, &c. By M. F. Cusack. 8vo., 6s.

Broken Chain. A Tale. 18mo., 6d.

BROWNE (E. G. K., Esq.), Monastic Legends. 8vo., 6d.

BROWNLOW (Rev. W. R. B.), Church of England and its Defenders. 8vo., 1st letter, 6d.; 2nd letter, 1s.

————— "Vitis Mystica"; or, the True Vine: a Treatise on the Passion of our Lord. 18mo., 4s.; red edges, 4s. 6d.

BUCKLEY (Rev. M.), Sermons, Lectures, &c. 12mo., 6s.

BULENS (F. Alexis, of the Monastery, West Gorton), Treatise on the Way of Sorrows, followed by a Practical Method of Blessing, Erecting, and Solemnly Performing the Stations of the Way of the Cross. 1s. 6d.; red edges, &c., 2s.

BURDER (Abbot), Confidence in the Mercy of God. By Mgr. Languet. 12mo., 3s.

————— The Consoler; or, Pious Readings addressed to the Sick and all who are afflicted. By Père Lambillotte. 12mo., 4s. 6d.; red ed., 5s.

————— Souls in Purgatory. 32mo., 3d.

————— Novena for the Souls in Purgatory. 32mo., 3d.

Burial of the Dead. For Children and Adults. (Latin and English.) Clear type edition, 32mo., 6d.; roan, 1s. 6d.

BURKE (Rev. T. N.), Lectures and Sermons. 3 vols., 36s.

BURKE (James), Travels of an Irish Gentleman in search of a Religion. 12mo., 3s. 6d.

BUTLER (Alban), Lives of the Saints. 2 vols., 8vo., 28s.; gilt, 34s.; 4 vols., 8vo., 32s.; gilt, 50s.; leather, 64s.

————— One Hundred Pious Reflections. 18mo., 1s. and 2s.

BUTLER (Dr.), Catechisms. 1st, ½d.; 2nd, 1d.; 3rd, 1½d.

CALIXTE—Life of the Ven. Anna Maria Taigi. Translated by A. V. Smith Sligo. 8vo., 2s. 6d. and 5s.

Callista. Dramatised by Dr. Husenbeth. 12mo., 2s.

CAMERON (Marie), The Golden Thought, and other Stories. 12mo. 1s. 6d.; gilt, 2s.; or cheap edition, separately, 6d. each.
  1. The Golden Thought, and The Brother's Grave.
  2. The Rod that bore Blossoms, and Patience and Impatience.

CARAHER (Hugh), A Month at Lourdes and its Neighbourhood. Two Illustrations. 12mo., 2s.
Catechisms—The Catechism of Christian Doctrine. *New edition*, No. 1, ½d., or 3s. a 100; No. 2, 1d. or 6s. a 100.
—————— *The Old edition of No. 2, is offered at Half Price.*
—————— made Easy. By Rev. H. Gibson. Vol. III., 4s.
—————— By Fr. Power. 3 vols., 10s. 6d. ; 2 vols., 7s. 6d.
—————— By Dr. Butler. 32mo., 1st, ½d.; 18mo., 2nd, 1d.; 3rd, 1½d.
—————— By Dr. Doyle. 18mo., 1½d.
—————— By Bishop Challoner. Grounds of Catholic Doctrine. 4d.
—————— Fleury's Historical. Complete Edition. 18mo., 1½d.
—————— Frassinetti's Dogmatic. 12mo., 3s.
—————— Keenan's Controversial. 2s.
—————— Lessons on Christian Doctrine. 18mo., 1½d.
—————— for First Confession. By Rev. R. G. Davis, 1d.
—————— of Confirmation. A very complete book. 18mo., 3d.
—————— of Perseverance. By Gaume. Vols. I. to III., 7s. 6d. each.
—————— of the Council. 12mo., 3d.
—————— of the History of England. By a Lady. 18mo., 1s.
—————— for the Use of Pupil Teachers. 6d.
Catherine Hamilton. By M. F. S. 12mo., 2s. 6d.; gilt, 3s.
Catherine Grown Older. By M. F. S. 12mo., 2s. 6d.; gilt, 3s.
Catholic Calendar for England. 6d.; Almanack, 1d.
Catholic Directory for Scotland. 1s.
Catholic Hours. By J. R. Digby Beste. 2s. 6d.
Catholic Piety. *See* Prayer Books, page 31.
Catholic Pilgrim's Progress—The Journey of Sophia and Eulalie to the Palace of True Happiness. 2s. 6d. Cheap edition, 1s. 6d.
Catholic Progress. A Monthly Magazine. Price 3d..
Catholic Sick and Benefit Club. By Rev. R. Richardson. 4d.
Ceremonies of Low Mass. 2s. 6d.
CHALLONER (Dr.), Grounds of Catholic Doctrine. 4d.
—————— Think Well on't. 18mo., 2d.; cloth, 6d.
Chats about the Rosary. By Miss Plues. 3s.
Chats about the Commandments. By the same. 3s.
CHAUGY (Mother Frances Magdalen de), Lives of the First Religious of the Visitation. 2 vols., 12mo., 10s.
Child's Book of the Passion of Our Lord. 32mo., 6d.
Child (The) of Mary's Manual. Second edition, 32mo. 1s.
Child's Picture Prayer Book. With 16 Illustrations. Cloth, tinted, 1s. and 1s. 6d. ; coloured, 1s. 6d., 2s., 2s. 6d., 3s., 3s. 6d. French morocco, 3s. 6d. and 4s. Calf, 5s. and 6s.
Children of Mary Card of Enrolment. Folio, 9d., post free on a roller, 1s.
Children of Mary in the World, Rules of. 32mo., 1d.
Christ bearing His Cross. A Steel Engraving from the Picture miraculously given to Blessed Colomba, with a short account of her Life. 8vo., 6d.; proofs, 1s.
Christian Doctrine, Lessons on. 18mo., 1½d.
Christian, Duties of a. By Ven. de la Salle. 12mo., 2s.
Christian Politeness. By the same Author. 18mo., 1s.
Christmas (The First) for our dear Little Ones. 4to., 6s.
CHRISTOPHER (S.) The Rose of Venice. A Tale. 5s.
Chronological Sketches. By H. Murray Lane. 2s. 6d.

Church Defence. By T. W. M. Marshall. 2s. 6d.
Church of England and its Defenders. 1s.
Cistercian Legends of the XIII. Century. 3s.
Cistercian Order: its Mission and Spirit. 3s. 6d.
Clare (Sister Mary Cherubini) of S. Francis, Life of. Preface by Lady Herbert. With Portrait. 12mo., 3s. 6d.
Clare's Sacrifice. By C. M. O'Hara. A Tale for First Communicants. 6d.
Cloister Legends; or, Convents and Monasteries in the Olden Time. 12mo., 4s.
COBBETT'S History of the Protestant Reformation. 4s. 6d.
COLLINS (Rev. Fr.), Legends of the XIII. Century. 12mo., 3s., or in 3 vols., 1s. 6d. each.
——— Cistercian Order: its Mission and Spirit. 3s. 6d.
——— Easy Way to God. Translated from the Latin of Cardinal Bona. 12mo., 3s.
——— Spiritual Conferences on the Mysteries of Faith and the Interior Life. 12mo., 5s.
COLOMBIERE (Father Claude de la), The Sufferings of Our Lord. Sermons preached in the Chapel Royal, St. James's, in the year 1677. Preface by Fr. Doyotte, S.J. 18mo., 1s.; stronger bound, 1s. 6d.; red edges, 2s.
Colombini (B. Giovanni), Life of. By Belcari. Translated from the editions of 1541 and 1832. With Portrait. 12mo., 3s. 6d.
Comedy of Convocation in the English Church. Edited by Archdeacon Chasuble. 8vo., 2s. 6d. *See* page 18.
COMERFORD (Rev. P.). Month of May for all the Faithful; or, a Practical Life of the Blessed Virgin. 32mo., 1s.
——— Pleadings of the Sacred Heart. 18mo., 1s.; gilt, 2s.; with the Handbook of the Confraternity, 1s. 6d. Hand-book, 3d.
Communion, Manual for. Meditations and Prayers. 2s. 6d.
Communion, Prayers for, for Children. Preparation, Mass before Communion, Thanksgiving. 32mo. 1d.
Compendious Statement of the Scripture Doctrine regarding the Nature and chief Attributes of the Kingdom of Christ. By C. F. A. 8vo., 1s.
COMPTON (Herbert), Semi-Tropical Trifles. 12mo., boards, 1s.; extra cloth, 2s. 6d.
Conferences. *See* Collins, Lacordaire, Mermillod, Matignon, Ravignan.
Confession and Holy Communion: Young Catholic's Guide. By Dr. Kenny. 32mo., 4d.; cloth, 6d.; red edges, 9d., French morocco, 1s. 6d.; calf or morocco, 2s. 6d.
Confidence in the Mercy of God. By Mgr. Languet. Translated by Abbot Burder. 12mo., 3s.
Confirmation, Instructions for the Sacrament of. A very complete book. 3d.
——— Order of Administering. 3d.
Consoler (The). By Abbot Burder. 12mo., 4s. 6d. and 5s.
Contemplations on the Most Holy Sacrament of the Altar; or Devout Meditations to serve as Preparations for, and Thanksgiving after, Communion. 1s. and 2s.; red edges, 2s. 6d.
Conversion of the Teutonic Race. By Mrs. Hope. 2 vols. 10s.

Convert Martyr; or, "Callista." By the Rev. Dr. Newman, Dramatised by the Rev. Dr. Husenbeth. 12mo., 2s.
Convocation, Comedy of. By A. J. P. Marshall. 8vo. 2s. 6d.
CORTES (John Donoso), Essays on Catholicism, Liberalism, and Socialism. 12mo., 5s.
Credentials of the Catholic Church. By Rev. J. B. Bagshawe, author of "The Threshold of the Catholic Church." 12mo., 4s.
Crucifixion, The. A large Picture for School walls, 1s.
CULPEPPER. Family Herbal, 3s. 6d.; coloured plates, 5s. 6d.
CUSACK (M. F.):—Sister Mary Francis Clare.
    Book of the Blessed Ones. 12mo., 4s. 6d.
    Case of Ireland Stated. 7s. 6d.
    Devotions for Public and Private Use at the Way of the Cross. Illustrated. 32mo., 1s.; red edges, 1s. 6d.
    Father Mathew, Life of. 12mo., 2s. 6d.
    Good Reading for Sundays and Festivals. 2s 6d.
    Handmaid of the Holy Ghost. 6d.
    History of the Irish Nation. Morocco gilt, 45s.
    Ireland, History of. 18mo., 2s.
    Jesus and Jerusalem. 4s. 6d.
    Jubilee of 1881. 3d.
    Knock; Apparitions, &c. 1s.
    Knock: Three Visits to. 2s.
    Life of the Blessed Virgin, 12s.
    Life and Times of the Liberator. 2 vols., 16s.
    Life of Most Rev. Dr. Dixon. 7s. 6d.
    Life of Mary O'Hagan. 6s.
    Lives of St. Columba and St. Brigit. 8vo., 6s.
    Meditations for Advent, 3s. 6d.
    Ned Rusheen; or, Who fired the first Shot. 5s.
    Nun's Advice to her Girls. 12mo., 2s. 6d.
    Patrick (S.), Life of. 8vo., 6s., gilt, 10s.; 32mo. 1s.
    Patrick's (S.) Manual. 18mo., 3s. 6d.
    Pilgrim's Way to Heaven. 12mo., 4s. 6d.
    Retreat for the Three Last Days of the Year. 1s.
    The Spouse of Christ. 12mo., vol. 2, 7s. 6d.
    Tim O'Halloran's Choice. 12mo., 3s. 6d.
    Tronson's Conferences. 12mo., 4s. 6d.
    Woman's Work in Modern Society. 4s. 6d.
DALE (Rev. J. D. H.), Sacristan's Manual. 12mo., 2s. 6d.
Dark Shadow (The). A Tale. 12mo., 3s.
Daughter (A) of S. Dominick: (Bells of the Sanctuary). By Grace Ramsay. 12mo., 1s. and 1s. 6d.; better bound, 2s.
DAVIS (Rev. R. G.) Garden of the Soul. *See* pages 30 and 32.
  ——— Catechism for First Confession. 1d
DECHAMPS (Mgr.), The Life of Pleasure. 12mo., 1s. 6d.
DEHAM (Rev. F.) Sacred Heart of Jesus, offered to the Piety of the Young engaged in Study. 32mo., 6d.
Diary of a Confessor of the Faith. 12mo., 1s.
Directorium Asceticum. By Scaramelli. 4 vols., 12mo., 24s.
DIXON (Fr., O.P.) Albertus Magnus: his Life and Scholastic Labours. From original documents. By Dr. Sighart. With Photographic Portrait. 8vo. 10s. 6d. Cheap edition, 5s.

DIXON (Fr., O.P.) Life of St. Vincent Ferrer. From the French of Rev. Fr. Pradel. With a Photograph. 12mo., 5s.
Dominican Saints, Sketches of the Lives of. By M. K. 3s. 6d.
Dominus Vobiscum; or, the Sailor Boy. By Rev. F. Drew. 1s.
DOWNING (Sister M. A.), Voices from the Heart. 2s. 6d.
DOYLE (Canon, O.S.B.), Life of Gregory Lopez, the Hermit. With a Photographic Portrait. 12mo., 3s. 6d.
———— Lectures for Boys. 2 Vols., 12mo., 10s. 6d.; or separately:—Vol. I., Containing—The Sundays of the Year, and Our Lady's Festivals, etc. 6s.—Vol. II., Containing—The Passion of Our Lord, and The Sacred Heart. 6s.; or may be had separately: The Sundays of the Year, 3s. 6d.; Our Lady's Festivals, etc., 2s. 6d.; The Passion of Our Lord, 3s.; The Sacred Heart, 3s.
———— Rule of our holy Father St. Benedict. Edited in Latin and English. 12mo., 4s. 6d.
DOYLE (Dr.), Catechism. 18mo., 1½d.
DOYOTTE (Fr., S.J.), Elevations to the Heart of Jesus. 3s.
———— Sufferings of Our Lord. By Fr. Columbiere. 1s.
DRAMAS. Bluebeard; or, the Key of the Cellar. A Drama in 3 Acts. 6d.
———— Convert Martyr; or, "Callista" dramatised. 2s.
———— The Duchess Transformed (Girls, 1 Act). Comedy. 6d.
———— The Enchanted Violin (Boys, 2 Acts). Comedy. 6d.
———— Ernscliff Hall (Girls, 3 Acts). Drama. 12mo., 6d.
———— Filiola (Girls, 4 Acts). Drama. 12mo., 6d.
———— Finola (Moore Melodies, 4 Acts). An Opera. 1s.
———— He would be a Lord (Boys, 3 Acts), a Comedy. 2s.
———— He would be a Soldier (Boys, 2 Acts) Comedy, 6d.
———— Reverse of the Medal (Girls, 4 Acts). Drama. 6d.
———— Shakespeare. Expurgated Edition. 8vo., 6s.
———— Shandy Maguire (Boys, 2 Acts), a Farce. 12mo., 2s.
———— St. Eustace (Boys, 5 Acts). Drama. 12mo., 1s.
———— St. William of York (Boys, 2 Acts). Drama. 12mo., 6d.
———— The Violet Sellers (3 Acts). Drama for Children. 6d.
———— Whittington and his Cat. Drama for Children. 9 Scenes. By Henrietta Fairfield. 6d.
———— *See* R. Washbourne's **American List.**
DRANE (Augusta Theodosia); Inner Life of Pere Lacordaire. Translated from the French of Père Chocarne. 6s. 6d.
DREW (Rev. F.), Little Books of St. Nicholas. Tales for Children, 1s. each. 1. Oremus; 2. Dominus Vobiscum; 3. Pater Noster. 4. Per Jesum Christi; 5. Veni Creator; 6. Credo; 7. Ave Maria; 8. Ora pro nobis: 9. Corpus Christi; 10. Dei Genitrix; 11. Miserere; 12. Deo Gratias; 13. Angelus Domini.
Duchess (The), Transformed. By W. H. A. 12mo., 6d.
DUMESNIL (Abbe), The Reign of Terror. 12mo., 2s. 6d.
DUPANLOUP (Mgr.), Contemporary Prophecies. 8vo., 1s.
———— The Child. Translated by Kate Anderson. 12mo., 3s. 6d.
Dusseldorf Gallery. 357 Engravings. Large 4to. Half-morocco gilt, £5 5s. nett.
———— 134 Engravings. Large 8vo. Half-morocco, gilt, 42s.
Dusseldorf Society for the Distribution of Good Religious Pictures. Subscription, 8s. 6d. a year.

R. Washbourne, 18 Paternoster Row, London.

Duties of Christian Parents. Conferences by R. Père Matignon Translated from the French by Lady Constance Bellingham. 5s.

Eagle and Dove. Translated by Emily Bowles. 5s. and 2s. 6d.

Easy Way to God. By Cardinal Bona. 12mo., 3s.

Electricity and Magnetism; an Enquiry into the Nature and Results of. By Amyclanus. Illustrated. 12mo., 6s. 6d.

Enchanted Violin, The. A Comedy in 2 Acts (Boys), 6d.

England, History of. By L. Evans. St. 3, 2d.; 4, 2d.; 5, 3d.

—————— A Catechism. For the use of Pupil Teachers, 6d. By a Teacher, 1s. By a Lady, 6d.

—————— By W. F. Mylius. 12mo., 3s. 6d.

Epistles and Gospels. Good clear type edition, 32mo., 6d.; roan, 1s. 6d.; larger edition, 18mo., French morocco, 2s.

——————, Explanation of. By Rev. F. Goffine. Illustrated, 8vo., 9s.

Ernscliff Hall. A Drama in Three Acts, for Girls. 12mo., 6d.

Eucharistic Year. 18mo., 4s.

Eucharist (The) and the Christian Life. 3s. 6d.

Europe, Modern, History of. 12mo., 5s.; cloth gilt, 6s.

Eustace (St.). A Drama in 5 Acts for Boys. 12mo., 1s.

EVANS (L.), History of England, adapted for Junior Classes in Schools. Part 1 (Standard 3) 2d. Part 2 (Standard 4) 2d. Part 3 (Standard 5) 3d.

—————— Chronological Outline of English History. 1½d.

—————— Milton's l'Allegro (Oxford Local Exam.). 2d.

—————— Parsing and Analysis Table. 1d.

FAIRFIELD (Henrietta), Whittington and his Cat. A Drama, in 9 Scenes, for Children. 12mo., 6d.

Fairy Ching (The); or, the Chinese Fairies' Visit to England. By Henrica Frederic. 12mo., 1s.; gilt edges, 1s. 6d.

Fairy Tales for Little Children. By Madeleine Howley Meehan, 12mo., 6d.; stronger bound, 1s. and 1s. 6d.; gilt, 2s.

Faith, Hope, and Charity; a Tale of the Reign of Terror. 2s. 6d.

Faith of our Fathers. By Most Rev. Archbishop Gibbons. 4s.

Fall, Redemption, and Exaltation of Man. 12mo., 1s.

Familiar Instructions on Christian Truths. By a Priest. 10d.

Fardel (Sister Claude Simplicienne), Life of. With the Lives of others of the First Religious of the Visitation of Holy Mary. 12mo., 6s.

FARRELL(Rev.J.), Lectures of a certain Professor. 7s. 6d

FAVRE (Abbe), Heaven Opened by the Practice of Frequent Confession and Communion. 12mo., 2s.; stronger bound, 3s. 6d.

Favre (Mother Marie Jacqueline), Life of. With the Lives of others of the First Religious of the Visitation of Holy Mary. 12mo., 6s.

Feasts (The) of Camelot, with the Tales that were told there. By Mrs. E. L. Hervey. 3s. 6d., or in 2 vols. 1s. 6d. each.

FERRIS (Rev. D.), Life of Sister Mary Frances of the Five Wounds. From the Italian. 12mo., 2s. 6d.

—————— Manual of Christian Doctrine; or Catholic Belief and Practice familiarly explained by Question and Answer. 6d.

FEVAL (Paul), The Jesuits. Translated from the French. 3s. 6d.
Filiola. A Drama in Four Acts, for Girls. 12mo., 6d.
First Apostles of Europe. By Mrs. Hope. 2 vols. 10s.
First Communion and Confirmation Memorial. Beautifully printed in gold and colours, folio, 1s. each, or 9s. a dozen, nett.
First Communion ; or, Clare's Sacrifice. By O'Hara. 6d.
First Religious of the Visitation of Holy Mary, Lives of. Translated, with a Preface, by Mrs. Bowden. 2 vols., 10s.
FLANAGAN (Rev. T.), History of the Catholic Church in England. 2 vols., 8vo., 18s.
FLEET (Charles), Tales and Sketches. 8vo., 3s. 6d.
FLEURIOT (Mlle. Zenaide), Eagle and Dove. Translated by Emily Bowles. 12mo., 2s. 6d. and 5s.
FLEURY'S Historical Catechism. Large edition, 12mo., 1½d.
Flowers of Christian Wisdom. By Henry Lucien. 2s.
Fluffy. A Tale for Boys. By M. F. S. 12mo., 3s. 6d.
Following of Christ. *See* A'Kempis.
For Better, not for Worse. By Rev. Langton George Vere.
Foreign Books. *See* R. W.'s Catalogue of Foreign Books.
FORMBY (Rev. H.), Little Book of the Martyrs. 1s. 6d.
Francis of Assisi (S.) Life of. By S. Bonaventure. Translated by Miss Lockhart. 12mo., 3s. 6d.
—— **Works of.** [*In the press.*
FRANCIS OF SALES (S.), Consoling Thoughts. 18mo., 2s.
—— **The Mystical Flora.** 4to., 6s.
—— **Necessity of Purifying the Soul.** By Fr. Blyth. 1s.
Franciscan Annals and Monthly Bulletin of the Third Order of St. Francis 5s. year, post free.
FRANCO (Rev. S.) Devotions to the Sacred Heart. 4s.
FRASSINETTI—Dogmatic Catechism. 12mo., 3s.
FREDERIC (Henrica), The Fairy Ching ; or, the Chinese Fairies' Visit to England. 12mo., 1s. ; gilt edges, 1s. 6d.
—— **Story of a Paper Knife.** 12mo., 1s.; gilt edges, 1s. 6d.
From Sunrise to Sunset. By L. B. 12mo., 3s. 6d.
GALLERY (Rev. D.), Handbook of Essentials in History and Literature, Ancient and Modern. 18mo., 1s. 6d.
Garden of the Soul. *See* page 32.
Garden (Little) of the Soul. *See* page 30.
Gathered Gems from Spanish Authors. By M. Monteiro. 3s.
GAUME (Abbe), Catechism of Perseverance. 4 vols., 12mo. Vols. 1, 2 and 3, each 7s. 6d.
GAYRARD (Mme. Paul) Harmony of the Passion. Compiled from the four Gospels, in Latin and French. 18mo., 1s. 6d.
German (S.), Life of. 12mo., 3s. 6d.
GIBBONS (Most Rev. Archbishop), The Faith of our Fathers; Being a Plain Exposition and Vindication of the Church Founded by our Lord Jesus Christ. 12mo., 4s. Paper covers, 2s.
GIBSON (Rev. H.), Catechism made Easy. Vol. III., 4s.
GILMOUR (Rev. R.), Bible History for the Use of Schools. Illustrated. 12mo., 2s.
God our Father. By a Father of the Society of Jesus. 12mo., 4s.

R. Washbourne, 18 Paternoster Row, London.

GOFFINE (Rev. F.), Explanation of the Epistles and Gospels. Illustrated. 8vo., 9s.
Golden Thought of Queen Beryl, and other Stories. By Marie Cameron. 1s. 6d.; or cheap edition, in 2 vols. 6d. each.
Grace before and after Meals. 32mo., 1d.; cloth, 2d.
GRACE RAMSAY. *See* O'Meara (Kathleen).
GRACIAN (Fr. Baltasar), Sanctuary Meditations for Priests and Frequent Communicants. Translated from the Spanish by Mariana Monteiro. 12mo., 4s.
Grains of Gold. 16mo., Series 1 and 2, cloth, 2s. 6d.
GRANT (Bishop), Pastoral on St. Joseph. 32mo., 4d. & 6d.
GRAY (Mrs. C. D.), Simple Bible Stories. 1s. and 2s. 6d.
GREEN (Rev. Dr.), Indulgences, Sacramental Absolutions, and the Tax Tables with New Preface and Index. 2s. 6d.
Gregory Lopez, the Hermit, Life of. By Canon Doyle, O.S.B. With a Photographic Portrait. 12mo., 3s. 6d.
Grounds of the Catholic Doctrine. By Bishop Challoner. Large type edition, 18mo., 4d.
GUERANGER (Dom), Defence of the Roman Church against F. Gratry. Translated by Canon Woods. 8vo., 1s.
HALL (E.), Munster Firesides. 12mo., 3s. 6d.
Harmony of Anglicanism. By T. W. Marshall. 8vo., 2s. 6d.
HAY (Bishop), Sincere Christian. 18mo., 2s. 6d.
——— Devout Christian. 18mo., 2s. 6d.
He would be a Lord. A Comedy in 3 Acts. (Boys.) 12mo., 2s.
Heart of Jesus at Nazareth. Meditations. 3s. 6d.
Heaven Opened by the Practice of frequent Confession and Holy Communion. By the Abbé Favre. 12mo., 2s.; stronger bound, 3s. 6d.
HEDLEY (Bishop), Five Sermons—Light of the Holy Spirit in the World. 12mo., 1s.; cloth, 1s. 6d. Revelation, Mystery, Dogma and Creeds, Infallibility : separately, 3d. each.
HEFELE (Rev. Dr. Von), Cardinal Ximenes. 10s. 6d.
HEIGHAM (John), A Devout Exposition of the Holy Mass. Edited by Austin John Rowley, Priest. 12mo., 4s.
HENRY (Lucien), Flowers of Christian Wisdom. 18mo., 1s. and 2s.; red edges, 2s. 6d.
Herbal, Brook's Family. 12mo., 3s. 6d.; coloured, 5s. 6d.
HERBERT (Lady), True Wayside Tales. 12mo., 3s.; or in 5 vols., cheap edition, 6d. each.
1. The Brigand Chief, and other Tales. 2. Now is the Accepted Time, and other Tales. 3. What a Child can do, and other Tales. 4. Sowing Wild Oats, and other Tales. 5. The Two Hosts, and other Tales.
HERBERT (Wallace), My Dream and Verses Miscellaneous. With a frontispiece. 12mo., 5s.
——— The Angels and the Sacraments. 1s.; gilt, 1s. 6d.
HERVEY (E. L.), Stories from many Lands. 12mo., 3s. 6d.
——— Our Legends and Lives. 12mo., 6s.
——— Rest, on the Cross. 12mo., 3s. 6d.
——— The Feasts of Camelot, with the Tales that were told there. 12mo., 3s. 6d.; or, separately: Christmas, 1s. 6d.; Whitsuntide, 1s. 6d.

HILL (Rev. Fr.), Elements of Philosophy, comprising Logic and General Principles of Metaphysics. 8vo., 6s.
—————— Ethics, or Moral Philosophy. 12mo., 6s.
HOFFMAN (Franz), Industry and Laziness. 12mo., 3s.
Holy Church the Centre of Unity. By T. H. Shaw. 1s.
Holy Communion. By Hubert Lebon. 12mo., 4s.
Holy Family Card of Membership. A beautiful design. Folio. Price 6d., or 8d., on a roller, post free; 4s. 6d. a dozen, or post free 5s.
Holy Family, Confraternity of. By Card. Manning. 3d.
Holy Places: their Sanctity and Authenticity. 2s. 6d.
Holy Readings. By J. R. Digby Beste, Esq. 3s.
Holy Week Book. New edition, with Ordinary of the Mass, Vespers and Complin, Blessing of the Holy Oils, &c. 1s.
HOPE (Mrs.), The First Apostles of Europe; or, "The Conversion of the Teutonic Race." 2 vols., 12mo., 10s.
Horace. Literally translated by Smart, 2s. Latin and English, 3s. 6d.
HUGUET (Pere), The Power of S. Joseph. 1s. 6d.
—————— On Charity in Conversation. 12mo., 2s. 6d.
HUMPHREY (Rev. W., S.J.), The Panegyrics of Fr. Segneri, S.J. Translated from the orignal Italian. With a Preface by the Rev. W. Humphrey, S.J. 12mo., 6s.
HUSENBETH (Rev. Dr.), Convert Martyr. 12mo., 2s.
—————— History of the Blessed Virgin. Translated from Orsini. Illustrated. 12mo., 3s. 6d.
—————— Life and Sufferings of Our Lord. By Rev. H. Rutter. Illustrated. 12mo., 5s.
—————— Life of Mgr. Weedall. 8vo., 5s.
—————— Little Office of the Immaculate Conception. In Latin and English. 32mo., 4d.; cloth, 6d.; roan, 1s.; calf or morocco, 2s. 6d.
—————— Our Blessed Lady of Lourdes. 18mo., 6d.; with the Novena, 1s.; cloth, 1s. 6d. Novena, separately, 4d.; Litany, 1d.
—————— Roman Question. 8vo., 6d.
HUTTON (Arthur W.), Vesper Psalms and Magnifica for all Sundays and Feast days throughout the year, set to harmonised Chants for alternate singing, with the Gregorian Tones. 3s. Nett, 10 copies for 25s.
Hymn Book (The Catholic). Edited by Rev. G. Langton Vere. 32mo., 1d.; larger edition, 204 pages, 2d.; cloth, 4d.
Iceland (Three Sketches of Life in). By Carl Andersen. 12mo., 2s., cheap edition, 1s. 6d.
IGNATIUS (S.), Spiritual Exercises. By Fr. Bellecio, S.J. Translated by Dr. Hutch. 18mo., 2s.
Ignatius (S.), Cure of Blindness through the Intercession of Our Lady and S. Ignatius. 12mo., 2d.
Imitation of Christ. *See* A'Kempis.
Immaculate Conception, Definition of. 12mo., 6d.
—————— Little Office of, Latin and English. 32mo., 2d.
—————— Little Office of. By Rev. Dr. Husenbeth. 4d.; cloth, 6d.; roan, 1s.; calf or morocco, 2s. 6d.
Industry and Laziness. By Franz Hoffman. From the German, by James King. 12mo., 3s.

Indulgences. *See* Green, 2s. 6d.; Matthews, 1d.; Maurel, 2s.
Infallibility of the Pope. By the Author of "The Oxford Undergraduate of Twenty Years Ago." 8vo., 1s.
In Suffragiis Sanctorum. Commem. S. Joseph ; Commem. S. Georgii. Set of 5 for 4d.
IOTA. The Adventures of a Protestant in Search of a Religion : being the Story of a late Student of Divinity at Bunyan Baptist College; a Nonconformist Minister, who seceded to the Catholic Church. 12mo., 3s. 6d. ; cheap edition, 2s.
Ireland (History of). By Miss Cusack. 2s. By T. Young. 2s. 6d.
Irish Board Reading Books.
Irish First Book. 18mo., 2d. 2nd Book, 4d. 3rd Book, 6d.
Irish Monthly. 8vo. Vol. 1882, cloth, 7s. 6d.
Irish Saints in Great Britain. By Bishop Moran. 5s.
Italian Revolution (The History of). The History of the Barricades. By Keyes O'Clery, M.P. 8vo., 7s. 6d. and 3s. 6d.
Jack's Boy. By M. F. S., author of "Fluffy." 12mo, 3s. 6d.
JACOB (W. J.), Personal Recollections of Rome. 6d.
Jesuits (The). By Paul Feval. Translated from the French, 3s. 6d.
Jesuits (The), and other Essays. By Willis Nevin. 2s. 6d.
Jesus and Jerusalem ; or, the Way Home. 4s. 6d.
Jew of Verona. 12mo., 4s. 6d.
John of God (S.), Life of. With Photographic Portrait. 12mo., 5s.
Joseph (S.), Life of. By Miss Cusack. 32mo., 6d.; cloth, 1s.
———— Manual of a Happy Eternity. 18mo., 2s. 6d.
———— Novena of Meditations. 18mo., 1s.
———— Novena to, with a Pastoral by the late Bishop Grant. 32mo., 4d.; cloth, 6d.
———— Power of. By Fr. Huguet. 1s. 6d.
———— A Word to, for every day in March. 4d., cloth, 1s.
———— *See* Leaflets.
Journey of Sophia and Eulalie to the Palace of True Happiness. (The Catholic Pilgrim's Progress.) From the French by Rev. Fr. Bradbury. 12mo., 1s. 6d.; better bound, 3s. 6d.
Kainer ; or, the Usurer's Doom. By James King. 1s.
KAVANAGH (Rev. P. F.), Insurrection of '98. 2s.
KEENAN (Rev. S.), Controversial Catechism. 12mo., 2s.
Keighley Hall, and other Tales. By E. King. Gilt, 2s.
KENNY (Dr.), Young Catholic's Guide to Confession and Holy Communion. 32mo., 4d.; cloth, 6d.; red edges, 9d. roan, 1s. 6d.; calf or morocco, 2s. 6d.
———— New Year's Gift to our Heavenly Father. 4d.
KERSHAW (Frances J. M.), Bobbie and Birdie ; or, Our Lady's Picture. A Story for the very little ones. 2s. 6d.
Key of Heaven. *See* Prayers, page 31.
Killed at Sedan. A Novel. By Samuel Richardson, A.B., B.L. 7s. 6d.
KINANE (Rev. T. H.), Angel of the Altar ; or, the Love of the Most Adorable and Most Sacred Heart of Jesus. 2s. 6d.
———— Dove of the Tabernacle. 1s. 6d.
———— Lamb of God. 18mo., 2s.
———— Mary Immaculate. 2s.

R. Washbourne, 18 Paternoster Row, London.

KING (Elizabeth), Keighley Hall, and other Tales.
18mo., 6d.; cloth, 1s.; stronger bound, 1s. 6d.; gilt, 2s.
—————— The Silver Teapot. 18mo., 4d.
KING (James). Industry and Laziness. 12mo., 3s.
—————— Kainer; or, the Usurer's Doom. 1s.
Kishoge Papers. Tales of Devilry and Drollery. 12mo., 1s. 6d.
Knock; Apparitions and Miracles. 1s.
—————— Three Visits to. 2s.
LA BOUILLERIE (Mgr. de), The Eucharist and the Christian Life. Translated by L. C. 12mo., 3s. 6d.
Lacordaire. The Inner Life of Pere Lacordaire. From the French of Père Chocarne. By Augusta Theodosia Drane. 6s. 6d.
Lady Mildred's Housekeeper, A Few Words from. 2d.
LAIDLAW (Mrs. Stuart), Letters to my God-child. No. 4. On the Veneration of the Blessed Virgin. 16mo., 4d.
LAING (Rev. Dr.), Blessed Virgin's Root traced in the Tribe of Ephraim. 8vo., 10s. 6d.
—————— Knight of the Faith. 12mo., 5s.
    Absurd Protestant Opinions concerning *Intention*. 4d.
    Catholic, not Roman Catholic. 4d.
    Challenge to the Churches. 1d.
    Descriptive Guide to the Mass. 1s. and 1s. 6d.
    Favourite Fallacy about Private Judgment and Inquiry. 1d.
    Protestantism against the Natural Moral Law. 1d.
    Shortcomings of the English Catholic Press. 6d.
    What is Christianity? 6d.
    Whence does the Monarch get his right to Rule? 2s. 6d.
LAMBILOTTE (Pere), The Consoler. Translated by Abbot Burder. 12mo., 4s. 6d.; red edges, 5s.
LANE-CLARKE (T. M. L.) The Violet Sellers. A Drama for Children in 3 Acts. 6d.
LANGUET (Mgr.), Confidence in the Mercy of God. Translated by Abbot Burder. 12mo., 3s.
Last of the Catholic O'Malleys. By M. Taunton. 18mo., 1s. 6d.; stronger bound, 2s.
Leaflets. 1d. each, or 1s. 2d. per 100 post free, (a single dozen 5d.).
    Act of Reparation to the Sacred Heart.
    Archconfraternity of the Agonising Heart of Jesus and the Compassionate Heart of Mary: Prayers for the Dying.
    Archconfraternity of Our Lady of Angels.
    Ditto, Rules.
    Christmas Offering (or 7s. 6d. per 1000).
    Devotions to S. Joseph.
    Divine Praises.
    Gospel according to S. John, *in Latin*. 1s. 6d. per 100.
    Indulgenced Prayers for Souls in Purgatory.
    Indulgences attached to Medals, Crosses, Statues, &c.
    Intentions for Indulgences.
    Litany of Our Lady of Angels.
    Litany of S. Joseph, and Devotions.
    Litany of Resignation.
    Miraculous Prayer—August Queen of Angels.

R. Washbourne, 18 Paternoster Row, London.

Picture of Crucifixion, "I thirst" (or 5s. per 1000).
Prayer for One's Confessor.
Prayers for the Holy Souls in Purgatory. By St. Ligouri.
Reasonings of Plain Common-Sense upon the Church (2s. 10d. per 100, post free).
Union of our Life with the Passion of our Lord.
Visit to the Blessed Sacrament. 2s. 6d. per 100.

Leaflets. 1d. each, or 6s. per 100, (a single dozen 10d., post free).
Act of Consecration to the Sacred Heart.
Concise Portrait of the Blessed Virgin.
Explanation of the Medal or Cross of St. Benedict.
Indulgenced Prayers for the Rosary of the Holy Souls.
Indulgenced Prayer before a Crucifix.
Indulgences, Short Explanation of. By Rev. A. J. Matthews.
Litany of Our Lady of Lourdes.
Litany of the Seven Dolours.
Office of the Sacred Heart.
Prayer to S. Philip Neri.
Prayers before and after Holy Communion.
Reasons showing there must be a true Church.
Why Roman Catholics disbelieve in Anglican Orders.

Lectures for Boys. By Canon Doyle. 2 vols., 12mo., 10s. 6d.
Legends of the Blessed Virgin. 12mo., 3s. 6d.
Legends of the Commandments of God. 12mo., 3s. 6d.
Legends of the Saints. By M. F. S. 16mo., 3s. 6d.
Legends of the Thirteenth Century. By Rev. H. Collins. 3s., or in 3 vols., 1s. 6d. each.
LEGUAY (Abbe), The Postulant and Novice. 2s. 6d.
Lenten Thoughts. By Bishop Amherst. 18mo., 1s.; stronger bound, 2s., with red edges, 2s. 6d.
Letters to my God-child. By Mrs. Stuart Laidlaw. 16mo., 4d.
Life of Pleasure. By Mgr. Dechamps. 12mo., 1s. 6d.
Light of the Holy Spirit in the World. Five Sermons by Bishop Hedley. 12mo., 1s.'; cloth, 1s. 6d.
LIGUORI (S.), Fourteen Stations of the Cross. 18mo., 1d.
——— Selva; or, a Collection of Matter for Sermons. 12mo., 5s.
——— Way of Salvation. 32mo., 1s.
Lily of S. Joseph: A little Manual of Prayers and Hymns for Mass. 64mo., 2d.; cloth, 3d., 4d., and 6d.; gilt, 8d.; roan, 1s.; French morocco, 1s. 6d.; calf or morocco, 2s.; gilt, 2s. 6d.
LINGARD (Dr.), Gunpowder Plot. 8vo., 2s. 6d.
——— Anglo-Saxon Church. 2 vols., 12mo., 10s.
Little Mildred, or Oremus. By F. B. Birkerstaffe Drew. 1s.
Little Prayer Book. 32mo., 3d.
Lives of the First Religious of the Visitation of Holy Mary. By Mother Frances Magdalen de Chaugy. 2 vols., 10s.
Lost Children of Mount St. Bernard. 18mo., 6d.
Lourdes, Our Blessed Lady of. By Rev. Dr. Husenbeth. 18mo., 6d.; with the Novena, 1s.; cloth, 1s. 6d.
——— Novena of, for the use of the Sick. 4d.
——— Litany of. 1d. each.
——— Month at Lourdes. By H. Caraher. 2s.

LUCK (Dom Edmund J.), Short Meditations for every Day in the Year. From the Italian. 12mo. Edition for the Regular Clergy, 2 vols., 9s.; edn. for the Secular Clergy and others, 2 vols., 9s.
——— **S. Gregory's Life and Miracles of St. Benedict.** 31s. 6d.; cheap edition, 10s. 6d.; small edition, 2s. and 2s. 6d.
LYONS (C. B.), Catholic Choir Manual. 12mo., 1s.
——— Catholic Psalmist. 12mo., 4s.
MACDANIEL (M. A.), Month of May. 18mo., 2s.
——— Novena to S. Joseph. 32mo., 4d.; cloth, 6d.
——— Road to Heaven. A Game. 1s. and 2s.
MACEVILLY (Bishop), Exposition of the Epistles of St. Paul and of the Catholic Epistles. 2 vols., large 8vo. 18s.
——— Exposition of the Gospels. Large 8vo., SS. Matthew, and Mark, 12s. 6d., S. Luke, 6s.
MANAHAN (Dr.), Triumph of the Catholic Church in the Early Ages. 12mo., 5s.
Manning (Card.) A Biographical Sketch; with some account of Catholicism since 1829. Cloth 1s. 6d., paper 6d.
MANNING (Cardinal): Confraternity of the Holy Family. 3d.
MANNOCK (Patrick), Origin and Progress of Religious Orders, and Happiness of a Religious State. Translated from the Latin of Rev. F. Platus. 12mo., 2s. 6d.
Manual of Catholic Devotions. *See* Prayers, page 31.
Manual of Devotions in honour of Our Lady of Sorrows. Compiled by the Clergy at St. Patrick's, Soho. 18mo., 1s. & 1s. 6d.
Manuel de Conversation. 12mo., 6d.
Map of London, with Alphabetical List of the Catholic Churches, and view of the proposed Westminster Cathedral. 6d.
Margarethe Verflassen. Translated from the German by Mrs. Smith Sligo. 12mo., 1s. 6d. and 3s.; gilt, 3s. 6d.
MARQUIGNY (Pere), Life and Letters of Countess Adelstan. 12mo., 1s. and 2s. 6d.
MARSHALL (A. J. P., Esq.), Comedy of Convocation in the English Church. 8vo., 2s. 6d. *
——— English Religion. 8vo. 6d.,
——— Infallibility of the Pope. 8vo., 1s. *
——— Oxford Undergraduate of Twenty Years Ago. 8vo., 2s. 6d.; cloth, 3s. 6d. *
——— Reply to the Bishop of Ripon's Attack on the Catholic Church. 8vo., 6d. *
——— Two Bibles. A Contrast. 16mo., 1s. 6d.
MARSHALL (T. W. M., Esq.), Harmony of Anglicanism—Church Defence. 8vo., 2s. 6d. *
The 5 (*) in one Volume, 8vo., Marshallianae, 6s.
MARSHALL (Rev. W.), The Doctrine of Purgatory. 1s.
——— A Squib for the Saints. 3d.
MARTIN (Rev. E. R.), Rule of the Pope-King. 8vo., 6d.
Mary Immaculate, Devotion to. By Rev. T. H. Kinane. 2s.
Mary, New Month of. By Bishop Kenrick. 32mo., 1s. 6d.
Mary Venerated in all Ages—Regina Sæculorum. 12mo., 3s., cheap edition, 1s.

Mass, Descriptive Guide to. By Rev. Dr. Laing. 12mo., 1s., or stronger bound, 1s. 6d.
Mass, Devotions for. Very *Large type*, 18mo., 2d.
Mass (The). By Müller, 10s. 6d. Tronson, 4d. O'Brien, 9s.
Mass, A Devout Exposition of. By Rev. A. J. Rowley. 4s.
MATIGNON (Pere) The Duties of Christian Parents. 5s.
MAUREL (Rev. F. A.), Indulgences. 18mo., 2s.
Maxims of the Kingdom of Heaven. 12mo., 5s.; red edges, 5s. 6d.; calf or mor., 10s. 6d. Old Testament, 1s. 6d.; Gospels, 1s.
May, Festivals. By Canon Doyle. 12mo., 2s. 6d.
May, Month of. By Rev. P. Comerford. 32mo., 1s.
May, Month of. By M. A. Macdaniel. 18mo., 2s.
May, Month of, principally for the use of Religious. 18mo., 1s. 6d.
May Readings for the Feasts of Our Lady. By Rev. A. P. Bethell. 18mo., 1s., stronger bound, 1s. 6d.
May Templeton; a Tale of Faith and Love. 12mo., 5s.
M'CORRY (Rev. Dr.), Monks of Iona. 8vo., 3s. 6d.
——— **Rome, Past, Present, Future.** 8vo., 6d.
MCNEILL (Rev. Mark), The Faith. 12mo., 5s.
Meditations for every Day in the Year. By Fr. Luck. 9s.
MEEHAN (M. H.), Fairy Tales for Little Children. 12mo., 6d. and 1s.; stronger bound, 1s. 6d.; gilt, 2s.
MERMILLOD (Mgr.), The Supernatural Life. Translated from the French, with a Preface by Lady Herbert. 12mo., 5s.
MEYRICK (Rev. T.), Life of St. Wenefred. 12mo., 2s.
——— **Lives of the Early Popes.** St. Peter to St. Sylvester. 4s. 6d. From the time of Constantine to Charlemagne. 5s. 6d.
——— **St. Eustace. A Drama (5 Acts) for Boys.** 12mo., 1s.
M. F. S., Catherine Hamilton. 12mo., 2s. 6d.; gilt, 3s.
——— **Catherine Grown Older.** 12mo., 2s. 6d.; gilt, 3s.
——— **Fluffy. A Tale for Boys.** 12mo., 3s. 6d.
——— **Jack's Boy.** 12mo., 3s. 6d.
——— **Legends of the Saints.** 16mo., 3s. 6d. [gilt, 1s. 6d.
——— **My Golden Days.** 12mo., 2s. 6d.; or in 3 vols., 1s. ea.,
——— **Out in the Cold World.** 12mo., 3s. 6d.
——— **Stories of Holy Lives.** 12mo., 3s. 6d.
——— **Stories of Martyr Priests.** 12mo., 3s. 6d.
——— **Stories of the Saints.** Five Series, 12mo., 3s. 6d. each.
————— First and Second Series; gilt, 4s. 6d. each.
——— **Story of the Life of S. Paul.** 2s. 6d. and 1s. 6d.
——— **The Three Wishes. A Tale.** 12mo., 2s. 6d. and 1s. 6d.
——— **Tom's Crucifix,** and other Tales. 12mo., 3s. 6d., or in 5 vols., 1s. each, gilt, 1s. 6d.
MILNER (Bishop), Devotion to the Sacred Heart of Jesus. 32mo., 3d.; cloth, 6d. [2d.
Miracle at Rome, through the intercession of B. John Berchmans.
Miraculous Cure of Blindness, through the intercession of Our Lady and S. Ignatius. 12mo., 2d.
Misgivings—Convictions. 12mo., 6d.
Missal. *See* Prayers, page 31. [12mo., 8s.
MOEHLER (Dr.), Symbolism. Translated by Professor Robertson.

Monastic Legends. By E. G. K. Browne. 8vo., 6d.
MOHR (Rev. J., S.J.), Cantiones Sacrae. Hymns and Chants. Music and Words. 8vo., 5s.
——— **Manual of Sacred Chant.** Music and Words. 2s. 6d.
MOLLOY (Rev. Dr.), Passion Play at Ober-Ammergan. 2s.; with Photograph, 3s.
Monk of the Monastery of Yuste. By Mariana Monteiro. 2s. 6d.
Monks of Iona and the Duke of Argyll. By M'Corry. 3s. 6d.
MONSABRE (Rev. Pere), Gold and Alloy. 12mo., 2s. 6d.
MONTAGU (Lord Robert), Civilization and the See of Rome. 8vo., 6d.
Montalembert (Count de). By George White. 12mo., 6d.
MONTEIRO (Mariana), Allah Akbar—God is Great. An Arab Legend of the Siege and Conquest of Granada. 12mo., 3s. 6d.
——— **Monk of the Monastery of Yuste**; or, The Last Days of the Emperor Charles V. An Historical Legend of the 16th Century. 12mo., 2s. 6d.
——— **Gathered Gems from Spanish Authors.** 12mo., 3s.
——— **Sanctuary Meditations.** By Fr. Gracian. 4s.
MOORE'S Irish Melodies. With Symphonies and Accompaniments by John Stevenson and Sir Henry Bishop. 4to., 3s. 6d.
Mora (Ven. Elizabeth Canori), Life of. Translated from the Italian, with Preface by Lady Herbert. With Photograph. 3s. 6d.
MORAN (Rt. Rev. Dr.) Irish Saints in Great Britain. 5s.
MULHOLLAND (Rosa), Prince and Saviour: The Story of Jesus. 12mo., 1s. 6d.; 32mo., 6d. and 2d.
MULLER (Rev. M.), The Holy Mass. 12mo., 10s. 6d.
Multiplication Table, on a sheet. 3s. per 100.
MURRAY-LANE (Chevalier H.), Chronological Sketch of the Kings of England and the Kings of France, 12mo. 2s. 6d.; or in 2 vols., 1s. 6d. each.
MUSIC: Antiphons of the B.V.M. (S. Cecilian). 3s. 6d.
    Ave Maria, for Four Voices. By W. Schulthes. 1s. 3d.
    Cæcilian Society. *See* Separate List.
    Catholic Choralist. 12 Numbers for 3s.
    Catholic Hymnal. By Leopold de Prins. 2s.; bound, 3s.
    Cor Jesu, Salus in Te sperantium. By W. Schulthes, 2s.; with Harp Accompaniment, 2s. 6d.; abridged, 3d.
    Corona Lauretana. 20 Litanies by W. Schulthes. 2s.
    Evening Hymn at the Oratory. By Rev. J. Nary. 3d.
    Litanies (36) and Benediction Service. By W. Schulthes. 6s. Second Series (Corona Lauretana). 2s.
    Litanies (6). By E. Leslie. 6d.
    Litanies (18). By Rev. J. McCarthy. 1s. 6d.
    Litany of the B.V.M. By Baronnesse Emma Freemantle. 6d.
    Mass of St. Patrick. For three equal voices. By F. Schaller. 2s. 6d.
    Mass of the Holy Child Jesus. In Unison. By W. Schulthes. 3s. The vocal part only, 4d.; or 3s. per doz. Cloth, 6d.; or 4s. 6d. per doz.

Missa, Jesu bone Pastor. By Schaller. 3s. 6d.
Moore's Irish Melodies. 4to., 3s. 6d.
Motetts (Five), S. Cecilian Society. 3s. 6d.
Ne projicias me a facie Tua. Motett for Four Voices. By W. Schulthes. 1s. 3d.
Oratory Hymns. By W. Schulthes. 2 vols., 8s.
Recordare. Oratorio Jeremiæ Prophetæ. By the same. 1s.
Regina Cœli. Motett for Four Voices. By W. Schulthes. 3s. Vocal Arrangement, 1s.
Six Sacred Vocal Pieces, for three or four equal Voices. By W. Schulthes. 4s.
Six Invocations, for four equal Voices. By W. Schulthes. 1s. 6d.
Twelve Latin Hymns. By W. Schulthes. 1s. 6d.
Veni Domine. Motett for Four Voices. By W. Schulthes. 2s. Vocal Arrangement, 6d.
Vesper Psalms and Magnificat. By A.W. Hutton. 3s.
˽ *All the above (music) prices are nett.*
My Conversion and Vocation. By Rev. Father Schouvaloff, 5s.
My Golden Days. By M. F. S. 12mo., 2s. 6d., or in 3 vols., 1s. each; or 1s. 6d. gilt.
My Lady at Last. A Tale, by M. Taunton. 5s.
NARY (Rev. J.), Evening Hymn at the Oratory. Music, 3d.
Natural Philosophy, Catechism of. 18mo., 3d.
Necessity of Enquiry as to Religion. By H. J. Pye. 6d.
Nellie Gordon, the Factory Girl; or, Lost and Saved. By M. A. Pennell. 18mo., 6d.
NEVIN (Willis, Esq.), The Jesuits, and other Essays. 2s. 6d.
NEWMAN (Cardinal), St. Athanasius: Select Treatise in Controversy with the Arians. 2 vols., 15s.
New Testament. 12mo., 2s. 6d. Persian calf, 7s. 6d., morocco, 10s. Illustrated, large 4to., 7s. 6d.
New Year's Gift to Our Heavenly Father. 32mo., 4d.
Nicholas; or, the Reward of a Good Action. 18mo., 6d.
Nina and Pippo, the Lost Children of Mt. St. Bernard. 6d.
NOETHEN (Rev. T.), Good Thoughts for Priests and People; or, Short Meditations for every Day in the Year. 8s.
—— Compendium of Church History. 12mo., 8s.
NOUET (Rev. J.) Meditations on the Life of Our Lord, for every day in the Year. 2 vols. 7s. 6d.
Novena to Our Blessed Lady of Lourdes for the use of the Sick. 18mo., 4d.
Novena of Grace, revealed by S. Francis Xavier. 18mo., 6d.
Novena of Meditations in honour of St. Joseph, according to the method of St. Ignatius, preceded by a new method of hearing Mass according to the intentions of the Souls in Purgatory. 18mo., 1s.
Novena of Meditations. By Sister Mary Alphonsus. 2s. 6d.
Occasional Prayers for Festivals. *See* Prayers, page 31.
O'CLERY (Keyes, K.S.G.), The History of the Italian Revolution. First Period—The Revolution of the Barricades (1796-1849). 8vo., 7s. 6d. Cheap edition 3s. 6d.

O'GALLAGHER (Dr.), Sermons in Irish-Gælic; with literal idiomatic English Translation. By Canon U. J. Bourke. 7s. 6d.
O'HARA (C. M.), Clare's Sacrifice. An impressive little Tale for First Communicants. 6d.
O'KEEFE (Rev. P.) Moral Discourses. 18mo., 2s.
O'MAHONY (D.P.M.), Rome semper eadem. 8vo., 1s. 6d.
O'MEARA (Kathleen), The Battle of Connemara. 12mo., 3s.
———— A Daughter of S. Dominick (Bells of the Sanctuary, No. 4). 12mo., 1s.; stronger bound, 1s. 6d. and 2s.
On what Authority do I accept Christianity? 12mo., 6d.
Op BROEK (Rev. A.), Search the Scriptures. 7s. 6d.
Oratorian Lives of the Saints. With Portrait, 12mo., 5s. a vol.
    I. S. Bernardine of Siena, Minor Observatine.
    II. S. Philip Benizi, Fifth General of the Servites.
    III. S. Veronica Giuliani, and B. Battista Varani.
    IV. S. John of God. By Canon Cianfogni.
O'REILLY (Rev. Dr.), Victims of the Mamertine. 5s.
———— A Romance of Repentance. 12mo., 3s. 6d.
Oremus; or, Little Mildred. By Rev. F. Drew. 1s.
Oremus, A Liturgical Prayer Book. *See* page 31.
Our Lady (Devotion to) in N. America. By Fr. Macleod. 7s. 6d.
Our Lady's Festivals. By Canon Doyle. 2s. 6d.
Our Lady's Lament. By C. E. Tame. 2s.
Our Lady's Month. By Rev. A. P. Bethell. 18mo., 1s. and 1s. 6d
Our Legends and Lives. By E. L. Hervey. 12mo., 6s.
Our Lord's Life, Passion, Death, and Resurrection. 1s.
———————— By Rev. H. Rutter. Illustrated. 12mo., 5s.
———————— Incidents. A Series of 12 Illuminations. 4to., 6s.
Out in the Cold World. By M. F. S., Author of "Fluffy." 3s. 6d.
OXENHAM (H. N.), Poems. 12mo., 3s. 6d.
Oxford Undergraduate of Twenty Years Ago. By a Bachelor of Arts. 8vo., 2s. 6d.; cloth, 3s. 6d.
OZANAM (A. F.), Protestantism and Liberty. Translated from the French by Wilfrid C. Robinson. 8vo., 1s.
PAGANI (Rev. J. B.), Science of the Saints. 4 vols., 12mo., 15s.
Panegyrics of Fr. Segneri, S.J. Translated from the original Italian. With a Preface, by Rev. W. Humphrey, S.J. 12mo., 6s.
Paradise of God; or the Virtues of the Sacred Heart. By Author of "God our Father," "Happiness of Heaven." 12mo., 4s.
Paray le Monial, and Bl. Margaret Mary. 18mo., 6d.
Passion of Our Lord. Lectures by Canon Doyle. 3s.
Passion of Our Lord, Harmony of. By Gayrard, 1s. 6d. Walsh, 2s.
PASSIONIST FATHERS: Christian Armed. 1s. 6d.
    Sacred Eloquence. 18mo., 2s.
    S. Joseph's Manual of a Happy Eternity. 2s. 6d.
    S. Paul of the Cross. 12mo., 3s.
    School of Jesus Crucified. 18mo., 2s. 6d.
Pater Noster; or, an Orphan Boy. By Rev. F. Drew, 1s.
Path to Paradise. *See* Prayers, page 31.
Patrick (S.), Life of. 1s.; 8vo., 6s.; gilt, 10s.
Penitential Psalms. By Rev. F. Blyth. 1s. 6d.

PENNELL (M. A.), Bertram Eldon. 12mo., 1s.
———— Agnes Wilmott's History, and the Lessons it Taught. 1s. 6d.
———— Nellie Gordon, the Factory Girl. 18mo., 6d.
Pens, Washbourne's Free and Easy. Fine, or Middle, or Broad Points, 1s. per gross.
Perpetual Adoration, Book of. By Boudon. 3s. and 3s. 6d.
Per Jesum Christum; or, Two Good Fridays. By Rev. F. Drew. 1s.
Peter (S.), his Name and his Office. By T. W. Allies. 5s.
Peter, Years of. By an ex-Papal Zouave. 12mo., 1d.
Philip Benizi (S.), Life of. 5s.
Philosophy, Elements of. By Rev. W. H. Hill. 8vo., 6s.
PHILPIN (Rev. F.), Holy Places; their sanctity and authenticity. With three Maps. 12mo., 2s. 6d. and 6s.
Photographs (10) illustrating the History of the Miraculous Hosts. (Cathedral, Brussels.) 2s. 6d. the set.
PILLEY (C.), Walter Ferrers' School Days; or, Bellevue and its Owners. 12mo., 2s.
Pius IX., from his Birth to his Death. By G. White. 4d.
Plain Chant. The Cecilian Society Music kept in stock.
PLATUS (Rev. F.), Origin and Progress of Religious Orders, and Happiness of a Religious State. 12mo., 2s. 6d.
PLAYS. *See* Dramas, page 10.
PLUES (Margaret), Chats about the Commandments. 3s.
———— Chats about the Rosary. 3s.
POOR CLARES OF KENMARE. *See* Cusack (Miss).
Pope-King, Rule of. By Rev. E. R. Martin. 8vo., 6d.
Popes of Rome. By Rev. C. Tondini. 3s. 6d.
Popes, Lives of the Early. By Rev. T. Meyrick. 2 vols. 10s.
Portiuncula, Indulgence of. 3d.; 12 for 2s.; 150 for 20s.
POTTER (Rev. T. J.), Extempory Preaching. 2s. 6d.
———— Farleyes of Farleye. 12mo., 2s. 6d.
———— Pastor and People. 12mo., 5s.
———— Percy Grange. 12mo., 3s.
———— Rupert Aubrey. 12mo., 3s.
———— Sir Humphrey's Trial. 12mo., 2s. 6d.
POWELL (J., Esq.), Two Years in the Pontifical Zouaves. Illustrated. 8vo., 3s. 6d.
POWER (Rev. P.) Catechism. 3 vols., 10s. 6d.; 2 vols. 7s. 6d.
PRADEL (Fr., O. P.), Life of St. Vincent Ferrer. Translated by Rev. Fr. Dixon. With a Photograph. 12mo., 5s.
PRAYER BOOKS. *See* page 31.
PRICE (Rev. E.), Sick Calls. 12mo., 3s. 6d.
PRINS (Leopold de). *See* Music.
Pro-Cathedral, Kensington. Tinted View of the Interior; 11 × 15 inches, 1s.; Proofs, on larger paper, 2s.
PROCTOR (John), A Lay Convert on the Catholic Church. Three Lectures. 12mo., cloth, 1s.
Prophecies, Contemporary. By Mgr. Dupanloup. 8vo., 1s.
Protestantism and Liberty. By F. Ozanam. 1s
Protestant Principles examined by the Written Word. 1s.
Prussian Spy. A Novel. By V. Valmont. 12mo., 4s.

R. Washbourne, 18 *Paternoster Row, London.*

Purgatory, A Novena in favour of the Souls in. 32mo., 3d.
Purgatory, Month of the Souls in Purgatory. By Ricard, 1s.
Purgatory, The Doctrine of. By Rev. W. Marshall. 12mo., 1s.
Purgatory, Souls in. By Abbot Burder. 32mo., 3d.
PYE (Henry John, M.A.), Necessity of Enquiry as to Religion. 32mo., 4d.; cloth, 6d.
———— Revelation. Being the substance of several conversations on First Principles. 6d.
———— The Religion of Common Sense. New Edition. 1s.
RAVIGNAN (Pere), The Spiritual Life, Conferences. Translated by Mrs. Abel Ram. 12mo., 5s.
Ravignan (Pere), Life of. 12mo., 12s.
RAYMOND-BARKER (Mrs. F.) Life of Countess Adelstan. 1s. and 2s. 6d.
———— Paul Seigneret. 12mo., 6d., 1s., 1s. 6d., gilt, 2s.
———— Regina Sæculorum. 12mo., 1s. and 3s.
———— Rosalie. 12mo., 1s., 1s. 6d., gilt, 2s.
Reading Books, by the Marist Brothers. 12mo., 1st, 4d.; 2nd, 7d.
Reasonings of Plain Common-Sense upon the Church. 2s. 10d. a 100, post free.
REDMAN (Rev. Dr.), Book of Perpetual Adoration. By Mgr. Boudon. 12mo., 3s.; red edges, 3s. 6d.
REDMOND (Rev. Dr.), Sermon Essays. 18mo., 1s.
REEVES' History of the Bible. 12mo., 3s. 6d. 18mo., 1s.
Reflections, One Hundred Pious. By Alban Butler. 1s.
Regina Sæculorum; or, Mary Venerated in all Ages. Devotions to the Blessed Virgin from Ancient Sources. 12mo., 1s. and 3s.
Rejection of Catholic Doctrines attributable to the Non-Realization of Primary Truths. 8vo., 1s.
Religion of Common Sense. By H. J. Pye, M.A. 12mo., 1s.
Religious Orders. By Rev. F. Platus. 2s. 6d.
Rest, on the Cross. By Eleanora Louisa Hervey. 12mo., 3s. 6d.
Revelation. By Henry John Pye, Esq. 6d.
Reverse of the Medal. A Drama for Girls. 12mo., 6d.
RIBADENEIRA—Life of Our Lord. 12mo., 1s.
RICARD (Abbe), Month of the Holy Angels. 18mo., 1s.
———— Month of the Souls in Purgatory. 18mo., 1s.
RICE (Rev. F. S.), Lina: an Italy Lily. 16mo., 1s. 6d.
RICHARDSON (Rev. Fr.), Catholic Sick and Benefit Club; or, the Guild of our Lady; and St. Joseph's Catholic Burial Society. 32mo., 4d.
———— Holy War against Drunkenness. Manual 6d. a dozen, Cards 2d. each.
———— Little by Little; or, the Penny Bank. 32mo., 1d.
———— Shamrocks. 6s. 2d. a gross (144), post free.
———— S. Joseph's Catholic Burial Society. 2d.
———— The Crusade. For the Suppression of Drunkenness. 1d.
RICHARDSON (Samuel, A.B., B.L., of the Middle Temple), Killed at Sedan. A Novel. Crown 8vo., 7s. 6d.
Ritus Servandus in Expositione et Benedictione. Red cloth, 7s. 6d., red morocco, 10s.
Road to Heaven. A Game. By Miss M. A. Macdaniel. 1s. and 2s.
`BERTSON (Professor), Edmund Burke. 12mo., 3s. 6d.

ROBINSON (Wilfrid C.), Protestantism and Liberty
Translated from the French of Professor Ozanam. 8vo., 1s.
Roman Question, The. By Rev. Dr. Husenbeth. 8vo., 6d.
Rome and her Captors: Letters collected and edited by Count Henri d'Ideville, and Translated by F. R. Wegg-Prosser. 4s.
Rome, Past, Present, and Future. By Dr. M'Corry. 8vo., 6d.
———— Personal Recollections of. By W. J. Jacob, 8vo., 6d.
———— The Victories of. By Rev. F. Beste. 8vo., 1s.
———— (To) and Back. Fly-Leaves from a Flying Tour. Edited by Rev. W. H. Anderdon, S.J., 12mo., 2s.
Rosalie; or, the Memoir of a French Child, told by herself. By Mrs. F. Raymond-Barker. 1s.; stronger bound, 1s. 6d.; gilt, 2s.
Rosary, Fifteen Mysteries of, and Fourteen Stations of the Cross. In One Volume, 32 Illustrations. 16mo., 2s.
Rosary for the Souls in Purgatory, with Indulgenced Prayer. 6d. and 9d. Medals separately, 1d. each, or 9s. gross. Prayers separately, 1d. each, 9d. a dozen, or 6s. for 100.
Rosary, Chats about the; Aunt Margaret's Little Neighbours. 3s.
Rose of Venice. A Tale. By S. Christopher. Crown 8vo., 5s.
ROWLEY (Rev. Austin John), A Devout Exposition of the Holy Mass. Composed by John Heigham. 12mo., 4s.
RUSSELL (Rev. M.), Emmanuel. 2s.; cheap edition, 6d.
———— Madonna. Verses on Our Lady and the Saints, 2s.
RUTTER (Rev. H.) Life and Sufferings of Our Lord, with Introduction by Rev. Dr. Husenbeth. Illustrated. 12mo., 5s.
RYAN (Bishop). What Catholics do not Believe. 12mo., 1s.
Sacred Heart. Act of Consecration to. 1d.; or 6s. per 100.
————————, Act of Reparation to. 1s. 2d. per 100.
————————, A Novena. 1s.
————————, A Spiritual Bouquet. 6d.; cloth gilt, 1s.
————————, Devotions to. By Rev. S. Franco. 12mo., 4s.
————————, Devotions to. By Bishop Milner. 3d.; cloth, 6d.
————————, Elevations to the. By Rev. Fr. Doyotte, S.J. 3s.
————————, Golden Treasury. 48mo., 1s. 6d.; French morocco, 2s. 6d.; calf or morocco, 3s. 6d.
————————, The Heart of Jesus at Nazareth. 3s. 6d.
————————, Hours with. 2s.
————————, Lectures. By Canon Doyle. 3s.
————————, Letters of Blessed Margaret Mary. 3s.
————————, Little Treasury of. 32mo., 2s.; French morocco, 2s. 6d.; calf, 5s.; morocco, 6s.
———————— offered to the Piety of the Young engaged in Study. By Rev. F. Deham. 32mo., 6d.
————————, Office. 1d.
———————— *See* Paradise of God, 4s.; Kinane (Rev. T. H.), 2s. 6d.
————————, Pearls from the Casquet. 3s.
————————, Pleadings of. By Rev. M. Comerford. 18mo., 1s.
————————, Treasury of. 32mo., 2s.; French morocco, 2s. 6d.; calf, 5s.; morocco, 6s. 18mo., 3s. 6d.; roan, 4s.
Sacred History in Forty Pictures. Plain, 5s.; coloured, 7s. 6d. mounted on cardboard, coloured, 18s. 6d. and 22s.

Saints, Lives of, for every day in the Year. Beautifully printed, within illustrated borders from ancient sources, on thick toned paper. 4to., gilt, 25s. *Only a few copies left.*

ST. JURE (S.J.) Knowledge and Love of Jesus Christ. 3 vols., 8vo., 31s. 6d.

———— **The Spiritual Man.** 12mo., 6s.

Sanctuary Meditations for Priests and Frequent Communicants. Translated from the Spanish of Fr. Baltasar Gracian, by Mariana Monteiro. 12mo., 4s.

SCARAMELLI—Directorium Asceticum; or, Guide to the Spiritual Life. 4 vols. 12mo., 24s.

SCHMID (Canon), Tales. Illustrated. 12mo., 3s. 6d. Separately:—The Canary Bird, The Dove, The Inundation, The Rose Tree, The Water Jug, The Wooden Cross. 6d. each; gilt, 1s.

Schools supplied with all School Books. 3d. taken off the 1s.

School of Jesus Crucified. By the Passionist Fathers. 18mo., 2s. 6d.

SCHOUVALOFF (Rev. Father, Barnabite), My Conversion and Vocation. Translated from the French, with an Appendix, by Fr. C. Tondini. 12mo., 5s.

SCHULTHES (William). *See* Music.

SEAMER (Mrs.), *See* M. F. S., page 19.

SEGNERI (Fr., S.J.), Panegyrics. Translated from the original Italian. With a Preface, by Rev. W. Humphrey. 12mo., 6s.

SEGUR (Mgr.), Books for Little Children. Translated. 32mo., 3d. each. Confession, Holy Communion, Child Jesus, Piety, Prayer, Temptation and Sin. In one volume, cloth, 2s.

———— **Three Roses of the Elect.** 16mo., 1s. 6d.

SEGUR (Countess de), The Little Hunchback. 12mo., 3s.

Seigneret, Seminarist (Paul), Life of. 6d., 1s., and 1s. 6d.; gilt, 2s.

Selva; a Collection of Matter for Sermons. By St. Liguori. 12mo., 5s.

Semi-Tropical Trifles. By H. Compton. 12mo., 1s.; cloth, 2s. 6d.

Sermon Essays. By Rev. Dr. Redmond. 12mo., 1s.

Sermons. Irish and English. By Dr. O'Gallagher. 8vo., 7s. 6d.

———— *See* Doyle, 2 vols., 10s. 6d.; Scaramelli, 4 vols., 24s.; Segneri, 6s.; O'Keeffe, 2s.; Buckley, 6s.

———— By Rev. J. Perry. First Series, 3s. 6d. Second Series, 3s. 6d.

———— **and Instructions, Programmes of.** 2 vols., 12s.

———— **The Light of the Holy Spirit in the World.** By Bishop Hedley. 1s.; cloth, 1s. 6d.

Serving Boy's Manual, and Book of Public Devotions. Containing all those prayers and devotions for Sundays and Holydays, usually divided in their recitation between the Priest and the Congregation. Compiled from approved sources, and adapted to Churches, served either by the Secular or Regular Clergy. 32mo., embossed, 1s.; French morocco, 2s.; calf, 4s.; with Epistles and Gospels, 6d. extra.

SHAKESPEARE. Tragedies and Comedies. Expurgated edition. By Rosa Baughan. 8vo., 6s. The Comedies only, 3s. 6d.

Shandy Maguire. A Farce for Boys. 2 Acts. 12mo., 2s.

SHAW (T. H.), Holy Church the Centre of Unity; or, Ritualism compared with Catholicism. 8vo., 1s.

———— **The McPhersons,** to which is added "England's Glory; the Roll of Honour." 8vo., 2s. 6d.

SIGHART (Dr.) Albertus Magnus. 10s. 6d. Cheap edition, 5s.
Silver Teapot. By Elizabeth King. 18mo., 4d.
Simple Tales—Waiting for Father, &c., &c. 16mo., 2s. 6d.
Sir Ælfric and other Tales. By Rev. G. Bampfield. 1s.
Sir Thomas Maxwell and his Ward. By Miss Bridges. 1s.
Sisters of Charity, Manual of. 18mo. 6s.
SMITH-SLIGO (A. V., Esq.), Life of the Ven. Anna Maria Taigi. Translated from French of Calixte. 8vo., 2s. 6d. and 5s.
—— (Mrs.) Margarethe Verflassen. 12mo., 1s. 6d., 3s., and 3s. 6d.
Solid Virtue. By Father Bellécius, S.J. With a Preface by Dr. Croke, Archbishop of Cashel and Emly. New edition, revised and corrected. Crown 8vo., 7s. 6d.
Sophia and Eulalie. (The Catholic Pilgrim's Progress.) From the French by Rev. Fr. Bradbury. 12mo., 1s. 6d., better bound, 3s. 6d.
Spalding (Archbishop), Life of. 8vo., 10s. 6d.
—— Sermon at the Month's Mind. 8vo., 1s.
Spiritual Conferences on the Mysteries of Faith and the Interior Life. By Father Collins. 12mo., 5s.
Spiritual Life. Conferences by Père Ravignan. Translated by Mrs. Abel Ram. 12mo., 5s.
Spiritual Life of Fr. Schouvaloff. 12mo., 5s.
Spiritual Works of Louis of Blois. Edited by Rev. F. John Bowden. 12mo., 3s. 6d.; red edges, 4s.
Stations of the Cross, Method of Blessing, &c. By F. Alexis Bulens, O.S.F. 1s. 6d.; red edges, 2s.
Stations of the Cross, Devotions for Public and Private Use at the. By Miss Cusack. Illustrated. 16mo., 1s. and 1s. 6d.
Stations of the Cross. By S. Liguori. 18mo., 1d.
Stations, and Mysteries of the Rosary. Illustrated, 2s.
STEWART (A. M.) St. Angela's Manual. 2s.; calf, 3s. 6d.
—————— Biographical Readings. 12mo., 3s.
—————— Cardinal Wolsey. 12mo., 6s. 6d.
—————— Sir Thomas More. Illustrated, 10s. 6d.; gilt, 11s. 6d.
—————— Life of S. Angela Merici. 12mo., 3s.
—————— Life of Bishop Fisher. 12mo., 7s. 6d.
—————— Life in the Cloister. 12mo., 3s. 6d.
—————— Life of Cardinal Pole. 8s. 6d.; gilt, 10s. 6d.
—————— Limerick Veteran; or, the Foster Sisters. 5s. and 6s.
—————— Margaret Roper. 6s.
—————— Yorkshire Plot. 6s. 6d. [1s.; gilt edges, 1s. 6d.
Stories for my Children—The Angels and the Sacraments.
Stories of Holy Lives. By M. F. S. 12mo., 3s. 6d.
Stories of Martyr Priests. By M. F. S. 12mo., 3s. 6d.
Stories of the Saints. By M. F. S. 12mo., Five Series, each 3s. 6d.; 1st and 2nd Series, gilt, 4s. 6d.
Stories from many Lands. Compiled by E. L. Hervey. 3s. 6d.
Story of a Paper Knife. 12mo., 1s.; gilt edges, 1s. 6d.
Story of Marie and other Tales. 12mo., 2s. 6d.; gilt, 3s.
Story of the Life of St. Paul. By M. F. S., author of "Stories of the Saints." 12mo., 2s. 6d., cheap edition, 1s. 6d.
Sufferings of our Lord. Sermons preached by Father Claude de la Colombière, S.J., in the Chapel Royal, St. James's, in the year 1677. 18mo., 1s.; stronger bound, 1s. 6d.; red edges, 2s.

Supernatural Life, The. By Mgr. Mermillod. Translated from the French, with a Preface by Lady Herbert. 12mo., 5s.
Supremacy of the Roman See. By C. E. Tame, Esq. 8vo., 6d.
Sure Way to Heaven. A Little Manual for Confession and Holy Communion. 32mo., 6d.; persian, 2s. 6d.; calf or morocco, 3s. 6d.
Taigi (Anna Maria), Life of. Translated from the French of Calixte by A. V. Smith-Sligo, Esq. 8vo., 2s. 6d. and 5s.
Tales and Sketches. By Charles Fleet. 3s. 6d.
Tales of the Jewish Church. By Charles Walker. 12mo., 2s. 6d., cheap edition, 1s. 6d.
TAME (C. E., Esq.), Early English Literature. 16mo., 2s. a vol. I. Our Lady's Lament, and the Lamentation of S. Mary Magdalene. II. Life of Our Lady, in verse.
———— **Supremacy of the Roman See.** 8vo., 6d.
TANDY (Rev. Dr.), Terry O'Flinn. 12mo., 1s.; stronger bound, 1s. 6d.; gilt, 2s. [1s. 6d.; stronger bound, 2s.
TAUNTON (M.), Last of the Catholic O'Malleys. 18mo.,
———— **My Lady at Last.** A Tale. 5s.
———— **One Hundred Pious Reflections,** from Alban Butler's Lives of the Saints. 18mo., 1s.; stronger bound, 2s.
TEELING (Mrs. Bartle), The Mission Cross. 2s.; cheap edition, in paper covers, 50 copies for 40s.
TERESA (S.), Book of the Foundations. Translated by Canon Dalton. 12mo., 3s. 6d.
———— **Letters of.** Translated by Canon Dalton. 12mo., 3s. 6d.
———— **Way of Perfection.** 12mo., 3s. 6d.
———— **The Interior Castle.** 12mo., 3s. 6d.
Terry O'Flinn. By Rev. Dr. Tandy. 12mo., 1s., 1s. 6d. and 2s.
Testimony; or, the Necessity of Enquiry as to Religion. By John Henry Pye, M.A. 32mo., 4d.; cloth, 6d.
Theobald; or, The Triumph of Charity. 12mo., 2s. 6d.
Three Wishes. A Tale. By M. F. S. 2s. 6d., cheap edition, 1s. 6d.
Threshold of the Catholic Church. By Fr. Bagshawe. 4s.
Tim O'Halloran's Choice. By Miss Cusack. 3s. 6d.
Tom's Crucifix, and other Tales. By M. F. S. 12mo., 3s. 6d., or in 5 vols., 1s. each; gilt, 1s. 6d.
TONDINI (Rev. Cæsarius), My Conversion and Vocation. By Rev. Fr. Schouvaloff. 12mo., 5s.
———— **The Pope of Rome and the Popes of the Oriental Orthodox Church.** An essay on Monarchy in the Church, with special reference to Russia. Second Edition. 12mo., 3s. 6d.
———— **Association Prayers in Honour of Mary Immaculate.** 12mo., 3d.
Transubstantiation, Catholic Doctrine of. 12mo., 6d.
TRONSON (Abbe), The Mass: a devout Method. 32mo., 4d.
TRONSON'S Conferences for Ecclesiastical Students and Religious. By Sister M. F. Clare. 12mo., 4s. 6d.
True Wayside Tales. By Lady Herbert. 12mo., 3s., or cheap edition, in 5 vols., 6d. each.
Two Friends; or Marie's Self-Denial. By Madame d'Arras. 1s., or
Ursuline Manual. *See* Prayers, page 32. [gilt, 1s. 6d.
VALMONT (V.), The Prussian Spy. A Novel. 12mo., 4s.

VAUGHAN (Bishop of Salford), The Mass. 2d.; cloth, 6d.
—————— Love and Passion of Jesus Christ. 2d.
Veni Creator; or, Ulrich's Money. By Rev. F. Drew. 1s.
VERE (Rev. G. L.), The Catholic Hymn Book. 32mo., 2d.; cloth, 4d.
—————— For Better, not for Worse. A Tale.
Veronica Giuliani (S.), Life of, and B. Battista Varani. With a Photographic Portrait. 12mo., 5s.
Village Lily. A Tale. 12mo., 1s.; gilt, 1s. 6d.
Vincent Ferrer (S.), of the Order of Friar Preachers; his Life, Spiritual Teaching, and Practical Devotion. By Rev. Fr. Andrew Pradel, O.P. Translated from the French by the Rev. Fr. T. A. Dixon, O.P., with a Photograph. 12mo., 5s.
VINCENT OF LERINS (S.). Commonitory. 12mo., 1s. 3d.
Violet Sellers, The; a Drama in 3 Acts, for Children. 12mo., 6d.
VIRGIL. Literally translated by Davidson. 12mo., 2s. 6d.
"**Vitis Mystica**"; or, the True Vine. By Canon Brownlow. 4s.
WALKER (Charles), Are you Safe in the Church of England? 8vo., 6d.
—————— Maggie Wilson, 2d.; **Joe Marks**, 2d.
—————— Tales of the Jewish Church. 12mo., 2s. 6d. and 1s. 6d.
—————— Why Roman Catholics disbelieve in Anglican Orders, 1d.
WALLER (J. F., Esq.), Festival Tales. 12mo., 3s. 6d.
Walter Ferrers' School Days; or, Bellevue and its Owners. By C. Pilley. 2s.; cheap edition, 1s.
Weedall (Mgr.), Life of. By Rev. Dr. Husenbeth. 8vo., 5s.
WEGG-PROSSER (F. R.), Rome and her Captors. 4s.
WELD (Miss K. M.), Bessy; or, the Fatal Consequences of Telling Lies. 1s.; stronger bound, 1s. 6d.; gilt, 2s.
Wenefred (St.), Life of. By Rev. T. Meyrick. 12mo., 2s.
WENHAM (Canon), The School Manager. 4s. 6d.
—————— The Catechumen. 3s. 6d.
What Catholics do not Believe. By Bishop Ryan. 12mo., 1s.
WHITE (George), Cardinal Wiseman. 12mo., 1s. and 1s. 6d.
—————— Comte de Montalembert. 12mo., 6d.
—————— Life of S. Edmund of Canterbury. 1s. and 1s. 6d.
—————— Pius IX., from his Birth to his Death. 12mo., 4d.
—————— Queens and Princesses of France. 12mo., 3s. 6d.
William (St.), of York. A Drama in Two Acts. (Boys.) 12mo., 6d.
WILLIAMS (Canon), Anglican Orders. 12mo., 3s. 6d.
WISEMAN (Cardinal), Doctrines and Practices of the Catholic Church. 12mo., 3s. 6d.
—————— Science and Religion. 12mo., 5s.
Wiseman (Cardinal), Life and Obsequies. 1s., cloth, 1s. 6d.
—————— Recollections of. By M. J. Arnold. 12mo., 2s. 6d.
WOODS (Canon), Defence of the Roman Church against F. Gratry. Translated from the French of Gueranger. 1s.
Young Catholic's Guide to Confession and Holy Communion. By Dr. Kenny. 32mo., 4d.; cloth, 6d.; red edges, 9d., French morocco, 1s. 6d.; calf or morocco, 2s. 6d.
Zouaves Pontifical, Two Years in. By Joseph Powell, Z.P. Illustrated. 8vo., 3s. 6d.

Garden, Little, of the Soul. Edited by the Rev. R. G. Davis. *With Imprimatur of the Cardinal Archbishop of Westminster*. This book, as its name imports, contains a selection from the "Garden of the Soul" of the Prayers and Devotions of most general use. Whilst it will serve as a *Pocket Prayer Book* for all, it is, by its low price, *par excellence*, the Prayer Book for children and for the very poor. In it are to be found the old familiar Devotions of the "Garden of the Soul," as well as many important additions, such as the Devotions to the Sacred Heart, to Saint Joseph, to the Guardian Angels, and others. The omissions are mainly the Forms of administering the Sacraments, and Devotions that are not of very general use. It is printed in a clear type, on a good paper, both especially selected, for the purpose of obviating the disagreeableness of small type and inferior paper. Twentieth Thousand.

32mo., price, cloth, 6d.; with Epistles and Gospels, 6d.; stronger bound, 8d., with clasp, 1s.; blue cloth, 1s.; with clasp, 1s. 6d. Roan, 1s.; with E. and G. 1s. 6d.; with rims and clasp, 1s. 6d. and 2s. French morocco, 1s. 6d.; with E. and G., 2s.; with rims and clasp, 2s. and 2s. 6d. French morocco extra gilt, 2s.; with E. and G., 2s. 6d.; with rims and clasp, 2s. 6d. and 3s. Calf or morocco, 3s.; with E. and G., 3s. 6d.; with clasp, 4s. and 4s. 6d. Calf or morocco, extra gilt, 4s.; with E. and G., 4s. 6d.; with clasp, 5s. and 5s. 6d. Morocco antique, 7s. 6d., 10s. 6d., 12s., 16s. Velvet, rims and clasp, 5s., 8s. 6d., and 10s. 6d. Russia, 5s., 5s. 6d., 6s., 6s. 6d., 7s. 6d., 8s. Russia antique, 17s. 6d. Ivory, with rims and clasp, 10s. 6d., 13s., 15s., 17s. 6d. Imitation ivory, with rims and clasp, 2s. 6d. Calf or morocco tuck (as a pocket book), 5s. 6d. With oxydized silver or gilt mountings, in morocco case, 25s.

  Illustrated edition, cloth, 1s.; with clasp, 1s. 6d.; roan, 1s. 6d.; French mor., 2s.; extra gilt, 2s. 6d.; calf or morocco, 3s. 6d.; extra gilt, 4s. 6d.

Catholic Piety; or, Key of Heaven, with Epistles and Gospels. Large 32mo., roan, 1s. 6d. and 2s.; French morocco, with rims and clasp, 2s. 6d.; extra gilt, 3s.; with rims and clasp, 3s. 6d.

Catholic Piety. 32mo., 6d.; rims and clasp, 1s.; French morocco, 1s.; velvet, with rims and clasp, 2s. With Epistles and Gospels, roan, 1s.; French morocco, 1s. 6d.; with rims and clasp, 2s.; extra gilt, 2s.; Persian, 2s. 6d.; morocco, 3s. 6d.

Key of Heaven, same prices as above.

Crown of Jesus. 18mo., Persian calf, 6s. Calf or Morocco, 8s.; with rims and clasp, 10s. 6d. Calf or morocco, extra gilt, 10s. 6d.; with rims and clasp, 12s. 6d; morocco, with turn-over edges, 10s. 6d. Ivory, with rims and clasp, 21s., 25s., 27s. 6d. and 30s.

Devotions for Mass. Very large type, 12mo., 3d.

Garden of the Soul. Very large Type. 18mo., cloth, 1s.; with Epistles and Gospels, 1s. 6d.; French morocco, 2s. 6d.; with E. and G., 3s. 6d. Best edition, without E. and G., 3s. 6d.; with E. and G., morocco circuit, 7s. 6d.; calf antique, with clasp, 8s.; French morocco, antique, with clasp, 6s. 6d.

  Epistles and Gospels, in French morocco, 2s.

Holy Childhood. 6d., 1s. and 1s. 6d.

R. Washbourne, 18 Paternoster Row, London.

Child's Picture Prayer Book. 16 tinted Illustrations. Cloth, 1s. and 1s. 6d.; with coloured Illustrations, 1s. 6d., 2s., 2s. 6d., 3s., and 3s. 6d. Roan, 3s. 6d. and 4s. Calf, 5s. and 6s.

Holy Week Book. New edition, with Ordinary of the Mass, Vespers and Complin, Blessing of the Holy Oils, &c. 1s.

Key of Heaven. *Very large type.* 18mo., 1s.; leather, 2s. 6d.

Lily of St. Joseph, The; a little Manual of Prayers and Hymns for Mass. 64mo., price 2d.; cloth, 3d., 4d., 6d., or 8d.; roan, 1s.; French morocco, 1s. 6d.; calf or morocco, 2s.; gilt, 2s. 6d.

Little Prayer Book, The, for Ordinary Catholic Devotions. 3d.

Manual of Catholic Devotions. Small, for the waistcoat pocket. 64mo., 4d.; with Epistles and Gospels, cloth, 6d.; with rims, 1s.; roan, 1s.; calf or morocco, 2s. 6d.; ivorine, 2s. 6d.

Manual of Devotions in Honour of our Lady of Sorrows. 18mo., 1s. 6d.; cheaper binding, 1s.

Missal (Complete). 18mo., roan, 5s.; Persian, 7s. 6d.; calf or morocco, 10s. 6d.; with rims and clasp, 13s. 6d.; calf or mor., extra gilt, 12s. 6d., with rims and clasp, 15s. 6d.; morocco, with turn-over edges, 13s. 6d.; morocco antique, 15s.; velvet, 20s.; Russia, 20s.; ivory, with rims and clasp, 31s. 6d. and 35s. A very beautiful edition, handsomely bound in morocco, gilt mountings, silk linings, edges red on gold, in a morocco case. Illustrated, £5.

Missal. Pocket edition. Roan, gilt edges, 2s.

Missal and Vesper Book, in one vol. morocco, 6s.; with clasp, 8s.

Occasional Prayers for Festivals. 4d. and 6d.; gilt, 1s.

Ordinary of the Mass. 32mo., 2d.; cloth, 6d.

Oremus, A Liturgical Prayer Book: with the Imprimatur of the Cardinal Archbishop of Westminster. An adaptation of the Church Offices: containing Morning and Evening Devotions; Devotion for Mass, Confession, and Communion, and various other Devotions; Common and Proper, Hymns, Lessons, Collects, Epistles and Gospels for Sundays, Feasts, and Week Days; and short notices of over 200 Saints' Days. 32mo., 452 pages, 2s.; cloth, 2s. 6d.; red edges, 3s.; embossed, 3s. 6d.; French morocco, 4s. 6d.; calf or morocco, 6s.; Russia, 8s. 6d., &c., &c., &c.

A Smaller Oremus. An abridgment of the above. Cloth, 9d., with red edges, 1s.; roan or French morocco, 2s.; calf or morocco, 3s.

Path to Paradise. 32 full-page Illustrations. 32mo., cloth, 3d. With 50 Illustrations, cloth, 4d. Superior edition, 6d. and 1s.

Public Devotions, and Serving Boy's Manual. Containing all those Prayers and Devotions for Sundays and Holidays, usually divided in their recitation between the Priest and the Congregation. Compiled from approved sources, and adapted to Churches served either by the Secular or the Regular Clergy, 32mo., Embossed, 1s.; with Epistles and Gospels, 1s. 6d.; French morocco, 2s., with Epistles and Gospels, 2s. 6d.; calf, 4s., with Epistles and Gospels, 4s. 6d.

S. Patrick's Manual. Compiled by Sister Mary Frances Clare. 3s. 6d.

Sure Way to Heaven. Cloth, 6d.: Persian, 2s. 6d.; morocco, 3s. 6d.

Treasury of the Sacred Heart. 18mo., 3s. 6d.; roan, 4s. 6d. 32mo., 2s.; French morocco, 2s. 6d.; calf 5s.; morocco, 6s.

Ursuline Manual. 18mo., 4s.; Persian calf, 7s. 6d.; morocco, 10s.

Garden of the Soul. (WASHBOURNE'S EDITION.) Edited by the Rev. R. G. Davis. *With Imprimatur of the Cardinal Abp. of Westminster.* Twenty-third Thousand. This Edition retains all the Devotions that have made the GARDEN OF THE SOUL, now for many generations, the well-known Prayer-book for English Catholics. During many years various Devotions have been introduced, and, in the form of appendices, have been added to other editions. These have now been incorporated into the body of the work, and, together with the Devotions to the Sacred Heart, to Saint Joseph, to the Guardian Angels, the Itinerarium, and other important additions, render this edition pre-eminently the Manual of Prayer, for both public and private use. The version of the Psalms has been carefully revised, and strictly conformed to the Douay translation of the Bible, published with the approbation of the LATE CARDINAL WISEMAN. The Forms of administering the Sacraments have been carefully translated, *as also the rubrical directions,* from the Ordo Administrandi Sacramenta. To enable all present, either at baptisms or other public administrations of the Sacraments, to pay due attention to the sacred rites, the Forms are inserted without any curtailment, both in Latin and English. The Devotions at Mass have been carefully revised, and enriched by copious adaptations from the prayers of the Missal. The preparation for the Sacraments of Penance and the Holy Eucharist have been the objects of especial care, to adapt them to the wants of those whose religious instruction may be deficient. Great attention has been paid to the quality of the paper and to the size of type used in the printing, to obviate that weariness so distressing to the eyes, caused by the use of books printed in small close type and on inferior paper.

32mo. Embossed, 1s.; with rims and clasp, 1s. 6d.; with Epistles and Gospels, 1s. 6d.; with rims and clasp, 2s. French morocco, 2s.; with rims and clasp, 2s. 6d.; with E. and G., 2s. 6d.; with rims and clasp, 3s. French morocco extra gilt, 2s. 6d.; with rims and clasp, 3s.; with E. and G., 3s.; with rims and clasp, 3s. 6d. Calf, or morocco 4s.; with best gilt clasp, 5s. 6d.; with E. and G., 4s. 6d., with best gilt clasp, 6s. Calf or morocco extra gilt, 5s.; with best gilt clasp, 6s. 6d.; with E. and G., 5s. 6d.; with best gilt clasp, 7s. Velvet, with rims and clasp, 7s. 6d., 10s. 6d., and 13s.; with E. and G., 8s., 11s., and 13s. 6d. Russia, antique, with clasp, 8s. 6d., 10s., 12s. 6d.; with E. and G., 9s. 10s. 6d., 13s., with corners and clasps, 20s.; with E. and G., 20s. 6d. Ivory 14s., 16s., 18s., and 20s., with E. and G., 14s. 6d., 16s. 6d., 18s. 6d., and 20s. 6d. Morocco antique, 8s. 6d.; with 2 patent clasps, 12s.; with E. and G., 9s. and 12s. 6d.; with corners and clasps, 18s.; with E. and G., 18s. 6d.; morocco, with turn-over edges, 7s. 6d.; with E. and G., 8s.

The Epistles and Gospels. *Complete,* cloth, 6d.; roan, 1s. 6d.

"This is one of the best editions we have seen of one of the best of all our Prayer Books. It is well printed in clear, large type, on good paper."—*Catholic Opinion.*
A very complete arrangement of this which is emphatically the Prayer Book of every Catholic household. It is as cheap as it is good, and we heartily recommend it."—*Universe.* "Two striking features are the admirable order displayed throughout the book, and the insertion of the Indulgences in small type above Indulgenced Prayers. In the Devotions for Mass, the editor has, with great discrimination, drawn largely on the Church's Prayers, as given us in the Missal."—*Weekly Register.*

R. Washbourne, 18 Paternoster Row, London.

www.ingramcontent.com/pod-product-compliance
Lightning Source LLC
Chambersburg PA
CBHW030732230426
43667CB00007B/690